The Accidental Immigrant

The Accidental Immigrant

A Quest for Spirit in a Skeptical Age

Kyriacos C. Markides

HAMILTON BOOKS
an imprint of
Rowman & Littlefield
Lanham • Boulder • New York • London

Published by Hamilton Books
An imprint of The Rowman & Littlefield Publishing Group, Inc.
4501 Forbes Boulevard, Suite 200, Lanham, Maryland 20706
www.rowman.com

6 Tinworth Street, London SE11 5AL, United Kingdom

British Library Cataloguing in Publication Information Available

Library of Congress Cataloging-in-Publication Data Available

ISBN 9780761872870 (pbk. : alk. paper) | ISBN 9780761872887 (ebook)

∞™ The paper used in this publication meets the minimum requirements of American
National Standard for Information Sciences—Permanence of Paper for Printed Library
Materials, ANSI/NISO Z39.48-1992.

For our grandchildren

Contents

Prologue

The idea for this book of memoirs first came from my friend Nikos Aivaliotis, alias "Stephanos" in my previous books. He passed away as "Father Nektarios," just days after his initiation as an Eastern Orthodox monk. As he lay dying, holding a large silver cross over his chest, he urged me in a whispering voice to write it "for the glory of God." He had offered these words to me previously, and perhaps he noticed my uncertainty about my purity of motives. I wondered, would I be writing this spiritual and intellectual odyssey more for the glory of God or for my own ego gratification? I still have no clear answer, but I do find it an emotional challenge to have myself as the principal subject of my writing after a lifetime of studying others. My hope is that these memoirs might be of help to those who are similarly seeking answers to life's perennial questions. The last words of my beloved friend still echo in my mind: "My dear Kyriacos, know that what we have gained in this life is never lost." In his frail and semiconscious state, he did not elaborate, and I did not press him for clarification. I think he probably meant that the love and knowledge we grow in and share with others stay with us in eternity. Nothing is lost.

For 60 years I have been an active member of the American academic community, first as a student and then as a professor of sociology. My research focus began in political sociology, but by virtue of a series of uncanny synchronicities, it shifted to the uncharted and enchanted world of unconventional healers and lay mystics. Later, I added charismatic Christian hermits, monks, and spiritual elders to this curious and colorful mix. The common denominator was that these were all extraordinary human beings who lived within worlds radically different from most of us. I became witness to phenomena that defied rational explanation, and to spiritual wisdom that seemed not unlike that which inspired the world's great religions. Gradually, that wisdom overwhelmed my conventional academic way of thinking. The purely materialist interpretation of reality that I had absorbed during my ten years of formal training at American universities no longer worked for me.

The Western Enlightenment left us a legacy of magnificent knowledge, along with an overdose of extreme rationalism. That legacy now requires a massive revision, a broader framework that leaves room for nonphysical, spiritual truths lying beyond the reach of the three-dimensional, time-space universe. Authentic mystical and transcendent experiences are real, not illusory. They are not the result of biochemical reactions in the brain or delusional fantasies of the mentally challenged. They open us to majestic and grand realities that are now getting the attention of some pioneering contemporary scientists. I have come to accept certain basic assumptions about the nature of the world that go beyond the taken-for-granted understanding offered by higher learning in North America and Western Europe. Observing and learning from the healers, seers, and luminaries I studied were a central piece of my own transformation of understanding. I do have some excellent company, coming from various corners of the scientific, philosophic, medical, and other worlds, and throughout this book I appeal to some of their contributions where appropriate.

In the chapters that follow, I lay out some of the synchronicities as well as the life events that I had expected or at least hoped for, all leading me step by step to the awareness of the deep spiritual wisdom lying within every human being. Ironically, this is the very wisdom that, unbeknownst to me, has found a well-organized expression in my own cultural backyard for centuries: the mystical spirituality of Eastern Christianity. At Mt. Athos in Greece, I met Father Maximos, a young and charismatic monk who introduced me to this different Christianity, one that was more experiential and that focused on healing the split between humanity and God. In chapter 6 I review my discovery and observation of this living wisdom.

Of course, it is the nature of synchronicity to be unpredictable or at least unplanned in its appearance. Sometimes "a quest for spirit" (borrowing from my subtitle) took me in directions that might appear anything but spiritual. I show in chapter 1 that I was born in Cyprus when the island was still under British colonial rule. I describe how my sister's involvement (six years my senior) in the anticolonial movement sometimes turned our home into a meeting place for underground guerrilla planning, and how as a 14-year-old, I had to negotiate what my own role in those activities would be. But that development and my ruminations about its aftermath probably led me later into political sociology, and not long after that, into writing my book about Cyprus politics and history that earned me tenure at the University of Maine (chapter 2).

In turn, that book and my academic credentials led to an invitation to participate in some peace work after the island was invaded by Turkey in 1974. Close to forty percent of the island had been taken over by the Turks, and chapters 3 and 4 include more than a few pages about that conflict and my efforts toward reconciliation. Daskalos, the Cypriot healer and clairvoyant I had recently started observing and studying on the island (chapters 3 and 4), had warned me that my attempts would likely lead to nothing, but I persisted regardless.

Did my unanticipated peace work interfere with my continued focus on Daskalos' world—the presumptive center of my spiritual quest at the time? I may have occasionally thought so during that period when the peace work was fraught with tremendous frustration and a sense of futility. The more my life unfolded, however, the more I learned that spirituality has no boundaries. It is everywhere, integrative, and ready to connect that which is presumed to be separate, such as Greeks and Turks. How could attempts at reconciliation be somehow more alien to a quest for Spirit than observing a great healer or a gifted monk on Mt. Athos?

This exploration is colored by my training as a professional sociologist. We are not only corporeal spirits. We are also embedded in a unique culture with its own history, one that informs the parameters and sets the limitations within which we experience our lives and develop our consciousness. My sociological background, therefore, is a formative part of the lens through which I view and think about the world. You will often find me invoking that knowledge as part of my story, and in many respects these memoirs are as much about my intellectual history as they are about the important events of my life. For example, early on in my career I encountered the life and works of Pitirim Sorokin, a lesser-known member of the celebrated club of "classic sociologists." At one point I summarize some of the elements of his unique and visionary perspective, along with the impact it had on me (chapter 2). I encourage you to resist any temptation to skim over it, because as my story continues, I often link some new development in my perspective to something I learned from Sorokin long before.

There is a fair amount of theology and metaphysics in these memoirs. None of it should require any background to understand it. I am neither a theologian nor an ordained member of the priesthood, but I am deeply interested in theology. The perennial questions—who am I and what am I here for?—are what brought me to it. But you will find me contemplating and reflecting on ideas that will not sit well with the more traditional members of the mainstream Christian establishment or other traditional establishments and constituencies, including mainstream academia. And in this age that is so replete with agnostics and atheists, some of you may fault me for not endorsing the neo-atheist resurgence following the tragedy of September 11, 2001, although

I do signal my appreciation of the renewed conversation about spirituality that the neo-atheists stimulated (chapter 6).

You will see that I have a checkered history regarding spirituality, and particularly Eastern Orthodoxy, the religion of my birth (chapter 7 and throughout the book). That history culminated in my embracing the fundamental tenets of Christianity, but even here, my attraction centers on those elements that I see as universal and life-enhancing. Being Christian never stopped me from identifying relevant non-Christian wisdom that I have encountered in other spiritual traditions, cultures, and confessions. I do not believe in syncretism—the meshing of religions and the creation of a superreligion—the fear of so many devout believers. Each religious tradition is unique, just as every language and culture is unique, offering alternative and often complementary perspectives on how to make sense of our lives. Being a sociologist and spending most of my life within a pluralistic and cosmopolitan social milieu, I am temperamentally and by training a strong proponent of interreligious dialogue and cooperation. I hope this sensibility helps to cultivate understanding and tolerance across religious and cultural traditions, and that it stimulates a deeper appreciation of your own spiritual inheritance. A final note: a few names in the text are pseudonyms.

Acknowledgments

I am deeply indebted to all the people mentioned in these memoirs who became part of my life's story. I am particularly thankful to the following: My sister Maroulla who played a key role in my crossing the Atlantic to America; my Aunt Eleni who generously invited me to Ohio for my undergraduate education; my wife Emily, loving companion of 49 years, critical first reader of everything I wrote, and full-time partner in this spiritual and intellectual adventure; my children Constantine and Vasia for the boundless support and love towards their Papa, and for their editorial assistance! I also thank the following for reading the manuscript and offering me their invaluable feedback: my artist friend Professor Michael Lewis, our department's administrative officer Laurie Cartier, and our writer son Constantine. In addition, I am grateful to my colleagues and friends in Sociology at the University of Maine who supported my work in various ways over the years. I am especially thankful to Steven Cohn, Steven Barkan, and Stephen Marks. Stephen has been not only a most beloved and lifelong friend but also a terrific editor for this work. I am the happy beneficiary of his generosity and his superb editorial skills developed over many years as an accomplished scholar and an editor of an interdisciplinary journal. This book is a better work because of Stephen's surgical interventions. Needless to say, for any shortcomings I alone bear responsibility.

Contents

Chapter 1

Coming of Age in Colonial Cyprus

EARLY YEARS

I was four years old when my mother died in 1947 at age 36. I have no memory of her except for some vague images that occasionally flash in my mind. Yet I *know* her on a deep visceral level—aided, perhaps, by some yellowish black and white photographs and from stories told by my father, sister, aunts, and some cousins old enough to remember her. Although my father had only ten years with my mother, he remained in mourning until his death at 86. Contrary to the sober advice of friends and relatives, he refused to remake his life with another woman. Each night before turning off the light next to his bed, he would kiss her photograph. He was a devout pilgrim honoring the icon of his beloved, hoping that sometime, somehow, they would reconnect. It took him close to a decade to step into a church again, and longer than that to overcome his bitterness and anger at God.

My father's devotion to my mother's memory was seen by some as a testament to true love, a rare phenomenon encountered only in romantic literature and artistic creations. His relationship with her was indeed remarkable when one considers that their marital union was the result of an arrangement, like most unions in Cyprus at the time. They met at a family picnic, and without consulting my mother, my father quickly asked my grandfather for his daughter's hand in marriage. My mother was flabbergasted when she learned from a friend the next morning that she was now engaged. The friend had read it in the morning press.

The only concrete memory I have of my mother is from the day of her repose. As was the custom, they placed the body facing east, turned around on the marital bed, with her feet on the side of the pillow. This is the image I remember vividly. Everyone who stood around the motionless body was weeping silently, while I was staring in confusion, having been reassured that my mother simply went to sleep. Why were they crying? Wouldn't she wake up soon, as I was promised? Several times during the 40 days of formal mourning, I pulled down the black cloth that hung over the entrance to our

1

house, suspecting that something was not right. My mother did not wake up, and my father wore a black band around his right arm for more than a year. I learned quickly that life was no rose garden. People suffer, grow old, get sick, die. To this day black is not my preferred color, so it is ironic that for more than twenty-five years I have been studying the world of black-clad monks and hermits. Perhaps my mother's early death is what prompted my fascination with metaphysical questions about human existence, along with speculations about a possible life beyond the grave.

I remember only one dream about my mother, just after I turned fifty. It was unusually vivid. She was young and beautiful, dressed in a brilliant all-white dress and smiling as she faded from my earnest gaze. It was a vision consistent with what I once heard—that the departed reappear only in images most flattering to themselves. And throughout my own life, every time I dream of a departed friend or acquaintance, they always appear young and vibrant, regardless of their age or physical condition at the point of their death.

My sister Maroulla and I were raised by my father and one of his sisters, Aunt Myrofora ("the Myrrh Bearer"). She left her mountain village to live with us in Nicosia, the capital city of Cyprus. It was a step away from the drudgery of village life, particularly for a young woman. By every objective measure Aunt Myrofora was the embodiment of selflessness. So deep was her love for Melpo, my mother that she promised her as she lay dying that she would postpone marriage for herself until we came of age. She kept her vow and did not marry until her mid-thirties, which was very late by the standards of the time. She never had children of her own.

Growing up I often felt something was missing from my life. Why did others have mothers and I did not? But in fact I was blessed with several women around me, having them as surrogate mothers who looked after my welfare. My glass was more than half full. Besides Aunt Myrofora, I had my sister, six years my senior, along with many cousins and aunts. Most lived within walking distance from our house. I learned that the real reason why my cousin Maro opened a kindergarten next door to us was to help me cushion the trauma of losing my mother. Maro was in her early twenties and had some training in child pedagogy. I was her first pupil, and her school served the needs of three generations of youngsters in our community. So I learned from experience what sociologists teach, that extended families are often best equipped to handle the vagaries and tragedies of life. I may have lost my mother but I had female nurture in abundance. I have always felt a certain comfort in the company of women, and it was not difficult later on to overcome my inherited patriarchy and embrace the women's movement for equal rights. To be sure, my wife Emily was a major influence in that direction.

My mother, I was told, had been exceptional. During the 1930s, Cypriot women were rarely educated beyond elementary school. Few were learned enough to read anything beyond the social columns of the local newspapers: engagements, marriages, baptisms, funerals. But my mother was a graduate of the Cyprus Pedagogical Academy set up by the British, who ruled Cyprus at the time. She taught elementary school children until her marriage. Being a literate person, she left behind a library that included a rich collection of classics. As I grew older, I found a storehouse of European literature in Greek translation to dig through: Victor Hugo's *Les Miserables*, Jane Austin's *Pride and Prejudice*, Leo Tolstoy's *War and Peace* and *Anna Karenina,* to mention a few. Left behind was also her mandolin. I was told that she was a virtuoso amateur performer, particularly of Greek Cantatas originating in the Ionian Islands off the western coast of Greece.

My mother's educational differences from my father were enormous. My father had just three years of elementary schooling, but what he lacked in formal training he made up for in social graces and good looks. He was socially educated through "the school of the Cypriot bazaar," as many of his generation were fond of saying about themselves. Most of his friends had more formal education than he did. Some were doctors, lawyers, teachers and government employees. Despite his grief of losing his beloved, his gregarious nature and keen sense of humor saved him from loneliness in old age. When I was a pre-adolescent he often carried me on his bicycle to his soccer club, where he met with his friends to play backgammon, cards, and chat about politics and sports.

Born in the mountainous village of Agros, my father was forced to migrate to Nicosia to earn his livelihood at the tender age of twelve. My grandfather could not feed a family of six children. One day he ordered his oldest son, my father, to join a caravan of fellow villagers who, after loading their donkeys with dried fruits and wine, walked the sixty miles to Nicosia to sell their goods. It was arranged that my father would work at a grocery store owned by a relative, but the day after his arrival he walked the 60 miles back to his village. The culture shock of city life was simply too much for this village boy. The story has it that my grandfather, upon seeing his wayward son, grabbed him by the ear, slapped him in the butt, and sent him back down the mountains. Hence began my father's urban career. From a peasant lad he eventually became owner of a busy grocery store in the heart of Nicosia. Had he stayed in the village he would have done what most of his fellow villagers did in those rugged Troodos Mountains: ride donkeys, look after goats, and attend vineyards and fruit trees to eke out a living.

I grew up in Ayii Omologites, a suburb of Nicosia. Aside from losing my mother, my childhood could not have been more idyllic. We had ample open spaces to fly kites, climb eucalyptus trees, and take part in epic battles between cowboys and Indians. We played soccer, hid in wheat fields, and engaged in water fights with youngsters from other neighborhoods. Strong community bonds were taken for granted; secrets were hard to keep. My closest friends lived within minutes of my house. The notion of personal alienation and feelings of meaninglessness—the bread and butter of sociologists—were totally unknown to us. Contemplating suicide was unheard of.

From the vantage point of the twenty-first century, our life was impoverished as far as material comforts were concerned. There were few cars in the streets, as Nicosia was a city of bicycles. Modern amenities were enjoyed only by a small minority of the relatively affluent. We had no refrigerators, only ice boxes and only for the summer months. The ice cream man pushing his cart, loudly and flamboyantly advertising his wares, was always a welcome sound, heralding the beginning of summer and the end of the school year. Only those who had businesses or were officials in the colonial administration had access to telephones. I do not remember any of my relatives owning a motorized vehicle. The bathroom for most households was an outhouse; in the heart of winter we ran shivering to empty our bladders at night.

Television was unknown during most of the fifties. The first T.V. sets were introduced to the Island by the British at the end of the decade. Nationalists campaigned against them on the spurious presupposition that the British colonialists planned to use television to brainwash the Greek population against the struggle to unite the island with Greece. Many a television set was randomly smashed in protest.

As children we entertained ourselves by watching shadow theater performances of *Karakiozis* in the public square. This was the cultural equivalent of Popeye the Sailor or Donald Duck. During my high school years, entertainment entered a more advanced stage: we began watching school-approved films—only Saturday matinees, and only after we had our weekly bath. Woe to those of us who got caught in a movie theater at any other time.

The school was a powerful force for social conformity and control. Critical thinking was discouraged, even when learning about ancient Greece. Our teacher of Modern Greek told us several times, "I don't care about your ideas and opinions. What I care about is that you learn how to write correctly." That meant right spelling and right grammar. Developing a creative imagination and learning about the meaning and philosophy of the classical texts we studied were of no importance. In our senior year we read only the first few pages of the Odyssey, not to hear of the exploits and adventures of the "man of many ways" but to learn the correct spelling and syntax of ancient Greek.

In school we had to wear special uniforms and a military-looking gray hat, which we were expected to raise with deference whenever we met a teacher on the street. We had to do the same for the school constable, who roamed the streets on his bicycle like a military policeman, hunting for undisciplined students who dared go to the movies at the wrong time or roamed without the school uniform or were guilty of other misdemeanors. Other than cigarettes, drugs were unknown. Drinking was not a problem. The really bad boys were those old enough to sneak into brothels and then talk with relish about their exploits. The rest of us, innocent of carnal knowledge, listened with open mouths.

Before the onslaught of development, our neighborhood was surrounded by orange groves, wheat fields, and a eucalyptus forest, intermixed with cypress and palm trees. Turkish-speaking Roma, or Gypsies, wearing their colorful dresses, periodically visited our area and set up camp under the eucalyptus trees. Their services ranged from tinning kitchen pots and pans to fortune telling.

During my elementary school years, thanks to aunt Polyxeni ("She who has many guests"), another sister of my father, we spent much of the summer by the sea. My aunt's house was in Kyrenia, the pristine coastal town of the north, immortalized in Lawrence Durrell's classic autobiographical novel *Bitter Lemons.*[1]

Her home, minutes from the sea, was surrounded by orange and lemon trees. Grape vines climbed the walls and covered the flat roof, providing a robust harvest and, most importantly, cool insulation from the intense summer heat. Jasmine and rose bushes decorated the front of the house. During late afternoons, when the heat receded and refreshing sea breezes began to blow, my aunt gathered with her women neighbors in front of her house to embroider. They passed the time knitting and chatting until their husbands came home from the coffee shops.

When the heat intensified in August my sister, aunt Myrofora and I would leave Kyrenia and board a bus for my father's village in the mountains. There, we stayed at the house of another of his sisters. It was a time for mountain hiking and donkey rides with my village cousins. It was during those excursions that they introduced me to the secrets and mysteries of human conception. I was twelve years old and still clueless about the origin of species. They on the other hand lived close to the animals and were eye witnesses to the rhythms and tempos of nature and the intricacies of biological reproduction.

Poor by modern standards, but spared from the traps of consumerism, the quality of our lives made up for the absence of creature comforts. We were not aware of being poor. We simply were never exposed to a lifestyle of owning unaffordable things. The majority of Cypriots were happily poor. Life was, on the whole, good. Whenever we went on an excursion, whether in a bus or in one of the few cars around, we all sang popular Greek songs. It was almost reflexive: being on an excursion requires you to erupt into song.

Most people we knew lived the same life of minimum consumption within the context of strong communal bonds. In contemporary sociological parlance we were members of the lower middle class, the *petit bourgeois.* Hunger was never a part of my experience, although it was for many of my generation living in villages. In our family, having a father who owned a grocery store meant that there was always food on the table. But buying a pair of shoes or pants was a major indulgence. Overseas travel was unthinkable, and owning a bicycle was a turning point in life, the equivalent of a seventeen-year-old driving a car in today's America.

The almost utopian life of my elementary school years—summers swimming in Kyrenia and then riding donkeys with my cousins in the mountains—ended when I turned thirteen. I began working at my father's grocery store during school recess and Saturdays after school. Visits to Kyrenia and the mountains were getting shorter and shorter. I often envied boys my age whose fathers were government employees and therefore did not have to work during summers selling vegetables and canned foods.

I wanted to escape the drudgery of working in a grocery store. My father supported this aspiration. Hoping I would become a successful entrepreneur, he sent me to a business high school where poorer segments of society went in hopes of climbing the social ladder. This upward mobility was fostered by the absence of rigid class divisions in mid-20th century Cyprus, a legacy of the Ottoman Turks having leveled the field of all economic and hereditary hierarchies prior to England's takeover of the island in 1878. The feudal Venetian aristocracy that controlled the Island during the Ottoman conquest in 1573 had three options: convert to Islam, join the Christian Orthodox population, or get beheaded. Few chose the last option.

The fluid social divisions of my youth were sometimes found even within families. One brother might be high up in the colonial administration, another a peasant tilling the land, and yet another working in construction in the cities. I grew up with a feeling that it was normal to have relatives from a variety of social classes.

As teenagers we had clear notions about who we were, and we never agonized about the meaning of life. I recall no one of my generation going through an identity crisis, perhaps because the Church was always there to answer the existential questions. Emotional security was a given, though surely at the expense of the critical thinking so highly prized in the modern democratic world. Of course, it was not only the school and the Church that ruled out critical thought and existential searching. Those two institutions simply reflected what communal life and extended family solidarity always try to accomplish, which is to keep us on the straight and narrow path of unquestioned obedience to tradition. I had to be ejected from that early utopia before I could develop the kind of awareness that could raise questions about God and ultimate reality.

GROWING UP IN A TROUBLED LAND

If the loss of my mother was the major turning point in my childhood, the second turning point was during my mid-teens, arguably the dark night of my soul. Suddenly I had to wrestle with agonizing questions about whether there could be a justification for committing homicidal acts for patriotic, revolutionary reasons. Is God's prohibition against killing fellow human beings absolute and irrevocable? Or are there circumstances that could justify such ghastly behaviors?

Teenage years can be difficult in any society, but going through them during the fifties in Cyprus was particularly challenging. Cypriots endured the outbreak of a violent underground movement that the colonial government deemed terrorist, while its participants saw it as selfless patriotism and freedom fighting. The goal of the movement was to force England to cede the island to Greece. The rebellion lasted four years. I was 13 when it began early in the morning on April 1, 1955, and 17 when it ended in 1959, the year I began preparing for the long voyage to America. Growing up during these years was extremely difficult. I became obsessed with fundamental questions of human existence—not theoretically, not via reading books or teachers but on the basis of direct, deeply painful experiences.

In my early teens I had a strong desire to become a boy scout and enjoy the outdoors with my friends on the pine-covered Troodos Mountains. But such activities were quickly suspended with the rise of the "Troubles," as the fighting years were called (the Irish used a similar term in their rebellion against England). The mountains became dangerous places whenever the EOKA underground (National Organization of Cypriot Fighters) was engaging the British army in ambushes and hit and run operations. In the towns and villages, a parallel form of combat—urban guerrilla operations—were taking place all around the island. We spent those years under martial law, which included curfews after sunset for teenagers, and major disruptions in our education as a result of mass arrests and school closings. Teenagers were often prohibited from riding their bicycles—an attempt to prevent them from tossing crude, homemade grenades at British troops. The majority of the hard-core participants in the underground (77 percent, I later confirmed empirically) were between the ages of 15 and 25.[2]

High school students were prime targets for induction into the underground. George Grivas, the retired fifty-five-year-old Greek colonel who clandestinely returned from Greece to his native Cyprus to set up the militant underground organization, describes how his recruitment efforts focused especially on the "passionate youth":

"It is among the young people that one finds audacity, the love of taking risks and the thirst for great and difficult achievements. It was to the youth of Cyprus that I made my main appeal and called on to give their all to the struggle. . . . I assigned young people the task of forming groups of saboteurs, the manufacture of explosives, and the supervision and execution of orders concerning passive resistance. . . . Schoolboys between the ages of fourteen and seventeen undertook dangerous missions such as the blowing up of aircraft at the British air bases, the laying of mines and the blowing up of police stations."[3]

This was neither the first nor the last time that youngsters were recruited to fight the revolutions and wars of adults, with disastrous consequences for the lives of young people. Cypriot high schools, dominated by Greek nationalist teachers, were breeding grounds for enthusiastic fighters. Our teachers indoctrinated us against British colonialism so intensely that we thought it was our patriotic duty to take up arms and fight for the union of Cyprus with "Mother Greece." We were primed for war, to kill if necessary, and to die for the sacred cause. We and our teachers believed that *Enosis* (union with Greece) was both inevitable and imminent. We ignored the inconvenient fact that 18 percent of the population were Turkish Cypriots who vehemently opposed it and that their "Mother Turkey" was only forty miles north of Cyprus, whereas mainland Greece was six hundred miles away. Of course, the colonial government sided with the Turkish minority to repress the fight for *Enosis* supported by the Greek Cypriot majority, which constituted eighty percent of the population. Turkish Cypriot civilians were recruited to patrol the streets alongside British soldiers, and British diplomacy invited Turkey to redouble its efforts to support the Turkish minority on the island.

During the fifties there were ample anticolonial struggles around the world to inspire some of our leaders to embrace violent methods of decolonization—the Irish IRA, the Kenyan Mau Mau, the Israeli Irgun, and the Algerian FLN, to name a few. There were nonviolent models as well, but none of our national leaders—not even the Archbishop of Cyprus—seemed to consider the peaceful resistance embodied in the life of political activists such as Mahatma Gandhi.

I never did join the boy scouts. Instead, I was approached by a classmate who asked if I was ready to join the underground movement. He was sixteen, two years older than I, and a member of EOKA. "If I join," I asked, "what exactly am I supposed to do?" He replied, "Well, you know: distribute revolutionary leaflets, paint slogans on walls, organize riots, and sometimes throw hand grenades against British soldiers." Thinking to entice me further, he added, "In the event you excel, you may be promoted by the sector chief to become a member of a fighting group." By that he meant shooting at British troops and tracking down and assassinating "traitors." I felt my heart speed up. After a deep breath, I replied, "Let me think about it. I'll let you know tomorrow." It was a difficult call because I was a nationalist and a Greek patriot, as most of my classmates were. That identity had been fostered by the Church, our teachers, and our families. Furthermore, I was seen to be aligned with Grivas's anticommunist proclivities because my father was not a communist.

Hardly able to sleep, I agonized over the offer all night long. In the end, I could not see myself throwing bombs or pulling a trigger to shoot at a human being. As a boy I had learned from our parish priest about the Ten Commandments and the Sermon on the Mount and had taken these teachings to heart. I therefore experienced a severe form of what psychologists call "cognitive dissonance." God was commanding one thing and our teachers were urging the opposite. Jesus taught us to love our enemies and turn the other cheek. Our teachers and the higher clergy, who glorified the armed uprising, kept reminding us of our warriors of the past—those at Marathon, Thermopylae, and the battle of Salamis. They quoted defiant Leonidas and his 300 Spartans, and they mesmerized us with the feats of the mustachioed heroes of the Greek War of Independence against the Turks in 1821 and the Greek resistance against the Nazis during the German occupation of mainland Greece. Nationalist poets urged the youth to imitate our heroic ancestors, and popular songwriters coaxed us to transcend ourselves and take part in the glorious struggle. We were constantly reminded that we were Greeks—proud members of a superior race—and it was therefore noble to kill and die for Greece, the idol of our worship.

Adding to my dissonance was the fact that the very same teachers—the Greek philologists, the theologians and the higher clergy who were teaching us about the Sermon on the Mount and "turning the other cheek"—were also propagandizing the holiness of the great, patriotic, armed struggle. To my mind, the teachings of Jesus and the ghosts of Marathon were in conflict, and because the adults to whom I looked for guidance were useless to help me, I felt alone in my dilemma. I had to figure things out for myself, including the meaning of life and death, the existence of God, and the prohibition against killing fellow human beings.

The next day I offered my answer and I felt a surge of relief. I was not willing to risk my own life, or to kill or hurt a fellow human being. I was a strong believer in an all-loving personal God, and I was deeply concerned about damaging my immortal soul if I committed acts prohibited by the Gospel.

I often look back and wonder how my life would have turned out if I had made a different decision. A simple "yes" could have drastically altered the trajectory of my life. Fortunately, I was still very young; I had an excuse to feel frightened. What if I had been two or three years older and a sense of manliness had risen within me to suppress my fears? I was shocked many years later when a man in his fifties reminisced with patriotic pride about his adventures in the underground. When he was sixteen and joined EOKA, he shot a police officer in the back of his neck at close range and in broad daylight. He still considered this killing to be a fully justifiable homicide, a "necessary" evil for his country's liberation. He was proud of his deed, and he felt no empathy for his victim.

Eventually, I was pulled into a more modest role in the underground by an unlikely recruiter, my sister Maroulla! It was a shock to me when I discovered that she was involved with EOKA. I thought that I was the patriot in the family, not her, even though young women did play an important role in the underground. Their tasks were primarily to help with the transport of fugitive EOKA fighters from one part of the island to another. The young British conscripts who were shipped to the island to serve their empire were less likely to conduct thorough searches at checkpoints when a young woman was present in the car. Women also served as mail carriers linking one sector chief to another and to Grivas himself. They hid the messages in their bosoms and panties. Our house became a hub of activity, often playing host to wanted men with a price on their heads. Unavoidably, I came to know many of them. They were only a few years older than myself, and they were inexperienced, so they saw no problem talking in my presence about things I shouldn't have been privy to.

One day I returned from school to find our home taken over by fully armed British commandos and police officers. I trembled in fear. The officer in charge asked me my age. When I told him that I was fourteen he never asked me another question. He apparently thought I was too young to be a terrorist. My youthful pride and sense of honor plummeted. My sister was taken to prison for interrogation, while I was dismissed as a harmless kid.

What would have happened to me had that officer realized how much I knew about the secret organization he was trying to dismantle? What if I had been subjected to severe ("enhanced" is the current euphemism) interrogation methods and began talking, thereby violating the values promoted by our teachers and church leaders who dominated the wider culture? What would have happened to my self-image had I confessed? The underground was merciless to "traitors," even if they provided information under torture or extreme duress. One glaring case as an example: When a brother of two wanted men betrayed the hideout of his brothers after being subjected to torture, the British soldiers surrounded the barn where they were hiding and the brothers were killed in the ensuing shootout, making them heroes in the eyes of Greek Cypriot nationalists. Their tortured and tormented brother, on the other hand, was branded a contemptible traitor. The colonial government flew him to London to prevent his execution. In London, however, he experienced extreme guilt for his betrayal. In despair, he returned to Cyprus and surrendered to the underground organization to be judged and executed if necessary. His former comrades took pity on him and they pleaded with Grivas to spare his life. But in his memoirs, Grivas pointed out that he did not hesitate to order his execution as an example to others. I learned early in my life that revolutionary justice has little to do with real justice and compassion as a habit of the heart.

My sister was released unharmed fifteen days after her arrest. It was my father who eventually paid the price. Two years later there was another major operation by the British to dismantle EOKA. They arrested hundreds of Greek Cypriots as suspects and sent them to concentration camps. My father had little to do with the underground, but it was his patriotic duty not to oppose what his daughter was doing in the secret organization, so he endured sleepless nights waiting for her to return home. It was the middle of that summer when he was rounded up with scores of others. Fortunately, our school was in recess. I was sixteen, and with the help of my sister, I had to become the breadwinner and take over the management of the grocery store.

We had no idea when our father would be released. I was desperate. In fifty days the school year was to begin. I would be in my senior year, hoping to move on to a university career somewhere outside Cyprus, as the Island had no university at the time. If I missed my senior year my fate was sealed. I would wind up a full-time grocer like my father. I dreaded that prospect, but lo and behold, my father was unexpectedly released the day before school started. Elated, I took it as a providential sign.

The underground years were not happy ones for me and most others of my generation. We felt robbed of our youth and forced to face life and death situations that could mark us for life. We spent our teenage years amid bomb explosions, assassinations, ambushes, riots, hangings and curfews. One of my cousins, two years older than I, became a wanted man. He left school in the nick of time in his senior year, running to the mountains to avoid arrest and join other wanted guerrillas.

On several occasions, having my sister as a member of the underground thrust me into the center of the action as a standby hand. Being a "kid," I was sometimes asked to assist in operations that didn't involve direct combat. I had to take a sacred oath and swear allegiance to the struggle for freedom "in the name of the Holy Trinity." I placed my right hand on the New Testament and swore that I would obey whatever orders I was given and never question or betray the underground organization, come what may. I swore that if I did betray any member of EOKA I would be condemned by both God and men in eternity, and I would be fully deserving to be executed as a traitor.

I was asked several times to hide homemade and crudely constructed hand grenades that could easily explode as I handled them. I stored them under my bed, oblivious to the risk, not only of being found out but also of the serious possibility of an accidental explosion. Before long, I dug holes deep in the ground under the lemon tree in our back yard, and I inserted large glass jars containing the grenades and other types of ammunition, covering them with a layer of rubber and dirt to prevent detection. On one occasion I was asked to distribute several hand grenades to three young women, still in high school. They were ordered to ride their bikes and toss the bombs at British patrols. It never occurred to me that somebody might get hurt when I handed them the deadly material. I was too scared and too eager to see the grenades removed from my custody to consider the possible consequences, so I was annoyed when the three 16-year-olds returned them to me and I had to rebury them.

I know of no other instance during the Troubles of teenage girls being asked to become bomb-throwing revolutionaries. I shudder now to think of the consequences if those three teenagers had decided to carry out their mission, which may have resulted in young British soldiers getting killed or maimed, and the impact that would have had on their loved ones and on my own inner world, my conscience, and my sense of self. "I feel a terrible burden in my conscience," a man who is now a grandfather told me. He was 22 when the underground organization initiated him as a leading member of his village. He and another EOKA operative planted a mine in an area of British troop movement. In the explosion, three young soldiers were killed. "At the time I thought I was doing my patriotic duty, but now I feel a terrible shadow, a blemish on my soul." I can easily sympathize with him; I might have been in the same predicament had those three young women kept the hand grenades and carried out their mission.

On another occasion I was asked by an active member of the underground, a local barber, to transport the empty shell of an airplane bomb. I had to carry it on my bike for three miles across Nicosia through narrow streets patrolled by the police and British paratroopers. It was so heavy I could hardly keep the bike straight. "You are only 15," he explained to me. "If you are arrested you are not likely to hang, but I am 20; if they catch me I will definitely face the gallows. So, I will ride in front of you with my own bike, and if I see a military block ahead I will signal with my left foot so that you can turn around in time." I was terrified but I agreed to do it. The colonial government did, in fact, hang several young men, including a 17-year-old, who was transporting a machine gun, empty of bullets, also on his bike.

One night I sneaked into the yard of our local elementary school and hastily replaced the British flag with the Greek one—another forbidden act. In the morning, to my great embarrassment and to the laughter of passersby, I noticed that the Greek flag was flying upside down. On another occasion I took part in a riot organized by older boys in my school. We intended to throw rocks at passing British patrols. That was the most violent act I directly committed. When a military jeep full of troops rounded the corner towards us, we threw our rocks and then ran as the soldiers chased us with shields and clubs. I remember closing my eyes as I threw the rock, making a wish that it would not land on anyone's head. As a result of that riot, our school was the first to be shut down. It remained closed for several weeks as a form of collective punishment. I carried out these "revolutionary" acts with neither pride nor fearlessness. It was a matter of obedience, patriotic duty, and peer pressure. I had not as yet developed enough critical thinking abilities to question those orders. We believed our leaders to be infallible no matter what they ordered us to do and no matter what choices they made.

I was greatly relieved when there were truces between EOKA and the colonial government in attempts to resolve the problem peacefully, and I was disappointed when the truces ended. I yearned for peace, but all around me there was violence that seemed never-ending, utterly unnecessary, and politically counterproductive.

PATRIOTS, TRAITORS, AND RULES

Grivas was the quintessential ascetic rebel, a fanatical moralist who left his wife in Athens and hid himself in Cypriot caves for four years, issuing orders to his fighters. He held steadfastly to certain rules and understandings, including the notion that the underground had no quarrel with the British people. The enemy was the colonial administration. Therefore, the fighters of EOKA rarely bothered or targeted British civilians. As a rule, Grivas and his young lieutenants adopted codes of military honor that precluded the killing of women, children and civilian noncombatants, much like the Irish Republican Army during the twenties under Michael Collins.

I was told that Grivas refused to allow women to join the mountain paramilitaries because he didn't wish "to seed the mountains with bastard babies." He enforced strict rules throughout the underground against sexual or romantic entanglements. Love and guerrilla warfare should not mix. Only love for the revolution should fill one's heart and mind. If you were a sworn member of the underground and contemplated engagement or marriage during those troubled years of 1955–1959, you had to resign from active duty. Single young men and women had to relate to each other purely as brothers and sisters.

If a member of EOKA got involved sexually with the daughter or the wife of a person offering hospitality and a safe house to guerrillas, the ultimate punishment was swift. I learned of an 18-year-old mountain guerrilla who had an extramarital affair with the wife of his host. The execution order from "the Leader" arrived promptly, and his comrades-in-arms had to carry out the killing. But the letter containing the order got into the hands of the prospective victim while the others were away from their hideout. Knowing there would be no mercy for violating the sex code, he set up an ambush of his own and waited for his friends to return. He shot them both and then surrendered at the nearest police station. To save his life the British flew him to London.

Many questions flooded my young mind when I learned about this instance, and not simply concerning the brutality of the leader's order. Why did this guerrilla have to kill his friends and former comrades? Why didn't he just surrender to the police and spare their lives? The total lack of compassion among these fighting heroes inflamed my doubts about the wisdom of the entire underground operation, with its bizarre moral codes. There was no one with whom I could talk about it, as everyone around me was certain of the infallibility of the "Leader." I once confided my reservations about the morality of such acts to an EOKA fighter who frequented our home, and I was severely reprimanded. To question orders or doubt the wisdom of the leader was an act of disobedience. Obeying orders was the sign of total commitment to the underground organization and its goals. Ironically, we had always prided ourselves as the inheritors of the greatness of our ancient ancestors, who elevated critical philosophical thought to the highest levels, yet now we were behaving like unquestioning conformists and killing robots.

Sexual misconduct apparently brought on the death penalty for another young EOKA patriot whom I knew personally. Lean and fragile-looking, lacking the features we might associate with a fearsome revolutionary or a Don Juan, he simply disappeared one day. His father, a priest, searched desperately and fruitlessly for his son's grave; he was hungry for justice. One morning he rushed into our church during Sunday service, climbed up on the throne reserved for visiting bishops, and began thundering with maniacal frenzy against his son's former comrades, naming them as his murderers. Even though he had interrupted the service, nobody tried to stop him, not even the presiding priest. Everybody listened in sadness and silence until the poor man stepped down from the bishop's throne, utterly exhausted. Compounding the tragedy, the son's legacy as a freedom fighter had become permanently tarnished. He was now a traitor, bringing shame to his entire family. There were unconfirmed rumors that his former friends and comrades, after receiving the order from "the Leader," forced him one night to dig his own grave and then beat him to death with shovels because their pistol did not work.

The principal targets of EOKA were British soldiers in uniform and Greek Cypriot traitors, including police officers who remained loyal to the colonial administration. The first known assassination of a "traitor" was a Greek Cypriot policeman, so my sister's friend Nikos, himself a policeman, could easily have become a major target, had he not joined the underground. Given his position as an employee of the Special Branch, the equivalent of the American FBI, he became a valuable mole for EOKA.

Like several other members of the underground organization, Nikos was a frequent visitor to our home. We became friends and I enjoyed a special relationship with him. He would pick me up on his motorcycle to go swimming with his friends at the northern coast, near Kyrenia. They all treated me like a kid brother. I learned later that Nikos's frequent visits to our home were prompted by more than friendship with our family and underground business. He was also coming to see Stella, my sister's close friend, with whom he was passionately in love. In spite of Grivas' ascetic moralism and punitive stance towards sexual relations, romances did, unsurprisingly, pop up on occasion. Stella often helped my sister escort wanted men from one part of the island to another. Nikos's romance with Stella's might have cost him his life because of a rival suitor who spread rumors that Nikos was a double agent. Had it not been for my sister who intervened just in time, Nikos would have been killed as a traitor. Instead, the dejected suitor, who became a wanted man, blew himself up while making homemade bombs. It was officially reported as an accident. Others claimed it may have been a suicide. Nikos never forgot that he owed his life to my sister.

Another episode that shocked me deeply was the case of Alex, a proprietor of a grocery store. Tall, handsome, impeccably dressed in his three-piece suits, and fluent in English, he could have passed for an English gentleman. Indeed, his clientele was mostly British. He frequented British pubs and spent his leisure time fraternizing with British expatriates. Apparently unaware of the dangers he faced, he never tried to hide his pro-British sentiments. In time, he developed a reputation among Greek Cypriot nationalists of being a *philanglos* (friend of the British), a deadly reputation in those dark years. When people warned him about the perils of his fraternizing, he replied with a defiant foolishness, "I am afraid of no one." One day an EOKA executioner came into his shop. Realizing what was about to happen, Alex ran frantically away from his shop, the gunman in close pursuit. Alex was found face down on the pavement some thirty yards away dying from three bullets in his back. He left a pregnant wife and an unborn son.

Alex's father was one of the two parish priests who served our community. He was universally loved by his parishioners. Every Easter, he would end the long celebratory service with the traditional proclamation of "*Christos Anesti*" (Christ is Risen) followed by the wish, "*Kai tou chronou eleftheroi*" ("May we be free next year!"). Like most Greek Cypriots he was mesmerized with the mantra that we were slaves, and our redemption would be the union of our island with "Mother Greece." But now his son had been marked and killed as a traitor, and no one came to the funeral other than the aging priest himself and his religiously devout and noted philanthropist daughter. Through their windows the frightened parishioners, including myself, watched mutely as the white-bearded priest walked slowly by, weeping profusely, his right hand on the casket pulled by two black horses on the way to the cemetery. No one came out of their front door to offer condolences to this exemplary man who had served his community with such devotion for decades. Within a year the grief-stricken priest was dead, never having recovered from the double tragedy of losing his son and the stigma of his execution as a traitor.

Alex's assassin, for his part, claimed to his comrades that he felt more remorse about the damage he had inflicted on his victim's tailor-made suit than about the life he had taken. Every time he killed a "traitor," he scratched a notch on the wooden handle of his revolver—much like a gunslinger of the American Wild West—to remind him of his prowess. His number of victims was 27 by the time the Troubles ended. Addicted to blood lust, he went around describing with relish his orgiastic feelings as he assassinated people and watched their blood spurt out. "When the struggle is over," he confided to a group of his horrified comrades, "I will have to cut the throats of chickens so that I can see the blood running."

REFLECTIONS ON KILLING AND DYING

None of the EOKA fighters I knew were bloodthirsty or clinically pathological like Alex's assassin, but being in a fighting group meant that you sometimes did have to make your peace with killing. Andreas was a 17-year-old who was recruited into one such group and took part in the killing of several Greek Cypriot "traitors." A senior and an athlete in high school when he began his underground career, Andreas was recruited by an activist priest who reassured him that the struggle was sacred. I asked him years later when he reached his forties and was a member of the emerging urban bourgeois class, "What was it like as a teenager to kill a human being?" He replied, "At first it was extremely difficult. On my first execution I was so tense that I felt like I was in a thick fog. I couldn't see clearly. I pulled the trigger, threw the gun away, and ran through the streets as fast as I could. I must have broken an Olympic record. After that it became easier." Once the Struggle was over his conscience was bothering him, and he made an appointment for confession with the same priest who had recruited him. When he described his work in the underground, the confessor told him somberly that he had committed mortal sins and needed sustained penances and prayers to wipe out the fatal blemishes on his soul. Andreas left the confessional disgusted, now seeing his former recruiter as a hypocrite. He resolved the contradiction by renouncing the Church altogether, remaining loyal to the memory of the Struggle as sacred, and never again questioning, as far as I know, the morality of what he had done as a Greek patriot.

Another former member of a fighting group dealt with these contradictions in the opposite way. He became devoutly religious after meeting Father Maximos, the young and charismatic spiritual guide who eventually became central to my study of Greek Orthodox spirituality. With nurturing guidance from the Father, this former urban guerrilla spent much of his time doing volunteer and philanthropic work at a monastery, and he lived like a lay monk, working towards the salvation of his soul.

My most complex understanding of living with killing, along with other challenges created by my EOKA experiences, came from Phidias Symeonides. He was the surrogate older brother I never had, and along with my sister and my father, his influence on me was enormous. Phidias was a migrant from the mountain village of *Lagoudera,* not far from my father's village. An exceptionally bright and promising student, he had ambitions to attend the University of Athens after graduation and study Greek literature. Coming from a poor family, however, he lacked the means to fulfill his dream. Deeply disheartened, the 18-year-old found employment as my father's helper at the grocery store. I looked up to Phidias. He tutored me in Greek, both ancient and modern, and he helped me with mathematics.

I never suspected that Phidias was also a member of EOKA while he was working for my father. I learned about it when his secret became known to the police and, as was the practice of those whose cover was betrayed, he fled and joined the mountain guerrillas. Despite a quiet and humble demeanor, he was highly regarded as an EOKA fighter. His guerrilla band was headed by the second-in-command of the organization, Gregory Afxentiou, a 28-year-old who, like Grivas, had served in the Greek army. Afxentiou's mountain hideout near the Macheras Monastery was eventually betrayed. During a major operation, thousands of British soldiers surrounded them. The officer in charge ordered all of them to surrender with their hands up. Afxentiou ordered his comrades to do so while he stayed behind to fight it out, knowing full well that his decision was hopelessly suicidal. The British soldiers, after several hours of exchanging shots, lost one of their own. As Afxentiou shouted back Spartan cries of defiance, they poured gasoline over his hideout and burned him alive. His sacrifice became a legend among Greek Cypriot nationalists, who honored him as a patriot worthy of emulation and the foremost hero of the four-year rebellion. When the Troubles ended, a huge statue was erected at the spot of his martyrdom, and it became a focal point of celebratory, patriotic rituals.

I was desperate and depressed when I heard the news. Phidias and his comrades were on the front page of the morning papers, shown with their hands up, facing the barrels of their captors' guns. The colonial government showed no mercy to those caught armed and fighting their troops. Routinely, after all appeals were exhausted for condemned EOKA fighters, the British military governor Sir John Harding would announce, "the law must follow its course." I dreaded that Phidias would suffer a ghastly fate, the same fate as the other young men who were sent to the gallows chanting hymns to the Holy Virgin and singing the Greek national anthem. Fortunately, and to my great relief, a ceasefire was declared soon after Phidias' arrest, and negotiations began to yield a solution to the Cyprus Problem. The British decided to leave Cyprus, and in accordance with the Zurich and London Agreements of 1959, the Republic of Cyprus was created—a new member of the United Nations (a "reluctant republic," as someone dubbed it). The *Enosis* dream of union with Greece was suspended once Turkish Cypriot and Turkey's opposition began to trigger vicious intercommunal violence in 1958 and Greek and Turkish Cypriots began killing each other. Most of those who fought for Enosis, however, lamented the loss of purpose in their lives. They felt that their sacrifices had amounted to nothing. Some of them blamed the Archbishop who, as head of the Greek community, signed the agreements. They accused him of treachery, opening the way for later political upheavals and tragedies.

Phidias and the other political prisoners were freed after the signing of the agreements. Those who were still hiding in the mountains were given unconditional amnesty. They came down from the mountains and were welcomed as heroes by deliriously enthusiastic and admiring crowds. The former fighters paraded in formation in downtown Nicosia wearing their black berets and guerrilla uniforms, many proudly displaying their revolutionary mustaches. They were showered with rose petals.

Unlike a number of leading EOKA guerrillas, Phidias refused to take advantage of his hero status. Other comrades enriched themselves in one way or another. Some, with no real administrative experience or maturity of age, acquired excessive power in the new state. Phidias barely survived in obscurity, however, unable to get assistance for an ailment that disabled him and that eventually cost him his life. The damp and harsh conditions of life in mountain caves and the severe beatings he received from the soldiers who arrested him affected his spinal cord. A few years after the end of the struggle he was found by a former comrade dead in his shack.

Back when he was released from prison, I asked Phidias why he joined the EOKA underground. He gave me two reasons—his love for Greece and his disappointment that he could not continue his studies. "Once I realized I couldn't go to university, I plunged wholeheartedly into the Struggle to forget my dream and find a new purpose in my life."

This thoughtful and deeply intelligent man might have ended up a professor of Greek literature had he not been poor, but he wound up only with a statue in his native village, honoring his legacy as a selfless freedom fighter. I could not control my tears when decades later, and for the first time, I visited the village on the Troodos Mountains and stood mute, contemplating his statue at the center of the square.

I never asked Phidias if he had participated in combat or caused the death of anyone. I could not fathom him doing so. I remember his sincere attempt while working for my father to calm down the anxieties of Mr. Donaldson, an expatriate Briton who lived next door to us, taught English, spoke impeccable Greek, and was a customer of my father. Phidias reassured Mr. Donaldson that "as far as he knew," the underground would not bother him because they did not target British civilians. In fact, Mr. Donaldson did survive the four-year emergency without harm, and he continued teaching English and riding his green bicycle in his white suit, sun grasses and straw hat.

I was surprised by the passing comment Phidias made to me one day as he reminisced about the tragic shootout that caused the death of his leader. "I wished," he said, "I stayed with Afxentiou and died with him." The dream of *Enosis* had become his only bedrock for a meaningful life. Another former EOKA fighter echoed this sentiment. "Those were glorious years," he lamented. "We knew who we were, why we lived, and why we were fighting. Our lives had meaning and each of us was ready to die for each other and for the cause we fought for. Look at me now! I am buying and selling land. How meaningful can that be?"

TAKING STOCK OF THE REBELLION

The official narrative of these underground warriors was that they were champions of their Greek heritage, driven only by selfless devotion to their just cause. But the dark underside of EOKA activities in those years continued to chip away at my own acceptance of the methods they used to fight the British. And later, as I integrated myself into multicultural America, it became easier to separate myself from what I now saw as massive and destructive collective delusions. I came to realize that there are certain values embedded in human existence that we violate only at the expense of our humanity, values articulated in the Golden Rule, in Jesus' teachings at the Sermon on the Mount, and within other great philosophical or religious traditions.

I do believe that under extraordinary circumstances, one must sometimes use force, as in the case of fighting Nazis during the Second World War. I can appreciate the heroic action of the German Lutheran pastor and theologian Dietrich Bonhoeffer, who resisted the Nazis and paid with his life after participating in the failed plot to assassinate Hitler and save millions of innocent lives. But other than in such extreme circumstances, the best way to fight injustice is to follow Gandhi's method of nonviolent resistance. The decolonization of Cyprus did not necessitate a violent uprising. The British were not Nazis, and sooner or later they would leave Cyprus, like they did in other colonial possessions such as Malta and Hong Kong. Our leaders, headed by none other than the Archbishop, were on the wrong side of history.[4]

The overwhelming majority of the young people who took part in the Cypriot underground were warm, selfless, idealistic and honorable young men and women who saw themselves as soldiers fighting for liberation from "the British yoke." Unfortunately, they received nothing but encouragement and even participation from leading Orthodox clergymen. The Archbishop, after all, was the chief conspirator, giving money and support early on for the creation of EOKA. He never openly renounced violence as a means of achieving nationalist goals, so it was curious, once the anticolonial struggle ended, that he commissioned and installed a statue of Mahatma Gandhi at the central park in downtown Nicosia. Several former EOKA chiefs were infuriated. Was this act a sign of the Archbishop's regret for decisions that unleashed so much violence and suffering in the lives of his fellow Cypriots? We will never know.

Coming of age in a troubled island left me with gnawing questions. How could my teenage generation find itself in an underground movement? How could we take lives away and give up our own for the sake of the dream of *Enosis?* How could we so unquestioningly follow orders issued by anonymous leaders who hid in caves and cellars, men whom we had never met and knew nothing about? Of course, the simple answer is that we were conditioned by our teachers, our religious leaders, and our overall culture to believe in the sacredness of the nationalist cause. *Enosis* offered direction and meaning to youth at the age when teenagers most need direction. The primary motivation of human beings, writes Viktor Frankl in his classic *Man's Search for Meaning,* is neither the pursuit of pleasure, as Freud claims, nor the will to power as Adler assumes, but the search for a meaningful existence.[5] Eric Fromm adds that we need a frame of orientation that transcends our limited ego attachments.[6] Young Cypriots were ready to kill and to die for what was a narrow tribal mindset, which triumphed for several years over the teachings of Christ. Years later, as I matured in America, I concluded that the only meaningful path is to follow the Socratic injunction to "know thyself," free of the cultural and ideological contaminants that we confuse for Reality. Ignorance of our own inner depths makes us vulnerable to destructive beliefs that masquerade as promises of a meaningful life.

Trying to explain the Holocaust, sociologist Fred E. Katz, a survivor himself of that ghastly episode in world history, wrote of the "cunning of governments"—their tendency to glorify their policies and seduce good people to commit horrendous acts that would be unthinkable under normal circumstances. I would add that all systems of domination have a tendency to sacralize their power. The greatest atrocities in history were committed not by sadistic and malicious psychopaths but by ordinary people convinced by their leaders to do extraordinary evil in the pursuit of tribal or nationalist goals.[7]

The tragedy of the Cyprus debacle was that it was ethically questionable and totally unnecessary. All that was needed was some elementary wisdom and some historical discernment on the part of the various power elites. It was difficult for me to forgive what the higher clergy in Cyprus did to the Island, consciously or unconsciously. I lost faith in my religion for some time, defining myself as "spiritual but not religious" until I realized that there is another, more mystical side to the Orthodox Christian religion. But I am getting ahead of the story.

MORAL RE-ARMAMENT

Growing up in Cyprus during the fifties had a lasting impact on my life, especially because of the intensity of my connections with the circle of people who went through similar experiences. Though I spent most of the rest of my life away from the Island, these connections cemented me emotionally to my native culture. As the German sociologist Georg Simmel noted, social conflict often leads to the integration of society by intensifying the attachments between human beings.[8] The American warriors who fought the Nazis continued to feel a close affinity for one another as "bands of brothers" decades after the war ended. A former Vietnam veteran, a colleague, once told me, "The people I feel closest to in my life are those who fought with me in the jungles of Vietnam. They are the only ones who can really understand me." A female veteran of the Cypriot rebellion, an aging friend of my sister, said: "I feel sorry for people who did not share the intensity of emotions that we felt fighting as members of EOKA for the liberation of Cyprus. Those were the best years of my life." They were not the best years of *my* life, but they did keep me emotionally attached to the Island and to the people with whom I shared intense, shattering, and often heartbreaking experiences.

Life is full of surprises and unexpected twists. My sister helped to turn me into a reluctant and unlikely freedom fighter, but she also was instrumental in triggering the preconditions for my life in America. Paradoxical as it may sound, the latter would not have happened without my life in the underground, and I am deeply grateful for that.

Soon after the EOKA struggle was over and the peace accord signed, several representatives of a quasi-religious and nondenominational international organization known as Moral Re-Armament (MRA) visited the Island. Their mission was to recruit Greek Cypriots who were involved in the EOKA uprising, and Turkish Cypriots who participated in the TMT, the Turkish counterpart whose members fought against the Greeks. The plan was to fly them to their two centers for a special international conference where Greek and Turkish Cypriots, along with others of different nationalities, would get to know one another. These religious peace activists wanted to expose traditional enemies to an alternative "Gandhian" way of solving political problems, one that centered on four moral absolutes: "honesty, unselfishness, purity and love." There was also a big dose of anticommunist propaganda. This was the height of the Cold War, following the death of Stalin and the ascent to power of Nikita Khrushchev in the Soviet Union.

One of the MRA centers was a mountain resort in Switzerland, and the other was on Mackinac Island in the middle of Lake Huron, bordering Michigan and Canada. MRA agents claimed that their organization helped negotiate the Zurich and London Agreements that ended British colonialism and established the Republic of Cyprus. None of us paid much attention to these claims, as we assumed they were just fanciful notions intended to help us take the group seriously. But Greeks and Turks alike welcomed the idea of a paid vacation to these distant and exotic-sounding centers.

My sister was one of the first recruits, along with several EOKA big wigs and their Turkish Cypriot counterparts. They spent time at both of these centers so that former enemies might become cooperative friends, a prerequisite for the Republic of Cyprus having a peaceful future. That was in 1959, just after the agreements were signed, when hostile feelings between the two ethnic groups were still alarmingly raw. I was about to enter my senior year in high school, and financial limitations stood in the way of my continuing with my schooling after graduation. My sister's visit to Mackinac Island changed everything, thanks to what happened after that conference ended.

We had relatives in America: three uncles who were brothers of my late mother, and a sister. They had begun migrating to the New World during the "Roaring Twenties." Two of them became small-scale entrepreneurs; one owned a florist shop in New York and the other a grocery in Youngstown, Ohio. Their younger brother became a well-paid steel worker, also in Youngstown. After the end of World War II and a year after my mother died, they brought over one of their sisters, my Aunt Eleni, from Cyprus. She joined her two brothers in Ohio where she married another Cypriot émigré, a baker. The only memory I had of Aunt Eleni was at the docks of Limassol as she was about to board the ship for her transatlantic voyage. As a five-year-old I remember holding my father with one hand and waving a white handkerchief with the other, bidding her farewell. Tearful relatives sang goodbye melodies as the boat left the harbor. Before the jet age, an immigrant's journey often meant separation from relatives for life, with little realistic hope of seeing them again. For example, I had never met my uncles who migrated to the USA before I was born, as they had never revisited their homeland. Our contacts with our American kin were sparse, formal, and limited to letters on special occasions related to marriages, childbirths, and funerals. It had never crossed my mind that I might join them and study in America. My ambitions for a university career went as far as 600 miles west to Athens and 100 miles east to Lebanon. The majority of Greek Cypriots went to Greece for university study, although those with economic means sometimes studied in England or, closer to home, at the American University of Beirut. As for me, I had no means to study anywhere. My father had no money to send me abroad and my prospects for a university career were more wishful thinking than realistic possibility. Following in the footsteps of my father—selling and delivering groceries—was the likely reality awaiting me after graduation.

My sister was invited by our relatives in Ohio to spend a few days with them after the MRA conference on Mackinac Island was over. She took the bus to Youngstown to meet them. While chatting about family matters they inquired about my age and my life plans. Because I was defined as an orphan, the son of their deceased sister, they were sympathetic to my situation. In no time, Aunt Eleni had filled out the necessary immigration papers to get me a student visa so that I could join them in Ohio and begin my studies at the local university. Without Mackinac Island, without my sister's visit to Youngstown, Ohio, and without the generosity of my relatives, particularly Aunt Eleni, I would never have crossed the Atlantic in 1960. And none of this would have happened if my sister had not joined the Cypriot underground!

In addition to this exciting turn of events there was another surprise. The MRA recruiters, while negotiating my sister's visits to America and Switzerland, reached out to me and Petros, a boyhood friend and neighbor who was just being released from the concentration camps. He had been locked up for several months as a terrorist suspect. The MRA agents offered us tickets, as former EOKA youth, to spend a couple of weeks at their center in Switzerland and learn about the Four Absolutes and the ways of Mahatma Gandhi! My friend was 18 and I was 16. For us it was an exciting opportunity for a trip to Switzerland. That was our real motivation, not learning about the objectives of MRA or how to make peace with the Turks, our primordial enemies. I had never been in an airplane before and had never traveled outside of Cyprus. The thrill of a magical journey to the center of Europe was nothing short of an Alice-in-Wonderland adventure. Fortuitously, it was also an opportunity to practice my high school English, which of course would be helpful once I arrived in America.

Moral Re-Armament became my baptismal experience into a multicultural, multireligious, and pluralistic world, the world that I was destined to inhabit for the rest of my life. In a magnificent grand hotel at the foothills of the Alps at *Caux sur Montreux,* overlooking Geneva Lake near Lausanne, we met representatives from just about all the troubled spots of the world. There were Africans wearing their native costumes, some of them former Mau Mau warriors from Kenya. There were Indians and Pakistanis with their turbans and saris, plus a music band of three brothers who gave up a lucrative singing career in California to join the organization and entertain participants with their peace ballads.

It was the period of the end of colonialism, although the Algerian revolt and the Battle of Algiers against France were still raging. There were representatives of both Algerian rebels and French generals who, before arriving at Caux, were busily working to exterminate one another. At the MRA hotel we saw them having tea and engaging in civilized conversation, trying to understand one another. It was surreal. There were also representatives from the conflicting sides of other African countries and from parts of the world that we had never heard of before our arrival to Switzerland.

Neither I nor my friend knew much at this point about the involvement and perhaps importance of this organization in world affairs, particularly for the process of reconciliation between the Germans and the French that had paved the way for a new and more peaceful Europe. The movement hosted many world leaders as well as ordinary youngsters like ourselves. Oxford University welcomed the movement so that the MRA people were often referred to as the "Oxford Group." Its American founder, Frank Buchman, a pastor who claimed he had a mystical epiphany on how to bring about world peace, hoped that the world would avoid war if individuals experienced a moral and spiritual awakening. MRA got impressive praises from a string of luminaries and hosted the likes of German Chancellor Konrad Adenauer and French Foreign Minister Robert Schuman that seemingly contributed towards Franco-German reconciliation after the war.

It surprised me to learn later on that in 1960, the year Cyprus became an independent state, Archbishop Makarios, the first Greek Cypriot president of the new republic, and Dr. Fazil Kucuk, his Turkish Vice-President, jointly sent the first flag of independent Cyprus to Frank Buchman. They did so in recognition of his behind-the-scenes help in establishing the new state. I realized then that our friends from the MRA who sent us to Caux were not boasting about their importance unjustifiably. But I could also understand why several hard-core EOKA chiefs who were guests at Caux were not happy with MRA's role in the peace accord and the ensuing formation of the new republic. They had fought for *Enosis*—union with "Mother Greece"—not a new and separate state. Independence was not their goal. Alas, intercommunal fighting between Greeks and Turks resumed on the island four years later, once again tormenting the lives of both Greek and Turkish Cypriots and continuing to this day.

The magnificent mountain resort hotel at Caux gave to me and my friend a crash course in international relations and global awareness. It also exposed us to strange and sometimes uncomfortable routines, such as daily morning meditation to open ourselves to "God's Guidance." It was a novel experience to see members of the organization voluntarily stand in front of hundreds of international strangers and publicly confess their past errors and sins. In graphic detail, they would reveal intimate aspects of their lives and the way that their participation in MRA had transformed them. The founder of MRA believed that peace on earth is possible only after one begins to systematically work on oneself, hence the daily practice of morning inner self-exploration based on the Four Absolutes of honesty, unselfishness, purity, and love.

I sensed as a teenager at Caux that I had encountered something important, but I realized only later just how significant it was for my development. This was my first exposure to reconciliation as a process, with my native Cyprus clearly in the spotlight, along with other war-torn and troubled regions of the world. Much later, after Turkey invaded Cyprus in 1974 and took over the northern part of the island previously inhabited by Greek Cypriots, I and my friend Petros became involved in further attempts at reconciliation and ethnic understanding. I also got involved in various organizations and forums to promote understanding between the world's religions and to bridge the rift between religion and science. It was as if the MRA kick-started my life's hidden agenda. It was also the beginning of cleansing my inner world from the darkness of the underground years. And little did I know that those strange morning meditation practices I observed back then foreshadowed my later attraction to meditation and healing practices, both personally and in the realms of research and teaching.

NOTES

1. Lawrence Durrell, *Bitter Lemons* (Edinburg, VA: Axios Press, 2009).
2. Kyriacos C. Markides, *The Rise and Fall of the Cyprus Republic* (New Haven: Yale University Press, 1977), p.18.
3. George Grivas, *Guerrilla Warfare and EOKA's Struggle: A Politico-Military Study*, trans A.A. Pallis (London: Longmans, Green 1964), pp.14–15.
4. For a sociological historical context of the Cypriot rebellion see my *Rise and Fall of the Cyprus Republic*. Op.cit.
5. Viktor Frankl, *Man's Search for Meaning* (Boston: Beacon Press, 2006).
6. Eric Fromm, *The Anatomy of Human Destructiveness* (New York: Holt Paperbacks, 1992).
7. Fred E. Katz *Ordinary People and Extraordinary Evil: A Report on the Beguilings of Evil* (Albany: State University of New York Press, 1993).
8. Georg Simmel, *Conflict and the Web of Group Affiliations* (New York: Free Press, 1955).

Chapter 2

Accidental Immigrant

THROUGH THE PILLARS OF HERCULES

Until the sixties, mass migration from Europe to the New World took place mostly via ocean liners. Unlike today, it was not the leisure class who crossed the Atlantic on passenger ships but the less affluent in search of a better life. Air travel was new, and too expensive for ordinary travelers. In July of 1960, a few months before Cyprus officially became an independent republic, I boarded a ship in Limassol for passage to America. The vessel docked first in Beirut, then passed by Port Said in Egypt, then Alexandria, and finally Piraeus in Greece. A brief stay with family friends in Athens enabled me to pay homage to the Parthenon, and then I boarded the ocean liner "*Queen Frederica*" for the big crossing. It was one of its last voyages before it was sold for scraps. In a couple of years jet travel would replace ships as the most economic mode of world travel.

Loaded with Greek immigrants, the *Queen Frederica* stopped by Naples to fill its remaining cabins with Italians before passing through the straits of Gibraltar, the mythic "Pillars of Hercules." There were few if any tourists on board. Unlike the tragic *Titanic*, the Greek ship was certainly not a luxury liner. I may have been the only passenger who headed west for strictly educational purposes, a "Non-Immigrant Alien," according to my visa status. Everyone else was earnestly looking forward to a new life in the Promised Land, as shown by the thunderous applause when a large American flag appeared on the boat's movie screen in a documentary about the United States. I thought, "These folks have become Americanized even before reaching New York!" This was my first glimpse of the extraordinary power of American society to assimilate its immigrants.

Crossing the Mediterranean and then the Atlantic was a bittersweet experience. During the almost three-week journey from Cyprus to New York, I vacillated between great expectations and gnawing anxieties about what awaited me in a foreign land. Can I make it in America? Do I know enough English to start university studies? Am I smart enough? Or am I destined for

27

failure, forced to return to Cyprus in utter humiliation for myself and my family? Coming from a "shame culture," as anthropologists would say, the thought of coming back home with no shiny credentials was chilling. I never dreamed that I was destined to spend the rest of my life away from Cyprus, my beloved "Ithaca."

I had no worries about meeting my American relatives, who would surely be much like my Cyprus aunts, uncles, and cousins who showered me with support and affection. My anxieties centered mainly on my separation from close friends and relatives I left behind. Switzerland had been a minor foretaste of this separation. Living with hundreds of international strangers never disrupted the certainty that I would soon return to the emotional safety of home. My Atlantic crossing changed everything. I would not see my friends and relatives in Cyprus for at least four years—the time needed to complete an undergraduate degree in America. I barely had enough money to get by. My American relatives would provide me food and shelter, but my father had to send me pocket money and cover tuition, books, and other university expenses, a big financial burden. Traveling back and forth to Cyprus during summers or holidays was out of the question.

Crossing the Atlantic in mid-summer was smooth and uneventful. The seas from Piraeus to Halifax, our first port of entry in the New World, were calm and balmy. What excitement I experienced was thanks to daily Greek and Italian dances in the evening and ping pong during the day, a skill I had acquired at my father's soccer club. I was the proud winner of the trip's tournament.

Another distraction from morbid thoughts of separation came from the antics of my two cabin mates. One was a short, bespectacled, balding young physician from Crete. Fresh out of medical school, he looked forward to a new life with his sister's family in Toronto. He always wore a summery three-piece suit and a tie, confirming his new status. I could empathize with his nostalgia for his island and his ambivalent feelings about abandoning Greece. He brought on board a large, tin pot full of high-quality olive oil from his native village in Crete, along with an equally large pot of water he had collected from the public fountain there. He treated it like an *agiasma*— holy water—used by Greek Orthodox priests to sprinkle the faithful during Epiphany and to exorcise demons.

My second shipmate was a longshoreman from Piraeus who never stopped cursing at the slowness of our *kolovaporo* (ass-of-a-boat) as he was fond of calling the *Queen Frederica*. A self-identified adventurer, he remained supremely confident of his seductive charms and his irresistibility. He had an unyielding obsession with Italian women of any age or status, though I never saw tangible evidence of his success as a Don Juan.

In their dissimilarity, my accidental companions teamed up to provide me ample amusement and comic relief, and I felt fortunate to have known them as my shipmates. They deflected my noxious thoughts about my separation from home and my future in a strange land. Relief and amusement also came from the excitable Greeks and Italians who considered each other cultural kinfolk, "*una fatsa, una ratsa*" (same face, same race) as the Italians put it. As groups, they constantly outdid each other in farcical encounters. Only a Federico Fellini could have captured in film the many episodes of hilarity unfolding on the *Queen Frederica* between the two geographical neighbors, briefly enemy combatants during World War II, and now aspiring fellow Americans.

ON THE DOCKS OF NEW YORK

There was a thick fog covering the Manhattan landscape the morning of our arrival at New York Harbor, so we were unable to marvel at the Statue of Liberty, that welcoming icon of Americanism. After passing through customs, I was warmly welcomed by my uncle Angelo, a lean, bespectacled gentleman with an effortless smile. I immediately felt comfortable with him, as if I had known him since childhood. I soon forged a close connection with Cousin Mary, three years my senior, and Aunt Loula, my uncle's wife, a native of Odysseus's Ithaca.

Uncle Angelo came to New York when ethnic differences and styles were not easily tolerated. There was prejudice and discrimination not only against African Americans and Latinos but also against Eastern and Southern Europeans. "No Greeks or Dogs Allowed," said a sign outside a Chicago restaurant in a documentary film I had seen about early 20th Century Greek Americans.

My uncles were burdened with difficult-to-pronounce names. As with many immigrants, anglicizing their names was a way of passing as members of the majority. From Vangelis Nicolaides my New York uncle became Angelo Nick. His younger brother from Soterios Nicolaides became Steve Nick while their oldest brother went from Nicolaos Charalambous to Nick Harry. That way they could more easily advance their careers and fulfill the American Dream of middle-class comfort.

Unlike my uncles' experience, I arrived in America after the Second World War, when American society was more pluralistic, culturally diverse, and tolerant of differences. I never experienced any prejudice or discrimination within the cultural perimeters of the American university. I felt no incentive to anglicize my name and begin introducing myself as "Charlie," the presumed American equivalent of "Kyriacos."

During my first night in New York, I shared family news with Uncle Angelo and his family. I conveyed greetings from his two Cyprus sisters whom he had not seen for decades. I could not answer his avalanche of questions about people he knew in Cyprus, all of them already dead when I was born. Before long we were watching *Gunsmoke*, the popular western TV serial of the sixties. This was my introduction to American television and pop entertainment. I then spent the rest of the evening going over black and white family photos saved by Aunt Loula over her years in America. These included a marriage photo of my parents with my mother's fond wishes to her brother and sister-in-law. Aunt Loula then reminisced about her life in New York. She migrated to America with her parents at the age of 17 and soon met and married my uncle Angelo. She spoke with nostalgia about Greece—her early life in Ithaca and her failed attempt to revisit it in the 1950s. Years later, she was still talking about it not long before she died at 100. As the boat entered the harbor a massive earthquake struck the legendary island, forcing the ship to turn back before any passengers had stepped on land.

STEEL TOWN, USA

The few days I spent with my New York relatives in Riverdale were enough to forge deep and lifelong bonds with them, and I would regularly revisit them. But now it was mid-August, and time to board the train to Youngstown, Ohio, my final destination. Uncle Steve, the steel worker, waited for me there at the station. He welcomed me with the same warmth as his older brother in New York and then drove me to the home of Aunt Eleni, who likewise received me as if I were her long-lost son. She had left Cyprus in 1948 when I was five and she was 35. That year she had married Uncle Jordan, a Cypriot immigrant living in Ohio and a friend of my uncles there. Jordan had come back to his native island just this once, in search of a bride. It was another arranged marriage; he arrived one morning at our house dressed in suit and tie, wearing a gentleman's hat, and carrying a letter of introduction drafted by her brothers in Ohio.

My relatives in Youngstown took turns housing and feeding me during the first three years of my life in America. They were like a second extended family; their daughters were much younger than I, and they became my surrogate sisters. Everyone made me feel like part of their family; I was a full participant in the rituals associated with Greek culture such as Christmas and Easter celebrations. I also joined them at gatherings with other immigrant Greek and Greek Cypriot families. It was soothing to be embraced by so many family and family-like people during my initial entry into American life.

But it was a rough landing. The America I encountered was not the America that fired my fantasies while watching Hollywood movies. During the early sixties Youngstown was a major steel-producing center, nicknamed Steel Town USA.[1] Its sky was chronically blocked out by a yellowish canopy of sulfur caused by fumes spilling furiously into the atmosphere. Faced with what appeared to be a hellish environmental calamity, my fears overtook me: in less than three months I would surely be diagnosed with lung cancer. I began imagining pains in my chest, telltale signs of the coming terminal illness. The dark mucus coming out of my nostrils every time I blew my nose was all the evidence I needed.

What a contrast to Cyprus, that legendary birthplace of Aphrodite—the goddess of love and beauty! We took for granted our world of pure air, pristine water, clean seas, sparkling blue skies, and abundant sunshine year-round. "Steel Town USA" was anything but that. I must summon a positive attitude, I thought; I must avoid all distractions offered by extracurricular life and focus exclusively on my studies, so that I can earn my degree and return as quickly as possible to the environmental utopia I left behind.

I never asked my uncles why they gave up Cyprus for such a challenging world. If they were lured by promises of suburban homes, brand new automobiles, and television sets, they did have these in abundance, but the price seemed hefty. Uncle Steve, the steelworker, earned his wages through the sweat of his brow. He swallowed salt pills daily because of the excessive loss of body fluids from working with molten steel day in and day out. His elder brother, Uncle Nick, spent his working life behind a counter running his grocery store, just a stone's throw from his house next to the steel mills. He was robbed at gunpoint on several occasions. Uncle Jordan, his brother-in-law, operated a bakery in the same neighborhood. He was also robbed at gunpoint. I marveled at the fact that all my uncles in Youngstown and their brother in New York were content with their lives and proud to be Americans. Perhaps the wellspring of their contentment was the communal ties they forged among other émigré Greeks who came in search of a more materially comfortable lifestyle. Polluted skies were more than counterbalanced by longstanding friendships with their coreligionists and fellow Greek Americans. My relatives' lives revolved around the three Greek Orthodox churches in the area, and like them, I found in these churches the emotional support that helped me assimilate into the wider culture. Church on Sundays was like vicariously visiting Cyprus for a few hours. I faced the familiar faces of the Orthodox saints painted on the walls and on wooden icons, listened to the chants that I'd been exposed to since infancy, heard the Greek language spoken during the liturgy, and smelled the familiar incense that triggered memories of home. As a sociologist I later learned that religion remained vibrant in America in large part because it facilitated the assimilation of its immigrants.

TRIALS AND TRIBULATIONS

The polluted air was not the only problem I faced in Ohio. I began my academic career at Youngstown University with an inadequate mastery of English. During the first week of classes I had no idea what the professor of my social science course was lecturing about. While my fellow students filled much of their weekends with dates, movies, and sports, I worked nonstop with a dictionary to translate dense reading material—filling the pages with the Greek equivalents of the English words. I feared that I might not make it. Fortunately, most of the other courses I was taking during the fall semester of 1960 were more technical, such as mathematics, economics, and accounting, and they did not require much language proficiency. The decent grades I got restored my self-confidence, and I had the breathing space to master English and preempt a panic attack. The next semester I was ready to tackle other linguistically challenging courses—American history, psychology, and English literature—but I soon declared a major in accounting and a minor in economics. As a graduate of a business high school, I thought I was destined to follow a business career. If I could develop the skills to earn a living in a white-collar job, I could then liberate myself from the prospect of inheriting my father's grocery store.

To cover some of my expenses I took odd jobs part-time. I worked on Saturdays at Uncle Jordan's bakery making donuts, apple pies, and cheesecakes. I also worked a few hours a week at the university library. I remember some tense moments with the chief librarian during the job interview, fielding his questions about my background and what I was studying. When I told him "accounting," he made a dismissive grimace and said, "My dear, you mean to tell me that you came all the way from Cyprus to study accounting? What a missed opportunity!" He suggested it would make more sense to get a liberal arts degree, perhaps in history, literature, or philosophy, something that would expand my horizons. He had a doctoral degree in philosophy himself, and from an Ivy League school. "Sir," I said, with some impatience, "I love subjects like philosophy, history, and literature, but what would I do with such a degree in Cyprus? I don't come from a well-to-do-family, so I don't have the luxury of those options. I have to think about making a living so I can create my own family!" He shook his head with a sigh. It must have sounded like a foolish argument on my part, a safe, conventional response. He asked no further questions. He simply signed my application form and hired me as a part-time library worker. I do not know if that simple and disagreeable exchange played any role in my later career choices, but I now carried a seed of doubt about my chosen field of study. His comments triggered a mixture of turmoil, self-doubt, and resentment. Perhaps these feelings came from a subconscious intuition that he might be right, that I was indeed in the wrong field, but I was not yet ready to face that fact.

I was quite successful as an accounting student, so much so that I earned the only "A" in one of the most difficult courses. Similar achievements in my economics classes, particularly in statistics, boosted my self-confidence still further. I no longer doubted that I could return to Cyprus with my head held high and a degree in hand, ready to make a living in something other than selling produce. My identity as a good student was sealed when I was initiated into the national Honorary Accounting Fraternity, reserved for students with high grade point averages. I was now eligible to become a lab assistant, which meant helping a faculty member teach an introductory course. I would have exclusive charge of the class once a week and solve accounting problems on the chalkboard, and this would have the side benefit of helping me overcome my shyness.

Shyness was a serious handicap at the start of my undergraduate career. I blushed with little provocation. At the time I thought I was suffering from a "girlish" affliction. My Aunt Myrofora told me that my mother also blushed easily, so maybe this was part of my biological inheritance. But I traced my phobic predicament to a specific incident when I was 14 and in my junior year in high school. It was a hot day in late May. Our teacher was lecturing on Greek history, and I was sitting on the far right of the room. As I leaned my head on the wall, I fell asleep. Apparently, the teacher stopped lecturing and stared at me for a few seconds, not saying a word. I woke up to the entire class giggling at me. After that, I could not face any class or audience without blushing and sweating profusely.

My blushing problem metastasized into a serious handicap in relationships with girls. Growing up in a homogeneous and insular culture, we had easy interaction with our mothers, grandmothers, aunts, sisters and cousins, but we were woefully unpracticed at connecting with girls and women outside those kinship boundaries. In public schools there was an iron curtain separating males from females. Within the same school teenage boys and girls were herded into different classrooms, and during intermission we played among ourselves in gender-segregated schoolyards. I once asked one of our teachers to explain the reasons for these rigid divisions. "When you bring fire and gunpowder together," he mused, "there is bound to be an explosion."

Within the American university world, it was a great shock to see that guys could simply ask a fellow student for a date, be alone with her, and go to dances, coffee shops and drive-in theaters. The "fire and gunpowder" metaphor was still active in my mind. I rationalized my dateless existence by holding to the belief that I had no time for dates; my goal was to survive academically and return to Cyprus, and I feared that asking a girl out was tantamount to making a marriage proposal.

I also told myself it would be wrong to fool around with someone when I knew I would be leaving for Cyprus once my education was completed. I was infatuated with several beautiful coeds sitting next to me in my classes, but I felt that, like Odysseus, I should resist the Sirens that could prevent me from reaching my "Ithaca." Having read somewhere that developing will power through various exercises would help me achieve my goals, I would come home sweating and thirsty from afternoon soccer, fill up a glass of cool water, and place it on the table. After contemplating it for fifteen minutes I would gobble it down, a masochistic little exercise that I would never recommend to my children.

By the end of my sophomore year, I knew that my blushing and sweating problem was serious enough to do something about it, but if counseling services were available at the university, I was not ready to use them. Instead, I drew inspiration from the ancient Athenian Demosthenes, who cured his stuttering handicap by putting sea pebbles into his mouth and, while walking up and down the beach, he practiced his oratorical skills by lecturing to the waves as if they were crowds listening to him in the Agora. He became the foremost orator of antiquity, if not of all history. Here was a golden opportunity to apply his strategy. I told my accounting professor that I wished to become a lab assistant, as I was now eligible for this position. She made the necessary arrangements, and I was now ready to execute my plan.

Before my first appearance in the class, I told myself, "I will deliberately sweat and blush to my heart's content. I will get red in the face as much as possible. I will then imagine myself part of the audience watching this idiot, and I will relish the bizarre spectacle." It worked! During that first encounter, I did not blush or sweat, and I never again had that problem in any classroom. And I could now easily interact and become friends with women other than my aunts and cousins. It felt like a miracle, although I learned later that I had innocently practiced a technique in psychotherapy for overcoming phobias, known as "paradoxical intention." Simply put, if you will yourself to do what you most want to stop doing, you cripple your capacity to keep doing it.

ACCIDENTAL SOCIOLOGIST

Now secure in my business major, I began to wonder if I was pursuing the wrong career. I thought, "Am I going to spend the rest of my life solving accounting problems and poring over balance sheets?" The words of the chief librarian haunted me more than he could have imagined. My exposure to the liberal arts and my three-year experience of American life had triggered an intense thirst for more knowledge and self-understanding. The new world I was living in had turned upside down the cultural baggage I had brought from

Cyprus. An avalanche of existential questions flooded my mind, and no business or accounting course could help me answer them.

As the 1960s unfolded, my issues of personal adjustment were often eclipsed by national and world events. This was the apex of the Cold War with the Soviet Union, and elementary school children were still being instructed to hide under their desks in the event of a nuclear explosion. It was also the time of the presidential elections: Kennedy vs. Nixon. I knew nothing about American history, only Greek history, taught within narrow and ideologically skewed contexts; we learned only what was compatible with Greek nationalism.

The fourth-year students in the business school were vocal and passionate in their support for the Republican candidate, proudly wearing "Nixon's the One" buttons. I was ignorant of the differences between Democrats and Republicans, but I did watch with my uncles the historic first televised presidential debates in the fall of 1960. Without understanding the issues, I was drawn to the young and charismatic Kennedy. Nixon appeared unappealingly awkward compared to his dashing and articulate opponent. Worse, Nixon's profuse sweating reminded me of myself at my worst moments. Those debates were the beginning of my acculturation into American society and a crash course in U.S. politics 101. I was a firm Kennedy fan by the time of his inauguration on January 20, 1961. The day before, I watched President Eisenhower's historic farewell address, warning his fellow Americans about the dangers of the "Military Industrial Complex."

I was frightened to my core by the 1962 Cuban missile crisis and the prospect of war with the Soviets. "Oh my God," I remember thinking, "did I come to America to get incinerated in a nuclear holocaust?" During those hair-raising days, humanity faced an Armageddon that dwarfed the problems of little Cyprus.

The assassination of President Kennedy a year later was devastating to me. Like most Americans, I was enchanted by his keen intelligence and charm, but I was especially grateful for his support of the newly established Cyprus Republic and his sympathy for the Greek Cypriots. I remember trying to solve an accounting problem with a classmate in the library when we heard the news. I could not control my tears. The world seemed to be falling apart, and here I was spending my life looking at balance sheets and tax forms. Now feeling myself to be a full participant in the wider life of my host country, I needed to find out what was going on.

Days later, I had a chance encounter with a student majoring in sociology. I soon realized that I had more in common with him than with most of my fellow business students. The more he shared his excitement about what he was learning, the more intrigued I became. I decided to pay a visit to Mrs. Pauline Botty, the chair of the sociology department and my professor in the introductory social science course I took my freshman year. Recalling that she had stroked my ego when she read one of my papers to the class, I was pleased that she remembered me. I told her that I was about to graduate with a degree in business administration, but I had come to the shocking realization that I was in the wrong field. She listened with a sympathetic ear. She suggested that I apply to as many graduate schools in sociology as possible, and she volunteered to write letters of recommendation for me.

All the graduate programs I applied to accepted me, but none of them offered me financial assistance, which I desperately needed to attend graduate school. A month later I went back to Mrs. Botty and told her mournfully what had happened. "I won't bother to fill out these last forms," I told her, showing her the application from Bowling Green State University in Ohio; "I know what the reply will be." Mrs. Botty, a no-nonsense version of my caring and openhearted aunts, fired back an impatient outburst: "Go home right now and fill out these forms. You are losing your chances!" "Okay," I said meekly, "but I just know that my chances are really slim."

A month later I got a phone call from the chairman of the sociology department at Bowling Green State. I was accepted with a full assistantship. That meant free tuition and a modest monthly stipend to cover my living expenses. After a semester of remedial courses in sociology, I would be teaching an introductory course all by myself. Thus began my graduate career, thanks in large part to Mrs. Botty's caring reprimand.

My years at Youngstown had widened my horizons, especially through encounters with my own limitations. I arrived in the United States a Greek nationalist. Only things Greek had positive value. It was shocking to discover that Americans felt likewise about their country. They saluted their flag and sang their national anthem with the same patriotic zeal as I did mine. This was perhaps my first encounter with cultural relativism.

Another humbling experience came with my attempt to join the university basketball team. In Cyprus I was captain of my high school team during my senior year, and I was under the illusion that I was a good player. But in my first appearance on the university basketball court, I was awestruck by how much better the American players were. I never played basketball again. I was learning that my skills and talents were only as good as the comparison group against which I measured myself.

At Youngstown I had continued to free myself emotionally from my underground experiences in Cyprus. I grew clearer that the movement was a horrendous mistake created by misguided patriots, self-serving political operatives, and unscrupulous demagogues. Freed from the rituals in Cyprus that kept celebrating "the Struggle," I could develop a more detached and critical outlook about it.

For the next two years I would be making my living as a full-time graduate student working on my master's degree in sociology. It was bittersweet. I was elated to finally be in a field that would help me tackle the big questions of life, but I would not be able to return to Cyprus until two more years. Despite my increasing Americanization, my passion for returning home remained undiminished.

Before moving to Bowling Green State, I worked for a month at a fast-food restaurant in New Jersey, hoping to save enough money for an adventure in the western United States. Petros, my companion at the Moral Re-armament conference in Switzerland and now studying in the U.S. had asked me to join him for a one-month camping excursion. This was my first trip west of Youngstown, and the contrast between "Steel Town USA" and the America we encountered on our journey could not have been bolder. The Rocky Mountains, Yosemite, the Red Wood Forest, the Grand Canyon, Mesa Verde—this was an experience bordering on the mystical. It further chipped away at my ethnocentrism, the feeling that natural beauty was confined to the sandy beaches and forest-covered mountains of Cyprus. Experiencing the American national parks was the visual preamble of my expanded awareness of a wider world.

Bowling Green was a small town in the middle of a vast sea of corn, with no industry other than its state university. The air was clean and crisp, the traffic typical of small town USA. A passenger train reliably whizzed by, its rhythmic sounds becoming an anticipated part of my everyday reality. With three other students I rented an old house within walking distance of campus. We lived a semicommunal existence. One of my roommates was a Parsee from India, a graduate student in Business Administration who practiced Zoroastrianism. Another was an Irish American and a graduate student in history. He had a passionate interest in the American Civil War and was a collector of every imaginable memento of that period—swords, Confederate and Union flags, rusted bullets, warn out military hats, and photocopied pictures of Lincoln and General Lee. His room was a mini museum of Civil War paraphernalia. Over morning coffee, he filled a gap in my knowledge of American history. My undergraduate U.S. history professor had skipped the Civil War, explaining that it was too painful for him to go over that subject. My third roommate was Jim, an affable Greek American from Cleveland and a senior in biology. He knew some Greek and never lost an opportunity to practice it with me.

Over the ten years of my American education, I had other roommates who came from diverse cultural and religious backgrounds. It was another form of education, helping me to get past my parochial worldview. There were Egyptian and Iranian roommates—"Non-Immigrant Aliens" like myself—and a herculean African-American football player, a Jehovah's Witness who praised the Lord in every sentence that exited his mouth.

My favorite professor at Bowling Green State was Dr. Joseph Albini, a specialist in organized crime who eventually became a leading authority on the Mafia. He was a popular teacher, a flamboyant, guitar-playing Italian with extraordinary humor. In addition to Italian opera, he was an enthusiastic lover of Greek music, particularly the work of Mikis Theodorakis, one of my favorite composers. With Joe, as he urged me to call him, I had a friend among the faculty, a relationship that became crucial in my subsequent graduate education and academic career.

My two years working on my Masters at Bowling Green State were my initiation into a different way of seeing the world. The first wisdom of sociology, Peter Berger wrote in his classic *Invitation to Sociology,* is that "things are not what they seem."[2] Sociology offers a special lens that allows its possessor to see through the official definitions of reality, which are very often forms of mystification that mask the true nature of social reality. As a form of consciousness, therefore, sociology is a debunking and liberating discipline. I was rapidly becoming a trained skeptic of all accepted orthodoxies and loving it. True liberation, Alan Watts claimed, presupposes overcoming our cultural conditioning.[3] Sociology was a powerful vehicle for my overcoming the cultural baggage I brought over from Cyprus.

The more I studied sociology, the more I saw its potency as a no-nonsense approach to unraveling the complexities of the social world. Teaching my own introductory course provided a boost to my new identity as a sociologist, and it gave me a believable vision of becoming a professor. Predictably, after two successful years at Bowling Green I began flirting with the idea of continuing my studies in a doctoral program. At that time Bowling Green had no such program, but with the encouragement of my professors I began applying to various programs around the country. The University of Kentucky at Lexington was the first to offer me a teaching assistantship, and without missing a beat or knowing where Lexington was on the map, I accepted. I was to start my doctoral work in September of 1966, but I felt the same ambivalent and bittersweet feelings as when I had begun my master's program. My goal of returning to Cyprus would once again be postponed, this time for another four years. After 1960, the only contacts I had with home were periodic letters from my sister and my father, who would mail me newspaper clippings to keep me posted about the ongoing political crisis with the Turks. We talked on the phone just once in those six years, when he let me know that my sister was getting married. Transatlantic telephone calls were still awfully expensive.

With my MA degree in hand, I longed for a visit. I did not have the money for a plane ticket, but a serious auto accident my father suffered made my trip possible. As he crossed a Nicosia road pushing his bicycle, a military truck carrying United Nations troops sent him to the hospital in critical condition for several days. Miraculously, he fully recovered. For reparations, the UN force offered him six thousand pounds. With the money left over after paying his medical bills, he bought me a plane ticket.

I expected to find a different Cyprus from the one I left behind in 1960. My sister was now married with three children. When I left, the island was still under British rule. Much political turmoil was unleashed during the first six years of its independence. In the summer of 1964, while I was camping out with my friend Petros in the Timpanogos Mountains in Utah, Turkey began bombing the northern part of Cyprus and threatened to invade it. The constitutional arrangements that were set up in 1960 fell apart, and ethnic conflict between the Greek Cypriot majority and Turkish Cypriot minority broke out. Before long, the United Nations forces arrived on the island to keep the peace, and they have remained there ever since.

I was not prepared for the depth of the culture shock I felt going back. My world turned upside down. Cyprus had changed radically, and America had irrevocably changed me. There was a huge gap there. I plunged into a deep state of melancholy, so much so that my father was concerned. During my two-month stay I found refuge under the lemon tree in the back yard of our house, the place where I used to hide home-made hand grenades for the underground. I escaped there for hours, losing myself in fiction, particularly the work of the celebrated Greek novelist Nikos Kazantzakis. It was comforting that he had similar ups and downs in his relationship with his beloved Crete. Reading his riveting autobiography had a temporary, calming effect on me.[4] But that difficult summer, I thought for the first time that I may not be able to return to make my life in Cyprus.

ECHOES FROM THE SUPRA-CONSCIOUS

I returned to the U.S. heartbroken. The dream had collapsed and for a while I was like a rudderless boat in the middle of the ocean. The idol and myth of Cyprus had provided purpose, focus, and direction throughout my first six years in America, and now it had collapsed. It took me years and more home visits to reach a new emotional equilibrium in my identity as a Greek Cypriot.

Given my volatile state, my arrival in Lexington, Kentucky in August of 1966 could not have come at a less auspicious time. I found myself in yet another strange place, and with no social support. The prospect of four years in Kentucky working on my doctoral degree depressed me terribly. The South felt like an alien land, with different ways and strange-sounding accents. I missed the North. I realized then that I had absorbed much of Yankee culture, and the old Confederacy seemed like enemy territory. My state of malaise heightened further when I learned that a Cyprus Airways flight from Athens to Cyprus was blown up over the Aegean. A terrorist had planted a bomb to kill a leading politician, and over a hundred people died, including my closest friend from high school.

Truth be told, there was no real problem with Lexington, Kentucky. The landscape was stunningly beautiful and the southern young women even more so. The university was a fine institution and the sociology department consisted of leading scholars who were very caring towards their students. The physical campus was one of the best I have seen. But I suffered from two problems that are at the core of the discipline I was studying: *alienation* and *anomie*, products of modernity. Human beings can lose their traditional moorings and feel like strangers in the world they inhabit. And without any norms to provide moral direction and guide everyday conduct, individuals can lose their connections with each other, with their society, and even with themselves. That is how I felt at the time.

Giving up and returning to Cyprus was not an option. I was determined to finish my doctoral program, even if I had to spend four more years in blue-grass Kentucky. At the same time, I began exploring other possibilities. I wrote an S.O.S. letter to my friend and former professor Joe Albini, explaining to him my predicament. He had given up his post at Bowling Green State and was now teaching at Wayne State University in Detroit, a school that had a well-established doctoral program in sociology. Joe vouched for me with his new colleagues, and I was soon offered a teaching assistantship beginning the following year. I felt immensely relieved, grateful, and unburdened. Joe would be my advisor, and Detroit had a vibrant Greek Town. Moving there was the perfect choice.

Now I could relax and even enjoy my remaining months at Lexington. I could not have known it yet, but I was about to have an experience that would reverberate throughout the rest of my life. In the spring of 1967, my second and last semester at the University of Kentucky, I signed up for an advanced course on classical sociological theory. The professor organized the course as a student-run seminar, and each of us had to choose a major sociologist and present what we learned to the rest of the class. We were given a list of the leading theorists who formed the canon of classical sociology, from which we were each to select one on a first-come-first-served basis. He gave us a week to decide which theorist we wanted to intensively explore. I had no difficulty making up my mind. I wanted to focus on one of the recognized leaders of the field—the Frenchman Emile Durkheim, either one of the Germans Max Weber or Georg Simmel, the American George Herbert Mead, or the German Karl Marx. These "Big Guns" created the foundation on which later sociological theory rested. When I informed my professor of my preferences, he replied that unfortunately, all these names were already spoken for, and the only ones left were the Russian-American Pitirim Sorokin and the nineteenth-century Englishman Herbert Spencer. At the time, I was prejudiced against Herbert Spencer, with his evolutionary theory of society and his social-Darwinist notions of "the survival of the fittest," so I was left with Sorokin. All I knew about him was that he was Russian, and the founder of the sociology department at Harvard. I envied my more enterprising classmates who were poised to sink their teeth into the real meat of sociological theory. But as I began to explore Sorokin's life and work, I became fascinated, so much so that I now honor him as one of my most important mentors. His genius had a decisive impact on my understanding of reality, both social and personal. And perhaps more than anyone, Sorokin saved me from a purely mechanistic, materialist, nonspiritual view of the world.

I was mesmerized as I learned the details of Sorokin's life, some of which were easy for me to identify with: he lost his mother during his childhood; he came from a country that was volatile and sometimes violent; he was Eastern Orthodox; he maintained his emotional connection with his home country; and as an immigrant he had to struggle and adjust to American culture.

Born in 1889 in Komi, a peasant village in northern Russia, Sorokin and his older brother followed their itinerant father from village to village fixing icons in Russian Orthodox churches. Their constant movement deprived young Pitirim of formal schooling, but his intense zeal for learning and his self-education ultimately caught the attention of a professor at the University of St. Petersburg. Encouraged to prepare for the entrance examinations there, Sorokin passed with flying colors and began his academic training. He eventually went on to earn a doctoral degree in sociology, specializing in crime and criminal justice. Upon graduation he was offered a teaching position at his alma mater.

In his extracurricular activities, Sorokin was an anti-establishment activist, which at times led to his incarceration. He joined the social-democratic Mensheviks, served for a short time as minister of culture in their provisional government, and fled to the Russian woods after the October 1917 coup by Lenin and the Bolsheviks. Eventually he surrendered and was immediately sentenced to death. A former student, a Bolshevik, pleaded with Lenin to spare Sorokin's life. The communist leader allegedly reacted by asking impatiently, "Who is this obscure bourgeois ass?" but in the nick of time he ordered his release; intellectuals like Sorokin who were "misguided" should not be executed but re-educated, Lenin argued in a newspaper article. Restored to his former teaching position, Sorokin's continued opposition to the communists led to his expulsion from Russia in 1923, and he migrated to the United States. Within five years he became recognized as a leading sociologist, and Harvard University recruited him to set up its first sociology department.[5]

Sorokin's life fascinated me, but I was most excited by his ideas, especially his views on human nature, on how we can know reality, and on the nature of sociocultural change. All three perspectives were radically at odds with the dominant worldview in American academia. About human nature, Sorokin claimed that people have not only a conscious and an unconscious mind, as Freud argued, but also a supraconscious mind, a concept not unlike Jung's "collective unconscious." Sorokin saw the supraconscious as the highest form of consciousness, attained by the great sages of humanity and experienced in mystical epiphanies of both ordinary people and great saints. He insisted that mystical illumination and other paranormal states should not be reduced to the unconscious part of the mind. They transcend "the skin-encapsulated ego,"[6] and we must see them as bona fide, authentic experiences, springing from a source transcending both intellect and the five senses. By the end of the Twentieth century, this theoretical position on the self was getting supported by strong empirical evidence.[7]

Parallel to his position on the self, Sorokin proposed a theory of knowledge that was also out of step with his academic peers. Their view was that authentic knowledge is the exclusive product of the five senses, aided by scientific instruments, laboratory experiments, and quantitative methodologies. Like Paschal before him, Sorokin argued passionately that human beings know the world through three strands: the senses, the intellect, and intuition. With our senses, amplified by scientific technology, we acquire reliable knowledge about how the material universe works. The second source of knowledge, the intellect, is rooted in our capacity for rationality. Unlike sense organs and the instruments that amplify them, the intellect is driven purely by our cerebral activity. Philosophy, logic, and mathematics are the domain of the intellect. Thus far the West has privileged the first two sources of knowledge—the senses and the intellect—but it has ignored the third source, intuition, which is the product of inner illumination. Sorokin saw intuition as a special form of knowledge *sui generis,* transcending the domains of both empirical science and rational philosophy. Its importance is paramount in Hindu philosophical and mystical tradition and the other great religious traditions including Christianity. It is also central to indigenous traditions of shamanism.[8]

Sorokin was passionate about honoring all three strands of knowledge (senses, intellect, and intuition) for any comprehensive understanding of Reality. He called his epistemology, "Integralist Truth." Like Paschal, Sorokin was an unrecognized precursor of thinkers like Ken Wilber and other founders of transpersonal theory.

It is Sorokin's cyclical theory of sociocultural change, however, that most marks his legacy as a visionary sociologist. At Harvard he embarked on a massive study of Western civilization and its future. Instead of "rise and decline" theories of civilization or "endless evolutionary progress" theories, Sorokin offered a "pendulum" or cyclical framework on civilizational change. Every culture is either religious or materialistic, either God-oriented or physical-matter oriented. He called the first "ideational" and the second "sensate." At the peak of the Middle Ages, Western civilization was ideational. The leading philosophers were religionists, and artists tried to portray spiritual themes in their works. The Nineteenth-century west became sensate, and all cultural manifestation—philosophy, art, social organization, legal arrangements—was now premised on the physical universe being all that there is. Philosophers became secular and atheistic in their outlook. They explained religion as "the opiate of the people," or the product of prescientific thinking, or even a form of infantile fixation. The artists focused on nature in all its physical grandeur and material detail.

Sorokin also pointed to a third, in-between stage, which he called "idealistic." Reality is seen as both spiritual and material, as in the Golden Age of ancient Greece and during the time of Dante. The focus of the idealistic integration is perfect form, as exemplified by the Parthenon of Athens, the Aphrodite of Milos and the Republic of Plato.

Sorokin claimed that Western civilization oscillated between the two extremes, from religiosity to materialism, and from materialism back to religiosity. He saw the violence and mayhem of the twentieth century as signaling the decline of the West's sensate phase. The carnage of the Second World War was its prime manifestation. As the sensate phase unravels, more extreme forms of violence may appear, and with modern technology and weaponry, the dangers are considerable.[9] Alarmed by the use of nuclear bombs against Japan at the end of the war, Sorokin created the Center for the Study of Creative Altruism at Harvard, believing that through love and altruism, we can avert a global holocaust.[10] But the movement of the pendulum swing back to the ideational integration is inevitable, and while most of his peers were predicting the eventual disappearance of religion, Sorokin was convinced that the West was on the verge of a massive religious revitalization.

I was so animated during my Sorokin presentation that my fellow students began to teasingly call me "Pitirim." This is fitting; I am forever indebted to this Harvard misfit professor who grew up a peasant boy in northern Russia. His work helped save me from the prevailing currents of reductionism and materialism. My year at Kentucky was a spiritual blessing, even with all its emotional turmoil, because after that seminar, no other professor of mine ever even mentioned Sorokin's name. Sorokin himself was saddened by the overall neglect of his work. I wrote to him the year before his death in 1968, and despite his election to President of the American Sociological Association in

1963, his letter back to me revealed a lingering disappointment that his work was not more appreciated by the wider sociological community.

THE ROAD TO SUSPICION

I arrived in Detroit on the day of one of the deadliest and most destructive race riots in the history of the United States. It was Saturday, July 23, 1967.[11] The riots lasted five days and 43 people died, almost 2,000 were injured, more than 7,000 arrested, and over 1,000 buildings were set on fire. As local authorities lost control, President Lyndon Johnson dispatched U.S. troops to restore order and prevent the violence from spreading.

I was at a loss when I stepped off the bus and was informed that a curfew was about to begin. For a moment I wondered whether I had made the right decision to leave the bucolic tranquility of Kentucky and land in the middle of a civil war. It was impossible to reach the Wayne State campus where I had reserved a room for my stay. Fortunately, a Greek family that I accidentally met at the bus station invited me to their nearby home. They graciously offered me hospitality for the next five days until the riots were over. This was a rude awakening to the problems plaguing inner city America, where I was to spend the last three years of the troubled sixties.

The African-American riots were rooted in extreme frustration and resentment about longstanding unemployment, underemployment, poverty, racial segregation, and lack of economic and educational opportunities. That was the conclusion of the report of the National Advisory Commission on Civil Disorder, with the warning that "our nation is moving toward two societies, one black, one white—separate and unequal."

My life in Detroit during the late sixties was a further immersion into the fabric of American society and culture. Growing up in Cyprus I had come face to face with the political turmoil and violence of the anticolonial movement raging all around me. At Wayne State my world was now rocked by the Civil Rights Movement and the ever-escalating Vietnam War. The difference was that here in America, I remained an insider/outsider during the convulsions in cities and college campuses. Unlike my classmates, I was not vulnerable to the dreaded military draft. As a "Non-Immigrant Alien" I could not be shipped to the jungles of South East Asia to fight "them Viet Cong," in the memorable words of Muhammad Ali, whose refusal to be drafted cost him his boxing championship but elevated him to hero status among antiwar protesters. I empathized with my classmates who were vulnerable to the draft, and I participated vicariously in the high anxiety they felt. Night after night, Walter Cronkite, the dean of television news and "the most trusted man in America," reported the "body count," the macabre way that military success was then measured. Those grim statistics, the televised sight of American soldiers screaming and dying in Vietnam, the flag-covered coffins of the dead soldiers unloaded from military cargo planes—all of this left me anguished and numb.

Those few years had an indelible impact on my American self-definition at Wayne State. I was deeply moved by the protests all over America, and like most of my age group I was riveted by the lyrics of antiwar troubadours and singer-songwriters like Peter, Paul and Mary, Joan Baez, Simon and Garfunkel, and Bob Dylan. But despite all the upheaval, I felt revitalized in Detroit. I no longer experienced that sense of personal disorientation, alone-ness, and alienation that I faced in Lexington. No doubt, the presence at Wayne State of some Greek and Greek Cypriot graduate students was impor-tant to my well-being. This was a group of peers with whom I shared a similar ethnic background and deep concerns about our troubled countries. Weekend visits to Greek Town, a thriving neighborhood of restaurants, grocery stores and Bouzouki lounges, helped us anchor ourselves within multicultural America. I rarely attended the Greek churches that previously had reminded me of home, but I shared with my fellow Greek students the political upheav-als of Greece and Cyprus—the 1967 catastrophic military coup in Greece and the never-ending ethnic problem of the island, with the constant threat of a Turkish invasion. These historic upheavals, the ones plaguing America and the very different ones plaguing Cyprus and Greece, intensified my sense of "double consciousness." I lived in two political and social worlds—one in America and the other a combination of Greece and Cyprus. It is little won-der that soon after my arrival at Wayne State I chose to specialize in political sociology.

Things were changing within me. I fully identified now with universal human values enlivened by the antiwar movement and other rights move-ments launched by disadvantaged minorities—African Americans, women, Native Americans and others. I learned to oppose values based on exclusion, xenophobia, and ethnic triumphalism. My heroes were no longer Archbishop Makarios and George Grivas, to whom I looked up during the fifties, but Mahatma Gandhi and Martin Luther King. I witnessed the emergence of the hippie movement with keen interest. Timothy Leary, the renegade psychology professor who was fired from Harvard for his work on psychedelics and LSD had urged youth to "turn on, tune in, and drop out," and he admonished them to "think for yourself and question authority." Some youth did drop out to join intentional communities, where they tried to live their revolutionary values of "free love" and free-spirited, psychedelic-inspired expressivity. Small wonder that President Richard Nixon could call Timothy Leary "the most dangerous man in America"!

By the end of that ten-year period, I felt completely liberated from the stranglehold of nationalism that had distorted my life experience as a youngster in Cyprus. There was no turning back. I had absorbed values that were part of the multicultural fabric of American society and were now central to my identity as a critical sociologist, dreaming of a fairer and more just world. Sociology at its best is a liberating and even radicalizing discipline, and it helped to fuel the revolution growing within me. My American experience and my training within the field of sociology had changed me in an almost total way.

My emotional attachment to Greek culture and Cyprus remained intact. My connection to my friends and relatives there remained fully alive within me. I still planned to return to Cyprus, despite the severe culture shock I suffered after visiting the island for the first time in 1966. I still preferred Greek food to any other food. I favored Greek music over any other music and preferred Greek dancing to any other dancing. Mikis Theodorakis, Manos Hajidakis, and Stavros Xarhakos remained my favorite composers, not Elvis Presley, the Beatles, or the Grateful Dead. But intellectually I was now and forever a self-identified American academic, a critical sociologist. By the end of the decade, I felt that my old way of thinking was singularly anachronistic and provincial. The political culture of blind faith and unthinking pride for "Mother Greece," the never-ending "struggles" for *Enosis* (union with Greece), the millenarian ideology that in my pre-American life had filled me with meaning—none of this was relevant anymore.

The biggest casualty of separating from Greek nationalism was my distancing from the Greek Orthodox Church. The two went hand in hand, packaged together and constantly reinforced by our nationalist teachers. The American tradition of separation of church and state seemed so much more appealing and less dangerous. When religion and politics become one, both get distorted. When patriotic rhetoric becomes encoded within exclusivist religious worldviews—the reality that marked so much of my early years in Cyprus—bad things happen. I developed an intensely negative reaction to populist and charismatic leaders cheered by adoring masses.

I became increasingly suspicious of the Church's role in Greek Cypriot society. I now saw its politics as largely responsible for the disastrous course that plagued the contemporary history of Cyprus. It was easy to reject organized religion altogether, and to forget Sorokin's inspiring understanding of its inevitability. I drifted into an agnostic position about the big questions of human existence. This was the outlook of all my professors in graduate school, and also of most university colleagues I have known in my fifty years in academia, perhaps a legacy of the Enlightenment-inspired worldview that religion was destined to disappear with the advancement of science and critical reason.

I learned that our most celebrated founding fathers of sociology—Karl Marx, Emile Durkheim, and Max Weber—were all pure secularists, oblivious to the spiritual truths at the core of all established religions. Marx was a militant atheist who saw religion as nothing but "false consciousness" ("the opium of the people") that keeps the oppressed classes in their place by promising them rewards in an imaginary afterlife. Durkheim saw religion in terms of its moral rules and rituals that promote social cohesion. Marx and Durkheim were both following a well-established atheist tradition going back to Voltaire, who would whisper tongue-in-cheek to his dinner guests to not speak too loudly about the absence of God, lest his servants hear them and cut their throats. That is, fear of God renders people peaceful (Durkheim) and keeps subordinates in their place (Marx).

Weber's position on religion was more historical, centering on how religious ideas can transform societies. Perhaps his most celebrated book is an essay about how the countries that adopted Protestant ideas at the time of the Reformation were the ones that gave modern capitalism its biggest push.[12] Weber joined Marx and Durkheim in their conviction that religion is central to understanding history, but he spoke of himself as religiously "unmusical."

I succumbed to the dominant secular outlook of my field, cooling off to Sorokin's cry in the wilderness about the truth of religion. I had been a God-fearing youngster and an altar boy during my early teens, and I took my faith for granted. When I arrived in the United States in 1960 at the age of 17, everything started changing. My experience at four universities gradually led me to question the entire fabric of that simple faith. By the time of my doctoral graduation in 1970, I saw myself as a reluctant agnostic.

MARXISTS AND FREUDIANS

Professor Don Strickland was a young political scientist at Wayne State when I arrived there. I signed up for one of his courses on political philosophy and theory—his favorite subject, I soon learned. The twenty-five graduate students in the class were mostly political science majors. Professor Strickland had a casual teaching style. In his sports jacket, he would sit on his desk cross legged, challenging his students in free-floating Platonic-style dialogues. I went to see him in his office, and we discovered that we had common interests. Don, as I began calling him at his insistence, became one of my closest friends and confidants as well as a member of my doctoral committee.

Don had a love for ancient Greece, particularly the works of Plato. So great was his admiration that on a pilgrimage to Greece, he traveled on foot all the way from Athens to the port of Piraeus. He wanted to vicariously follow in the footsteps of Socrates, who paced that distance two and a half millennia ago, exploring the big questions. It bothered Don not a bit that the road was now congested with noisy traffic and the air was filled with suffocating smog.

His mind was squarely trained on the spirit of Socrates, as if he were walking along with him. Don's love for classical Greece and for Mediterranean cultures apparently got projected onto a relationship with a Greek woman he dated briefly. Alas, his longing for a lasting relationship failed to materialize. A few months after I completed his course, Don was in a turmoil over the romance that might have been. He told me he had been going through intensive psychoanalysis, and he found the practice to be quite valuable, both for his psychological well-being and his professional work.

It was trendy during the fifties and sixties for academics and other cultural elites to be drawn to the thought of Sigmund Freud, either as patients themselves or through reading his works. Leftist intellectuals seemed to find in Freud an outlet for their angst regarding the failure of Marxism's Soviet expression. Instead of the utopian promise of equality, they had witnessed the first totalitarian superstate of the twentieth century. The chilling revelations of terror in the gulags following Stalin's death prompted a crisis of faith among the rank and file of the Marxist intelligentsia. Many concluded that socialism cannot be constructed simply by changing the political and socio-economic structures of society. What was also needed was a parallel struggle to transform the consciousness of human beings. Eric Fromm, a neo-Marxist sympathizer and a trained psychoanalyst, was in the forefront of this school of thought.[13] Fromm argued that Proletariats who were socialized within a capitalist culture of unfettered greed could not automatically transmute into selfless, altruistic, and loving neighbors, once they had power. They would likely follow the old pattern of corruption and exploitation, and the state would *not* "wither away," in Marx's famous words.

Leftists could find an unlikely similarity between Marx and Freud, as both had expressed a militant opposition to religion. If for Marx, religion was a dope-like distraction from oppression, for Freud it was a lingering infantile fixation destined to wither away in the life of humanity. Psychoanalysis, Freud's famed invention, was the way to human liberation and the triumph of reason. It would render the unconscious conscious, freeing humanity from superstition and ignorance.

Freud's unique strategy of turning inward could gain legitimacy within a variety of secular circles in a way that the teachings of mystics could not. After all, mystics through the ages had likewise promoted the value of turning inward as a way of transcending one's inherited egotism, but their teachings were discounted by secularists. Unwittingly, Freud may have advanced the mystics' agenda and helped to usher in a spiritual resurgence among the cultural elite. His discovery of the unconscious had signaled the existence of layers in the psyche that ran much deeper than ordinary consciousness, and these layers could be accessed, which is precisely what the mystics had been saying all along. Freud's former disciple Carl Jung advanced this very notion through his concept of the "collective unconscious." It is high irony that mystic Carl Jung had been schooled by his atheist mentor and former friend Sigmund Freud.[14] And this whole development is consistent with Sorokin's predictions about the future of the West and the inevitability of the historical pendulum swinging back toward religion, spirituality, and intuition.

My friend Don was not a Marxist. Some of my other professors did flirt with Marxism, partly as a reaction against Vietnam and the fires fueled by the Civil Rights movement, and partly as a reaction against mainstream sociology. Don was in fact a liberal political scientist who recognized the need to understand the human unconscious if we are to make sense of our lives. After all, Socrates taught that very principle: *know thyself*, the unexamined life is not worth living. Freudian psychoanalysis was now becoming the modern version of that Socratic ideal. Don not only studied Freud but practiced his theories experientially, and the electric energy of the sixties counterculture must have fueled him further. Coming from a family of Northwest Calvinists whose legacy, Don felt, had handicapped him emotionally, his primary concern was to kill the Calvinist within him. He lived the "Protestant ethic" of relentless hard work and repressed physical and emotional pleasure, but he longed to loosen up. For that reason, he was attracted to the Dionysian spirit he found in cultures of the Mediterranean and Latin America. I remember his excitement when on a visit to Cyprus he witnessed an uncle of mine in his 60s who, after a few shots of locally brewed brandy during a family picnic at a remote sandy beach, started dancing wildly. In a state of intoxicated exuberance, my uncle then plunged into the sea. For Don, it was as if he had witnessed an ancient ritual performance of Dionysus.

I too became interested in psychoanalysis, and not solely because of Don's influence. Talcott Parsons was the leading sociological theorist of the fifties and sixties, the rival of Sorokin at Harvard. Interested in integrating psychoanalytic with sociological theory, Parsons himself had undergone psychoanalysis. Allegedly, it had a decisive impact on unleashing his extraordinary creative powers and productivity. I became convinced that psychoanalysis was the modern equivalent of the Socratic injunction to "know thyself," and I became a convert.

Don informed me that the Detroit Psychoanalytic Institute was offering graduate students at Wayne State a unique opportunity to experience psychoanalysis for a nominal fee. The Institute was seeking subjects to serve as "guinea pigs" for the training of young doctors in psychotherapy, and we graduate students would be the beneficiaries. Without a second thought I volunteered. For the next six months I underwent intensive psychoanalysis: 50 minutes every day, five times a week. It was classic. I lay down on a Freudian couch, the young doctor behind me puffing on his pipe and listening to my "free associations" and to the dreams I had the night before. He took copious notes and on occasion he would offer some casual remark about the meaning of my dreams and my personal reflections. Thanks to Don, I was now becoming comfortable examining my inner thoughts and feelings, a process that was to serve me well when I later encountered the spiritual traditions—the true wellspring of knowledge about inner space and deeper self-discovery.

INTERLOCKING PROJECTS

During the summer of 1969 I traveled to Cyprus for the second time. I was making enough money to buy a plane ticket, and I was in a better frame of mind than during my visit three years earlier. I had no exaggerated expectations of what I would face on the island. Besides, I had two exciting projects that I was involved with. The first was the gathering of material for my dissertation. I got approval from my doctoral committee to study the nationalist movement in Cyprus, which I had experienced in my teenage years. Almost ten years had passed since that troubled period in my life, and through my training as a sociologist I felt I could write a dissertation about it with the necessary detachment and objectivity. I also believed that such a study could be psychologically therapeutic, even healing for me. Studying the Cyprus problem might help me to integrate the two poles of my double consciousness—the part of me that was intellectually American and the part that was emotionally Greek. My psychoanalyst agreed with that assessment.

The second project that summer unfolded organically with my friend Don. We would often join other friends at an Irish pub near the Wayne State campus. It was a warm place with pleasing furniture, a fire place with a piano next to it, juicy hamburgers, and plenty of beer on tap. Patrons were invited to crack the free peanuts and toss their shells on the marble floor. It was a joint for get-togethers and intellectual discussions, often related to Vietnam and the state of the Union. We would often hear dramatic news there, most notably about the assassinations of Martin Luther King and Robert Kennedy, back-to-back national tragedies that filled me, my classmates, and my professors with a deep sense of despair about the fate of America and the world.

It was in that beer parlor that Don and I spawned the idea that the world needed international universities, free of nationalist controls. The focus of such institutions would be to train students to become engaged global citizens for the sake of world peace. We decided to write letters to all living Nobel laureates, asking them to join a board of trustees that would govern this system of global institutions. A few answered positively, calling our suggestion a noble idea, but with no commitment on their part. Most of those we wrote did not respond. To our great surprise, however, Bertrand Russell did reply. He wrote a brief note, dryly saying that all universities should become universal in scope, and there was no need to create new international institutions. That killed our appetite to pursue the issue further.

We did do something smaller in scope. Without any financial support, we organized an ad hoc conference in Cyprus. We knew some leading academics who traveled during the summer to that part of the world. We invited them and some other prospective participants to come and give presentations on any topic related to peace and the future of the world, or just attend, listen, and participate. All presentations by bona fide academics would be accepted. It was an open forum for the sharing of ideas, and with the added lure of a summer vacation that could be tax deductible.

The main problem was to find an appropriate venue for our ten-day conference. At that time there were no colleges or universities on the Island to collaborate with. I made some preliminary contacts during the summer of 1969, while I was busy gathering data for my dissertation. Don agreed to complete the effort by coming later that year when he would be on sabbatical. Once there, he was greeted with deep suspicion. Don was not gifted with diplomatic abilities, and he was routinely suspected of being a spy for the State Department, or worse, the CIA. Our intention to include Turkish academics raised many an eyebrow, giving cause for further alarm that it was all some plot hatched by the "Anglo-Americans." Perhaps Dr. Strickland was an advance scout for an imposed solution to the Cyprus problem. These paranoid attitudes would have made good, farcical material for after-dinner laughter, but they were ill-served for poor Cyprus.

We were finally given permission, albeit reluctantly, to use the facilities at the Kyrenia gymnasium, the sea resort where I spent my summers as a youngster. Don had been cleared of any links to spy agencies, and the Cypriot bureaucrats who gave us the green light seemed to have redefined him as just a harmless, naïve American. The northern coast of Kyrenia, with its imposing Venetian castle overlooking an idyllic harbor, was the perfect location to attract participants. In attendance was a small but intimate gathering of about thirty people, a couple of whom were from Turkey. Our meetings were open to the public, but very few attended. Among the few was Christos Ioannides, who later became director of Byzantine and Hellenic Studies at Queens College in New York. A native Kyrenian, he was then a young graduate from the University of Athens. He attended our conference in the hope of a possible graduate education in America, and Don did help him land a scholarship at an Ivy League university. Thus began the professional career of a scholar with whom I established a long, close friendship. It pleases me that the impromptu conference in Kyrenia changed Christos' life in much the same way as the Moral Re-Armament conference in Switzerland changed mine.

After the presentations of the day, all participants, that included Professor Herbert Kelman of Harvard, a peace activist, would go to a local restaurant or visit "Clito's Bar," frequented by Lawrence Durrell and described in great detail in his classic novel *Bitter Lemons* about the fifties in Kyrenia. None of the participants could have imagined the tragic nightmare that was to unfold in this heavenly, beautiful town four years later when Turkey invaded Cyprus, and all Kyrenians who survived the onslaught became refugees in their own country. That included my aunt, who had hosted my sister and me during summers, some cousins and their families, and many friends.

ANONYMOUS HIPPIE

After I completed two years of course work at Wayne State, I took my doctoral exams and breathed a sigh of relief, vowing never again to take a written or oral examination. The written exam was excruciating—seven hours every day for four days. The stakes were high, the tensions that built up along the way were enormous, but I survived. The next step was to write the dissertation. Having Joe Albini as my friend and dissertation advisor was a great bonus. He gave me free rein to write on a topic of my own choosing, forgoing the typical expectation in sociology that the advisee normally would work within the advisor's research projects, and they would then publish articles together from the student's dissertation.

The major hurdle I encountered for my dissertation was its missing theoretical context. I had gathered great data on the rise and decline of the nationalist movement for the union of Cyprus with Greece, the movement I had participated in as a teenager, but I had no theoretical umbrella for integrating my empirical data. One day an anonymous hippie appeared as the catalyst I needed, as if, like so many people in the past, he was sent by some invisible force to help me out.

Despairing over not yet having a relevant dissertation framework, I took a stroll one night on campus. It was a hot July night close to midnight and the Detroit sky was unusually clear. I sat on a bench looking at the stars and contemplating my predicament. A friendly-looking hippie came by and sat next to me. We began a casual conversation as he lit a marijuana cigarette. My dissertation woes retreated to the back of my mind as we began contemplating the vastness of the universe with its billions of galaxies. He kept smoking and I kept inhaling his secondary smoke. I relaxed. Suddenly it was as if the heavens opened and the light hit me: I saw my dissertation encased within the appropriate theoretical framework in every detail. Some work of the great German sociologist Max Weber flashed through my mind, offering me the explanatory framework I needed to integrate my data. I felt like running around the campus screaming *Eureka*, but I restrained myself until morning when I met with Don and then with my dissertation advisor, Joe

Albini. They both liked my breakthrough insight. That quasi-mystical experience had helped me complete my dissertation and graduate with the Ph.D. degree. Thinking ahead, I also realized that with further elaboration of the theme of my thesis, I could have my first book publication, a development that happened later that launched my academic career. I sometimes wonder what would have happened if that anonymous hippie had not appeared next to me on that hot July night in Detroit. If I could find him, I should send him a thank-you note!

The decade of the sixties was pivotal in my life. It was a period of my rapid intellectual and emotional maturation within academia and the wider American culture. Crossing the Atlantic was not just a migration in space, a movement to a new country and continent. I earned the degrees that propelled me into a profession that I thoroughly loved. I embarked on my socialization as a sociologist, and I began my liberation from a myriad of prejudices and collective illusions. And perhaps most important, I had begun to feel within myself a quantum leap toward broader forms of consciousness and awareness, a process that continued at an accelerated pace in the next decades of my life.

NOTES

1. Sherry Lee Linkon & John Russo, *Steel-town U.S.A.: Work & Memory in Youngstown,* (Lawrence, Kansas: University Press of Kansas, 2002).
2. Peter Berger, *Invitation to Sociology: A Humanistic Perspective* (New York: Anchor, 1963).
3. Alan Watts, *Psychotherapy East and West* (New York: Vintage, 1975).
4. Nikos Kazantzakis, *Report to Greco* (New York: Simon and Schuster, 1965).
5. B.V. Johnston, *Pitirim A. Sorokin: an Intellectual Biography* (Lawrence, KS: University Press of Kansas, 1995); the story of Lenin's reaction was based on oral communication with Professor Emeritus of Sociology Lloyd Rogler.
6. Larry Dossey, *Healing Words: The Power of Prayer and the Practice of Medicine* (San Francisco: HarperOne, 1995).
7. Of course, it really depends on how we define science. After all, bona fide mystical phenomena, including inexplicable healings, have been reported all over the world by scientific researchers. As I discuss later, one can legitimately argue that science may indeed be an instrument in the discovery of spiritual realities.
8. An excellent source about this perspective is Dean Radin's *Supernormal: Science, Yoga, and the Evidence for Extraordinary Psychic Abilities* (New York: Crown Publishing, 2013).
9. Pitirim A. Sorokin, *Social and Cultural Dynamics* (Boston: Sargent Publishers, 1957).
10. Pitirim A. Sorokin, *Ways and Power of Love: Techniques of Moral Transformation* (West Conshohocken, PA: Templeton Foundation Press, 2002).

11. A Hollywood film, *Detroit*, based on those events, appeared in the theaters in the summer of 2017.
12. Max Weber, The *Protestant Ethic and the Spirit of Capitalism* (Mineola, NY: Dover Publications, 2003).
13. Eric Fromm, *The Sane Society* (Hollywood, CA: Fawcett Books, 1965).
14. Carl Jung, *Memories, Dreams, Reflections* (New York: Random House, Vintage, 1965).

Chapter 3

Family in Maine,
Tragedy in Cyprus

TURNING POINTS

I had just finished my oral defense of my dissertation. What a relief when my advisor Joe Albini came out of the faculty meeting with the news that the committee had unanimously accepted it! It took ten years and four universities, but I could now place the Ph.D. acronym next to my name—a quantum leap in my emerging self-definition. I was a fully socialized member of American academia, radically different than the "me" who arrived at the docks of New York in the summer of 1960.

My goal was still to return home to Cyprus, but what would I do there? My training had prepared me for an academic career, but Cyprus had no functioning university that might hire me. Perhaps I should seek a temporary position in the U.S., where I could fine-tune my teaching skills while scouting for other possibilities in Cyprus.

I called my friend James Kiriazis, the new sociology chair at Youngstown State, my alma mater. Jim was a second generation Greek American. His parents had migrated from Rhodes, the Greek island not far from Cyprus. We had developed a strong cultural chemistry when I was an undergraduate, and I asked him if there was a chance for me to teach in his department. By the fall of 1970 I was a tenure-track assistant professor there and loving what I was doing.

The pull of Cyprus remained fixed in my mind. My teenage years on the edges of the underground had left me with a sense of unfinished business. I still yearned for "normal" community life on the island, even if briefly. The fluidity of relationships in modern America bothered me. I found it too unsettling to establish new friends at one university, only to abandon them and repeat the process elsewhere. I remember my nostalgia as I watched the Russian film version of Tolstoy's *War and Peace.* I felt jealous of Tolstoy's characters, who were filled with intense feelings for one another as they defended their community from the invading Napoleonic armies, while my own fate was to leave my friends in Detroit and start over yet again.

After a year of teaching at Youngstown State, I asked for a leave of absence to turn my dissertation about the Cyprus turmoil into a publishable book. The semester back on the island turned out to be academically productive and emotionally therapeutic. I nurtured my cultural roots that had atrophied over the decade I was gone, and I strengthened old friendships and family ties. I helped set up the Cyprus Sociological Association with some new acquaintances and friends with whom I shared a sociology background. Unlike my first return in 1966 when I was still feeling that my teenage years had been hijacked by the underground movement, I was now feeling at home again.

As my leave wound down it dawned on me that I might regularly visit Cyprus during summers while maintaining my academic position in Ohio. I could have my cake and eat it too. Unlike my uncles who were tied to their shops in America, I was in a profession that allowed me time for travel. And living in the jet age, it no longer mattered how far you were from a given destination but only that you could afford a plane ticket.

EMILY

I made up my mind. I would keep my job in America and visit Cyprus in the summers. Sometimes, however, life unfolds in mysterious ways. As I began preparing for the return trip to Youngstown, my friend Eleni asked me to give a lecture at the *Kypriaka Chronika* (Cyprus Chronicles), a literary organization in which she served as a member of its governing board. Eleni broke through my initial resistance, and my introductory lecture in Greek on the history of sociology turned out to be the most important talk I had ever given.

I began by introducing my audience to the basics of the history of sociology, starting with the ideas of Auguste Comte, the nineteenth century French "Father of Sociology" who coined the term for the new discipline. His passion was to create a new science that would produce real knowledge about the workings of society. That science could then be harnessed to solve the intractable problems created in the aftermath of the French and industrial revolutions.

The small room was crowded. I was flattered that so many showed up to hear a talk on a subject so little known or understood on the island. My eyes honed in on a beautiful young woman who was sitting in the middle of the room, copiously taking notes. It was an effort to keep my focus on the lecture. I felt extremely drawn to her face—a strange feeling, unlike anything I had ever experienced. It was as if I had known her before. I hoped there would be an opportunity to have a chat with her after the lecture.

During the question-and-answer period she continued taking notes. When it was all over, she stood up and began walking towards the podium, but alas, a group of other participants surrounded me first, and they began firing their own questions. I saw her turn around and exit the room, and a sense of profound disappointment came over me. I was hardly able to focus on the others' queries, but five minutes later she was back. What a relief! I found out later that she had left the room feeling cold, rushed out to her car, and turned on the ignition to leave. But seconds later she changed her mind and came back. Apparently, I had made a remark about the Cyprus problem that she found problematic, and she wanted further clarification. "Your question can't be easily answered," I replied with a grin. "It would require some elaboration, and my friends are waiting for me." I pointed at the door where my friends were standing. "We are going for coffee at a nearby café. Why don't you join us, and we can continue the conversation there?" Blessedly, our conversation has continued for 50 years.

I knew on an intuitive level that Emily was the woman I was waiting for all my life. I could easily have asked her to marry me the next morning, but I realized that had I done so she would have dropped me like a hot potato. I was 29, she was 22. She was a Greek Cypriot, but she had just returned from England where she had lived with her parents for the last seven years, two of which were devoted to studying languages in Germany and Switzerland. She had just started working at the Cyprus Tourism Organization, and my lecture was the first event she had attended since her return from Europe three weeks prior. Fluent in five languages and steeped in English literature, she was poised for a promising career within that organization. Conversation with her at the cafe flowed effortlessly, and her extraordinary good-natured energy, her *élan vital*, and her shining, easy smile were infectious. I was surprised that she was still unattached. Finding an excuse to meet with her again and trying to impress her, I mentioned that my dissertation could offer more answers to her queries. Intellectually curious, she was eager to read it.

I lost no time. I borrowed my uncle's old bicycle and by morning I was at her office with the 300-page manuscript under my arm. I dared not express my true feelings to her yet. Perhaps I thought it important to maintain a sense of mystery. Her background in romantic European literature, her familiarity with the novels of Jane Austen, Emily Bronte, and Somerset Maugham demanded it. Our relationship remained platonic, with the understanding that I would be back in Cyprus in five months, and I dropped hints that I might stay on the island for good. In fact, I had already made up my mind that I was coming back to propose marriage, but I was the only one who knew that. Leaving her now felt like an awful risk; surely, many suitors would be after her, and we did not yet have the deep connection that Penelope had with her warrior husband Odysseus that would render me secure in our relationship.

We kept up a frequent correspondence. Every few days I would write her a long letter on a variety of subjects except for my true feelings for her. I wrote about everything from the condition of Native Americans to the politics of Richard Nixon—his "Tricky Dick" reputation among his enemies and his historic visit to Beijing with Henry Kissinger. I dredged up my most clever self in those letters, doing my best to avoid sounding ridiculous. I would often cut out some of the more amusing cartoons that appeared in the pages of the *New Yorker* and include them in my letters. Always, my feelings could only be inferred through carefully reading between the lines. I did ask her for a photo, a not-so-subtle move on my part; she readily mailed it to me, hopefully a sign of encouragement. I have kept that picture in my wallet to this day. It was taken the previous summer in Andalusia on her 21st birthday, while taking lessons in Spanish.

I was certain that our Platonic romance would progress to marriage within months. I had long ago concocted a mental image of what I wanted in a marital partner, probably using that image to screen potential partners, and Emily matched it perfectly. Maybe it was a composite of my late mother, my sister Maroulla, and my cousin Maro who started the kindergarten next door to us after my mother died. Who knows? But Emily arrived in my life as the harbor that my soul was craving for, a new endpoint that rendered much of my past more sensible.

I had decided that I would probably give up my career in America. When I got back to Ohio, Emily constantly on my mind, my dominant goal was to return to Cyprus. During the Spring break of 1972, I went to Chicago to visit Don Strickland, who had left Wayne State and was now teaching political philosophy at Northwestern University in Evanston, Illinois. We reminisced about old times in Detroit and our adventures in Cyprus, and we laughed about the sardonic rejection letter we received from Bertrand Russell about our idea to create international universities. It was our way of saying farewell.

Don mentioned in passing that the chair of the sociology department at Northwestern was Charlie Moskos, a Greek American whom I once met briefly at a sociology conference. He made a name for himself as a military sociologist by risking his life in the jungles of Vietnam to study the lives of American combat troops. Charlie also spent a year in Cyprus and wrote a book about the United Nations forces that had been keeping the peace since the outbreak of intercommunal fighting in 1964.[1]

I called Charlie and he immediately invited me to his office. We had an instant connection followed by dinner at his home, where I was introduced to his wife Ilka, a German-American language teacher. After dinner, Charlie asked me about my career plans. When I told him that I was determined to return to Cyprus, he questioned the wisdom of my decision. Why not consider the possibility of getting a position at a good research university in the U.S.?

I had made no mention of Emily, and he knew that Cyprus had no university. I simply replied that I was not looking for a job in the U.S. Before I left Chicago to return to Ohio, I gave him a copy of an article I had just written, which was eventually published in the *American Ethnologist*.[2]

A month later I received a call from Dr.Herbert Maccoby, professor and chair of sociology at the University of Maine, asking me if I would be interested in a position there. I was stunned. I later learned that the department was in a rebuilding process, and Professor Maccoby had been hired to recruit new faculty. He had sent letters to heads of sociology departments with doctoral programs asking for possible candidates. When Charlie received that letter, he suggested my name and sent along the copy of the article I had left for him before returning to Ohio. Another twist of fate!

Professor Maccoby was in something of a hurry. Spring semester would soon end, and decisions for hiring had to be made as soon as possible for the fall semester. I promised to let him know in a couple of days, and I immediately fell into a state of emotional turmoil. Do I go for an interview, and what if they offer me the position? And what about Emily? Would she leave Cyprus to join me in faraway Maine? I had never been there, but I had heard talk of its extraordinary beauty—its forests and lakes, its pristine coastal region, its lobsters of course. But Orono was neither London nor Munich, where Emily had lived before returning to Cyprus, and certainly no cosmopolitan hub. The symbol of the university was the black bear, and road signs of deer and moose crossings were everywhere. Could she be happy in such a place?

I called Emily at the Cyprus Tourism Organization, the first time I had phoned her. I asked only for her opinion, not her hand in marriage. Should I accept the job interview or not? Her reply was a quick: "Sure, go ahead." And I did. I did not know yet that she had no idea why I would ask her such a question, and she knew nothing about Maine. While I was implicitly signaling a coming marriage proposal, she was more focused on cutting the conversation short and ending the gossipy whispers of her nearby coworkers, who knew in those days that an overseas call was a big deal.

Suppose I had not traveled to Chicago that time to visit my friend Don, or simply called him on the phone and never went to see Charlie Moskos, or failed to leave Charlie a copy of my soon-to-be-published article? Would I still have been courted for that position in Maine through some other uncanny circumstance? If not, my life would have been utterly different. And what if I had refused Eleni's request to give that lecture, and therefore missed the chance to meet Emily? Mysterious coincidences often appear to shape our lives. Are they part of some larger plan? When they happen, we typically see them as unremarkable, or we fail to notice them at all. Whatever they are, here I was, perched on one of these almost-magical circumstances.

I looked at the map of Maine again, and I asked around. Friends used words like "isolated," "boondocks," "end of the earth," "Siberia," and "backwoods." The day before my interview, I strolled down Main Street in downtown Bangor, eight miles from the University of Maine campus. I felt as if I was in a frontier town, and I pictured John Wayne riding his horse up Main Street and chasing the bad guys.

My talk at the university was well received, and interviews with potential colleagues went smoothly. The campus was beautiful. I felt totally relaxed, neither eager nor anxious to make a good impression. My mind was on Emily and Cyprus, and I would have accepted either verdict. But I fully remember the moment at my hotel when Professor Maccoby sat next to me on a black leather couch, yellow pad and pen in hand, and he offered me the job. I accepted. The whole process was almost dizzying.

When I arrived in Nicosia in May of 1972, University of Maine contract in hand, Emily was waiting at the footsteps of the aircraft. As an official of the tourism organization, she had a permit to be on the tarmac to welcome special guests. In a month's time we were engaged, and a month later we had our wedding ceremony in Famagusta, her hometown. We then left Cyprus for Maine, with assurances to her inconsolable parents that we would be back permanently when Emily finished her undergraduate languages program at the University of Maine. Our ultimate plan was to settle in Famagusta—the tourist hub of the island and the fabled location of Shakespeare's Othello. It was also the home of arguably the most extraordinary sandy beach in the Mediterranean. This was our vision of the bright future awaiting us.

TUNING IN

Once we had settled into our new world in Maine, the old existential issues reappeared in my mind. I thought I had fulfilled my deepest yearnings: getting a doctorate, falling in love and marrying the woman of my dreams, and devoting my working life to what I considered the perfect occupation. But the gnawing questions about the meaning of life and the tragedy of our mortality resurfaced, the totally secular climate of academia offering me no real comfort. Should I not simply get over these unanswerable questions?

But how could I? Everything that gave me joy would be gone sooner or later. Death is the great equalizer, our ultimate destiny lurking in the background. It was the same realization that overwhelmed the Persian king Xerxes who, according to Herodotus, began weeping profusely as he watched his mighty army crossing the Dardanelles in his unsuccessful campaign to conquer Greece. "I cried," he explained to his horrified advisor, "when the thought crossed my mind that none of my thousands of soldiers will be alive a hundred years from now."

Not long after these morbid thoughts crossed *my* mind, I discovered meditation. I knew that it had surfaced widely in America in the sixties and that a guru named Maharishi Mahesh Yogi had disseminated the practice called Transcendental Meditation (TM). At that time, I was exclusively focused on my doctoral program, and I never paid much attention to this exotic fruit from the Far East.

My indifference soon changed. One day I noticed a peculiar sign stuck on the door of one of my new colleagues, Stephen Marks: "I'm meditating; please don't disturb." Like me, Stephen was a product of the sixties. We were both the same age, got our doctoral degrees around the same time, and began our career at the University of Maine the same year. We faced the same challenges of surviving the probationary period and getting tenure. I learned that Stephen had been doing TM for several years, and this struck me as strange. How could a trained sociologist like Stephen, steeped as he was in classic sociological theory, be drawn to this nonsensical mumbo jumbo? I was intrigued enough to ask him about it.

Our conversation had a watershed effect on my life, another one of those signal turning points and synchronicities that have shaped my life—Emily's as well. Stephen became one of my closest friends, sharing values, personal matters, and intellectual interests, along with common career concerns. We became confidants and counselors to each other. For close to four decades, we met every Wednesday morning for coffee at a local café. This was our weekly ritual of free-floating conversation and catching up with each other.

Stephen convinced us that meditation was beneficial for well-being, physical as well as emotional and spiritual.[3] It gave practitioners a deep state of relaxation, deeper than sleep, and it made them more productive and energetic in their daily lives. That very first semester, Emily and I picked up the practice of TM—twice a day, every day for twenty minutes. Eventually TM became a household word in America and was introduced as a psychotherapeutic practice into prisons, hospitals, and schools. With a little help from the Beatles having taken it up, TM was a major contributor to the counterculture watershed.

Maharishi claimed that through years of practice, one could attain "cosmic consciousness," a state of union with Ultimate Reality—a notion that reminded me of the "supraconscious" of Pitirim Sorokin and the "collective unconscious" of Carl Jung. I learned later that the concept of cosmic consciousness was first introduced to the West in 1901 in the work of the Canadian psychiatrist Richard Maurice Buck in his celebrated book *Cosmic Consciousness*.[4] I wondered if attaining such states could resolve the existential problems faced by ordinary people such as myself as they struggle with the meaning of life and death.

The combination of total relaxation during deep states of meditation and full awareness as the mind becomes silent is difficult to describe. If the six months of intensive Freudian psychoanalysis that I underwent at Wayne State initiated a habit of turning inward and focusing on my subjective world, TM opened my mind to possible realities that lay beyond my intellect and my Freudian unconscious.

The philosopher Peter Russell neatly summarizes this prospect in his "definitive overview of meditation."[5] Along with the three ordinary states of consciousness—waking, dreaming, and sleeping—meditation can open us to a fourth state, in which there is awareness of nothing but consciousness itself. It is awareness that is pure, transcending the consciousness of objects.[6]

Meditation practice changed my worldview in a fundamental way. Although TM is not itself the practice of a religion, Stephen explained to me, it is friendly to all religions and in many ways their fulfillment. It started my liberation from the ingrained agnosticism of ten years of secular education dominated by antireligious and anticlerical values. If the sixties turned me from a simple believer in a transcendent God into a secular doubter, the seventies was the beginning of my liberation from unbelief. I became suspicious of my skepticism, and I began to see agnosticism as another form of "false consciousness," an intellectual malady afflicting the way of thinking of most modern intellectuals and academics. Within the context of that new awareness, I began to reassess my sixties educational experience. Cosmic consciousness may have eluded me, but the systematic practice of meditation sensitized me to the possibility of transcendence and to realities that were unmistakably spiritual.

A RETROSPECTIVE GLANCE

I now realized that in academia I had unwittingly absorbed a syndrome I call reductionist materialism. It was pervasive in most of the courses I was exposed to, the lectures I listened to, and nearly all the textbooks and journal articles I was assigned to read. It is still too much with us. Its basic tenet is that gross matter is the totality of reality.[7] It is governed by immutable physical laws, and it operates like a huge machine of interdependent parts. There is no mind independent of the material machine, no God, no angels, no demons, no transcendent realities, only sensate, observable nature.

This syndrome left me with a sense of spiritual malaise, an existential angst that is probably an inevitable byproduct of any hypersecular understanding of reality. Once I understood the source of my unease, I felt liberated from it. I rekindled my attraction to Sorokin's perspective, in large part because meditation practice gave me experiential confirmation of some of his central convictions. I had a new appreciation of his perspective that we have a conscious mind, an unconscious mind, and a supraconscious mind. And I marveled once again at his notion that true knowledge of reality comes to us through three channels: the senses (science), the mind (reasoning, philosophy, logic, mathematics), and intuition (clairvoyance, precognition, meditation, contemplation, and so on). Sorokin's "Integralist Truth" was closer to the nature of Truth than the strictly cerebral approaches of positivistic science and reductionist, analytic philosophy.

Modernity is truly a Janus-headed phenomenon, having fostered both positive and negative consequences for Western civilization, the world at large, and for individuals. Reductionism is more than a simple narrowing down of reality. On the positive side, it dramatically heightened our perception of the material *part* of reality, with the help of scientific instruments. Paradoxically, I could begin to see reductionist materialism as a form of spirituality in disguise; it is just one of many ways that Spirit manifests itself in history. I was beginning to wonder if modernism's hostility to religion might usher in a more mature religiosity and a richer, deeper spirituality. Inspired by my rediscovery of Sorokin, I began to explore a different kind of literature that included intuition and inner contemplation as a central part of the pursuit of knowledge.

TROUBLES EXPLODE AGAIN

My emerging spiritual interests soon got relegated to the back burner. Just as Emily and I were adjusting to our new lives in Maine, I received an urgent call from Professor John Peristiani, an Oxford anthropologist with Cypriot roots. He asked me to join him for a maximum of two years to assist in the creation of a social science research center in Cyprus. The project was funded by UNESCO, the Ford Foundation, and the Cyprus Government. It would include a study of the urbanization of the island, a process which had accelerated since the establishment of the Republic of Cyprus in 1960. This was a call I could not ignore. Emily agreed to temporarily interrupt her studies, and my department gave me a full-year leave of absence, seeing the invitation to be a great research opportunity.

The unexpected turn of events was at first a positive development in our lives. We were together, and we were meditating twice a day, supremely happy in our Mediterranean paradise. I felt comfortable working at the research center and commuting the half hour with my research team to do interviews in the Messaoria region. Emily found a job at the British Council, a library and cultural institution. We rented a house in Nicosia, conveniently located near both of our jobs. During weekends we drove to the coast in Famagusta, where Emily's parents lived and where she grew up. We frequently made the three-hour trip to Rizokarpasso, the stunningly beautiful coastal village at the tip of the long Karpass peninsula, where Emily spent childhood summers with colorful relatives on her father's side. We often visited friends there. We would fish with nets and spears, followed by feasts at night with the day's catch. Life could not be more idyllic, so much so that thoughts of remaining on the island resurfaced in my mind.

But trouble was brewing in paradise, and our presence in Nicosia (the capital city) enabled me to closely follow the political volcano that was soon to erupt. Extreme nationalists, headed by former EOKA chief George Grivas, organized a new underground campaign, now called EOKA B, to fight the government of Archbishop Makarios—the first president of the Republic. He and his supporters accused Makarios of betraying the struggle for uniting the island with Greece, and they began blowing up police stations and terrorizing opponents. To make matters worse, this new civil strife was happening while the disputes between Greek and Turkish Cypriots were heating up with unresolved ethnic resentments.

Sensing the seriousness of the political situation, I kept a journal and took copious notes on events as they developed. I created a large file of newspaper clippings, personal notes, and data related to the political storm engulfing the island. It was as if I was working on two projects simultaneously—the village study of urbanization on the microlevel and the politics of the island on the macrolevel.

On the morning of July 15, 1974 madness broke loose. The Greek Cypriot national guard, headed by extreme right-wing officers loyal to the military dictatorship then ruling Greece, carried out their long-planned violent coup d'état against the government of Archbishop Makarios. Hundreds if not thousands were killed. We were devastated, watching the tanks roll by our office as they headed towards the presidential palace. One of my colleagues at the Center collapsed with uncontrollable sobbing. She feared for the life of her father, a leading politician and then president of the House of Representatives. It took the rebels several days to consolidate their power, and the situation was to become much worse. On the morning of July 20 Turkey invaded the island under the legal pretext of reestablishing constitutional order. With overwhelming force, Turkish troops captured a patch of land on the northern coast that included Kyrenia, the small town where I spent my summers as a child and where my friend Don Strickland and I had organized our conference four years earlier.

The U.S Sixth fleet rushed to the area and anchored near the eastern coast. The American embassy in Nicosia issued instructions to all U.S citizens to gather at the long Famagusta beach, where helicopters would pick them up and land them on the decks of American carriers. My new friend Leonard Doob, a distinguished retired American social psychologist who had come to the island to organize a reconciliation project among Greek and Turkish Cypriots, was forced to abort his project and leave. I was concerned that my file of notes and newspaper clippings would be confiscated by agents of the new military regime, and Leonard graciously agreed to take it with him.

Leaving Cyprus became extremely difficult for us. We were not yet American citizens, and the Nicosia airport was shut down. It was an arena of heavy fighting, eventually taken over by UN peacekeeping troops. It was difficult to move out of Nicosia, as Turkish planes were strafing the highways with their machine guns. We found refuge in the basement of a grocery store owned by a cousin. We could hardly sleep. Our adrenalin was surging; we feared that the nearby fighting would eventually reach us. During those agonizing days I tried to do my TM practice to calm my nerves, and using a portable transistor radio, I was glued to the reports monitored by the international service of the BBC. The national radio, now in the hands of the rebels, was blasting military marching songs and fabricated news of triumphs and victories.

There was a window of opportunity to leave the island during a ceasefire, but there was no way out of the island by air. We managed to get a couple of tickets on a passenger ship that docked in Limassol, the southern port of the island. It was coming from Haifa on the way to Venice via Piraeus. I will never forget the scene the day we boarded, along with wounded Greek Cypriot soldiers on stretchers. They were being shipped to Greece for medical treatment because the facilities on the island could not handle the load of casualties. On board were relaxed-looking and curious tourists enjoying their afternoon drinks, while a band was playing soft jazz. It was surreal.

Unlike the tourists, we were in a continuous state of emotional turmoil about what would happen to the Island, especially our loved ones. We were unable to say goodbye to my in-laws in Famagusta. We have few memories of our days in Venice, that majestic city of poets, writers, and high culture. We walked the streets like zombies, awaiting train passage to France and then a boat and bus ride to London. Our minds were still in Cyprus. We could hardly notice the gondolas and all the architectural marvels, remnants of a great empire. I recall a haunting passage from the poetry of George Seferis, one of Greece's leading poets and a Nobel laureate: "Everywhere I go," he lamented, "Greece always wounds me." Being a diplomat, he was fully engrossed in the troubled history of his country, and it was all too easy for me to apply his words to my own country.

In London we stayed with Emily's brother and his family, nurturing our emotional wounds from the double shock of the coup and the Turkish invasion. We assumed that the ceasefire in Cyprus would hold, but just as we were about to board the flight at Heathrow Airport for New York, we heard more devastating news. The diplomatic efforts had collapsed and Turkey broke the ceasefire, sending its tanks south to conquer more territory in Cyprus. Their forces were heading towards Famagusta. Emily sobbed almost nonstop during the seven-hour flight to New York. She finally fell asleep, exhausted from the agony of what might be happening to her parents and our other relatives and friends. I felt emotionally drained myself, but I could not sleep. I could not free my mind from flashbacks of what we had just gone through. I kept thinking of the last time we visited Kyrenia. My cousin Tryfon had invited us for a picnic at his brother-in-law's orange grove by the sea. It was the Sunday before the Greek coup and the Turkish invasion. We enjoyed a lovely day swimming, and then we had lunch under the canopy of orange trees. His 65-year-old father-in-law, feeling energized from the red wine, had suddenly stood up, placed a Turkish red fez on his head, and begun a solo dance in the middle of the grove. Nobody knew where he found that fez, banned in Turkey since the time of Kemal Ataturk in the twenties. His performance was infectious, everyone erupting in laughter. Like an intoxicated Delphic oracle he began singing and rhythmically jumping up and down, prophesying that "everybody will be wearing fezzes soon!" His drunken precognition came to fruition a week later. Tryfon's brother, present at the orange grove feast, went missing and was presumed dead. Tryfon and other members of his family including his father-in-law were taken prisoner by the Turks, while other Greek Cypriots were either killed or put under house arrest.

While Emily slept, I remembered the urgent telephone call I had made to my in-laws in Famagusta right after the coup. It was late afternoon. I implored them to take a taxi and come right over to Nicosia so that by morning I could drive them to the mountains, which seemed a safer place to be. The BBC reported that Famagusta, because of its long sandy beach, was a likely spot for the Turkish invasion. My in-laws had not been particularly worried. They were having tea with neighbors on their veranda, talking about the day's events. It was summertime, and the afternoon breezes mixed in with the smells of jasmine offered a false sense of normalcy. "Don't worry," my father-in law, a schoolmaster, reassured me over the phone. "Everything is quiet here. Nothing is happening." I asked him to promise me that by morning, he would take a taxi and come to Nicosia for a ride up the mountains to some village hotel. He agreed. By morning, however, life changed radically on the Island. The invasion had begun, and my in-laws found refuge in the basement of their house. Turkish aircraft were bombing the city and machine-gunning the highways.

Once we found a way to leave Nicosia and Cyprus, we could only connect with my in-laws by phone. They remained in Famagusta when the ceasefire was announced, and the invasion took place on another beach in the north, near Kyrenia, giving a false sense of security to the Famagustians. While we were flying over the Atlantic and the second phase of the invasion began, my in-laws fled to the south, as did all other Famagustians. But their belief that this was a temporary situation was unshakable; in just two or three days they would be able to get back to their homes. Risking an encounter with the approaching Turkish army, my father-in-law furtively returned home to change his clothes and pick up some cheese and bread. They expected to camp under olive trees outside of the city and wait for the dust to settle. He left his wife's jewelry and other valuables, on the illusory assumption that they would soon return home and find everything intact. This was my first exposure to the thinking that happens repeatedly in history—people feeling comfortable in their routines and never believing that their taken-for-granted worlds could collapse in a matter of days if not hours or minutes. It happened to Jews in Germany, to the people of ancient Pompeii, and to the victims of Hiroshima and Nagasaki. It is still happening to millions of people around the world.

Arriving in New York, we soon learned that our friends Stanley Kyriakides, a political scientist at Paterson State University, and his wife Helen were on a hunger strike outside the United Nations, joined by other Greeks and Greek Cypriots. It happens regularly in New York for any number of reasons and political causes. We met them there as they held placards protesting the Turkish invasion of Cyprus. They broke their three-day fast to offer us hospitality while sharing our common agony about the fate of Cyprus. On the drive to Wayne New Jersey, it felt strange to pass by carefree youngsters playing baseball, while at that very moment people were dying seven-thousand miles away in Cyprus under the weight of a mighty invading army. When we arrived at their home, we turned on the 6:30 news and we gasped. Turkish tanks were entering and capturing Famagusta, Emily's hometown.

Heartbroken, we reached Maine in time for me to resume my teaching responsibilities and Emily to continue her undergraduate work. This was the fall semester of 1974. The trauma of the events in Cyprus haunted us. I remember waking up one evening drenched in sweat as I heard explosions and what sounded like gunfire. It was fireworks at the University. Students were celebrating the start of the school year. Later in the semester while working late in my office, the janitor rushed in, asking with excitement if I had heard the news. My mind immediately went to Cyprus. "Oh my God," I moaned, "what are the Turks up to now?" The janitor looked at me curiously and asked, "What do you think about the coming blizzard?" I was constantly on pins and needles, but I laughed with relief.

Many of our relatives became refugees including Emily's parents, who ended up in London staying temporarily with their son. Their home in Famagusta was now under Turkish control. My aunt Polyxeni from Kyrenia became a refugee and fled south to Nicosia, staying with my sister and leaving behind her home, where we had spent our summers as children. A first cousin was missing and presumed dead, and other relatives were captured as prisoners of war and sent to concentration camps. Turkey ended up controlling 36 percent of the island's territory, while one-third of the Greek Cypriot population fled to the south, becoming refugees in their own country. Six thousand Greek Cypriots were killed in a population of a little over half a million. There was hardly a household without someone missing.

I notified Leonard Doob of our return, and in a week's time I received the large file of notes and paper clippings that I had handed him for safe keeping. Right away I began working with intense energy on what I considered to be the social and historical conditions that led to the Cyprus debacle. It was not merely an academic exercise on my part; it was a form of catharsis, a way to get it off my chest. Finishing a fifty-page paper and having no idea what to do with it, I sent it to Leonard for feedback and as a thank you for rescuing my file. Unbeknownst to me, he passed it on to the editor of Yale University Press with the note, "I recommend that you encourage Markides to write a book on the crisis in Cyprus." The editor, who had published several of Leonard's books, sent it to various experts on the Middle East for their opinion. Their consensus was quite positive, and they added some suggestions of their own about how to proceed with a book-length manuscript.

For the next several months, while teaching full time I plunged furiously into writing about the sociological and historical dynamics that led to the Greek-engineered coup and the Turkish invasion of the island. I did my utmost to put aside my own emotional investment. The whole exercise had a healing and bittersweet effect on my life, and it was decisive for my getting tenure at the University of Maine.

When I heard from Yale Press that my book was unconditionally accepted for publication, I could hardly contain my feelings. I donned my shorts and running shoes for a long jog through the woods that surround the University. *The Rise and Fall of the Cyprus Republic* came out in 1977.[8] A year later the study of the village in the Messaoria region, entitled *Lysi: Social Change in a Cypriot Village*, was published as a co-authored monograph by the Social Science Research Centre in Nicosia.[9] Tragically, Lysi was yet another place overrun by Turkish troops. Its people were displaced refugees, longing for the day of their return. Our study became a historical record of life in their village before it was taken over. Remote Rizokarpasso, where my friend Michael Attalides, a Princeton-trained sociologist had been doing his part of the overall study of urbanization, was likewise cut off by the Turkish army during the second phase of the invasion. Michael was able to flee south just in the nick of time.

The Yale book on the sociological context of the Cyprus tragedy kick started my academic career. There was a great deal of irony surrounding this success. We lost our home in Cyprus and lots of inherited property. Just before the invasion, we had borrowed money from an uncle to buy a piece of land in Kyrenia with nine robust olive trees on it. Now it was under Turkish control, but the debt to our uncle-turned-refugee remained. It took us nearly ten years to pay it all back. Still, that disaster became an important part of my life's journey, both spiritually and academically. We were "fortunate" refugees; we lost no member of our immediate family. In Cyprus, 200,000 people were trying to restart their lives as refugees just miles from their homes, while we were able to continue our lives in Maine.

The invasion of Cyprus sealed our decision to stay in America indefinitely. We had lost Famagusta and Emily's inherited family home there, where we had planned to eventually settle. The economy of the island was in shambles, and it would take years to recover. The places we loved most—Kyrenia, Famagusta, and Rizokarpasso—were no longer accessible. We felt forever evicted from our earthly paradise. That feeling still lingers decades later, but we were beginning to call Maine our home, thankful for a life in a pristine environment within the privileged context of university life. When our children were born, I felt great relief that they could grow up in a peaceful place, with activities no more risky or violent than competitive swimming, tennis, canoeing and soccer playing—this in sharp contrast to my life as a young teenager, when I was recruited to fight the British Empire.

My politically troubled background led me to focus my academic research on the sociology of violence, war, revolution, and terrorism. I designed a course entitled "Problems of Violence and Terrorism" to study and teach these age-old phenomena. Parallel to this focus, my hunger to make sense of life remained lively. In addition to daily meditation practice, I began exploring the world's wisdom traditions, from Zen Buddhism to the yoga methods of India and the mushrooming literature on tribal shamanism, particularly the work on native American spirituality. I also became aware of physicist Fritjof Capra's efforts in *The Tao of Physics* to find common ground between modern science and mystical spirituality.[10] The sixties counterculture had opened many new doors, at least for the middle-class American intelligentsia, and I was attracted to them.

BECOMING MAINERS

By the end of the seventies many things had changed in our family life. In 1976 Emily gave birth to Constantine and in 1978 she was pregnant with Vasia. She had earned both a bachelor's and a master's degree in German literature, and in the early eighties she added an MA in French. I was given tenure at the University in 1977, and a year later, I became a naturalized citizen like my uncles before me. That put an end to my lifelong struggle to resist America.

We no longer yearned for the extended-family relationships of my youth in Cyprus. My tenure provided us long-term security and stability and we had a fine place to raise our children, whose regular school routines seemed to ground us. We were sinking roots, and by tenure time I had gotten fully engaged in several meaningful quasi-communities—the sociology department, the wider University of Maine community, and the Greeks of the Bangor area. These communities helped to cushion the extreme grief we still felt in the aftermath of the Turkish invasion and our loss of Famagusta.

The Department of Sociology turned out to be my home away from home. Several of my colleagues became my close friends. Stephen Marks, whom I introduced earlier, was one of them. Steven Cohn was another, a Columbia-trained sociologist who was hired a year before my arrival. Steve had a big hand in my getting hired, having read my dissertation, and persuading the Chairman, Herb Maccoby, to bring me to the campus for an interview. With Steve I shared parallel theoretical interests in sociology, leading to several co-authored publications.

Five of us in the rebuilt department were of the same generation, all of us intellectual products of the sixties. We had grown into our discipline at a critical period of American history: the Civil Rights Movement, the turbulent years of the Vietnam War, and the rise of the counterculture. Those experiences inspired us to develop a pronounced humanistic orientation to sociology. We were not simply detached observers of American society but also its critics, spotlighting issues of social inequality, minority rights, gender equality, foreign policy, civil liberties, and the like. We bonded with each other around these shared perspectives. The Sociology Department was a safe haven for the free-floating exploration of unorthodox ideas. Within that intellectual milieu, I had free rein to explore areas I may not have pursued without that institutional support and protection.

The overall University was a second meaningful quasi-community for myself as well as for Emily. Over the years we forged friendships with colleagues across disciplines and from different ethnic backgrounds. This was a mini multicultural world within which we were destined to spend most of our lives. Its cosmopolitan flavor made it impossible to sustain narrow and xenophobic views of the world, the hallmark of the kind of homogeneous, traditional societies from which some of us had come.

Our third quasi-community was the small group of Greeks in the Bangor area. In my job interview I had learned that there was an active Greek Orthodox Church, just a 15-minute drive from Orono. The mayor himself was a second-generation Greek. At the time it made little difference to me. I was no longer traditionally religious. I was not a regular churchgoer. I was prejudiced. I inherited from my sixties' education an aversion to organized religion—an outgrowth of my encounter with the anticlerical values of the Western Enlightenment. I still had a chip on my shoulder toward the Greek Orthodox hierarchy in Cyprus; they had promoted the nationalistic fervor that unwittingly paved the way for the 1974 Greek coup and the Turkish invasion of the island. But in Maine, far away from the troubled world of Cyprus, the Greek Orthodox Church had a different and very positive impact on our lives. It offered us a meaningful community anchorage within the context of multicultural America. Most importantly, it provided for our children the foundation of a subcultural Greek identity, and it enlivened that identity for Emily and me.

The Greek community of the Bangor area was created during the 1910s by a handful of immigrant families. They arrived with their wagons selling fruits and vegetables, eventually buying a former Protestant church. They decorated it with Byzantine icons, created a consecrated Orthodox altar, and nurtured a strong community. It has been the center of Greek-American activities—not only weekly religious services but also major cultural events such as a yearly Greek dinner dance that became a big attraction for the entire state.

We were warmly welcomed. The church was a place to meet other Greeks and forge new friendships outside of the University. Over time these friendships evolved into family-like connections that were not unlike those we had in Cyprus. Some were employed by the University of Maine or other academic institutions in the area. Originally from the island of Lesbos was Dora, a leading nutritionist, and her civil engineering husband Miltos, who taught in the Engineering department. From Thessaloniki was Lambros, a clinical therapist and professor of psychology at Husson University in Bangor. He introduced us to the exquisite joys of authentic Byzantine chanting, which became a big factor in our attachment to the church as regular participants. Lambros also introduced us to the joys of sailing, with adventures up and down the Atlantic American coast, sailing to Bermuda and the Bahamas, and crossing the Mediterranean from Gibraltar to Greece.

OF GUERILLAS AND MYSTICS

I was scheduled to have my first sabbatical leave in the spring of 1979, freeing me from all teaching responsibilities during that semester. My time would be exclusively focused on research and writing. I had already gathered material for a book on international terrorism and presented papers on that topic at the American Sociological Association meetings of 1978 and at the International Political Science Association meetings in Mexico City. At that time hardly any sociologists were studying terrorism, which was beginning to emerge as a major concern in the affairs of modern states. At the conference presentations, I suggested that terrorism was proliferating because it was becoming the functional alternative to both conventional revolutions and conventional wars. Would-be revolutionaries opt for terrorism as a weapon against more powerful foes against whom they could never prevail in an open revolutionary war. Modern states have become too powerful and thus invulnerable to revolutions. Conventional armies of the sort George Washington mobilized against the colonial government could not possibly triumph over the powerful modern state, with its huge arsenal of technologically sophisticated weaponry. Modern states themselves often opt for terrorism when other means, such as diplomacy or conventional war, are not viable options. Paradoxically the world has become more peaceful in the age of terrorism![11]

I was encouraged to continue in this line of research when my paper was accepted pending revisions by the leading journal on terrorism. I felt I was poised to make a career as an expert on this subject. In addition to historical data I had assembled for the monograph, I had access to other exciting material that could help flesh out how ordinary people become terrorists, a pioneering project. Once again, however, my life was to take an unexpected turn, one that would radically change my life as well as Emily's.

In the summer of 1978, four years after the tragic events of 1974, we went back to Cyprus for a visit. The Turkish army was still on the Island occupying close to forty percent of the territory. Emily's parents had returned from London and settled in Limassol, the coastal city in the south of the island. They remained there in fruitless anticipation of the day they could return home. Famagusta was now a barb-wired "ghost city," fenced off by the Turkish army.

We rented an apartment in Nicosia. Emily was pregnant with our daughter Vasia, and she stayed with our son Constantine. She also taught at a local college while I went back to Maine for the fall semester. I planned to rejoin our family in Cyprus when the semester ended in December and begin working on the terrorism project during my sabbatical in the spring semester of 1979.

Back in Maine during the fall of 1978, I gathered more research material on terrorism. I also constructed a questionnaire for the in-depth interviews I planned to do with former Greek Cypriot underground guerrillas. But one night as I was lying in bed, my mind in that half-asleep, half-awake zone, I was literally jolted by a beam of light that seemed to hit me on the top of my head. I instantly sat up, exclaiming to myself, "Oh my God, mystics are more interesting than terrorists!" Of course, there was more than a little context for this bolt of insight.

Soon after Emily and I began practicing TM, my now close friend Stephen Marks introduced us to Carlos Castaneda's books about a Yaqui Indian medicine man named Don Juan. His work had quickly become must-reading for counterculture enthusiasts, and I devoured them.[12] Controversies soon arose about the authenticity of these allegedly anthropological works, but what was far more important to me was their heuristic value. They alerted me to phenomena such as nonmedical healing, mystical spirituality, and tribal shamanism, and they sparked a keen interest in comparative religions—all topics that have remained central to my work and my life.

I vividly remember reading another suggestion by Stephen in that period, a book on American shamanism entitled *Rolling Thunder: A Personal Exploration into the Secret Healing Powers of an American Indian Medicine Man*, by Doug Boyd.[13] Like the Castaneda books, it provided vivid material about tribal shamanism and "nonordinary" phenomena. But more important for the direction my life would soon take, it reminded me of a reputed healer and mystic whom I had met in Cyprus during the summer of 1974, just before the Turkish invasion.

I met the Cypriot shaman through one of those coincidences that seem to shape my life. I was walking in downtown Nicosia when I bumped into my old friend Vera, whom I knew from my teenage years when she was a comrade-in-arms with my sister Maroulla. As young women they had worked together in the EOKA underground. Our excitement about reconnecting was followed by a dinner invitation. We met Vera's husband, exchanged our personal news, and talked about the perennial "Cyprus Problem." Somehow, our conversation turned to philosophical matters about the nature of life and human existence. Emily and I were both impressed with their uncommon wisdom. Curious, I asked about their philosophical pursuits. "We have a master," they told us, "a spiritual teacher." "And who is that teacher?" I asked with great interest. "Daskalos," they replied.

I knew of that person while growing up. He lived only two miles from my house and had a reputation as a specialist of the spirit world. As children we were warned to keep our distance because he was dangerous. I never met him back then, but now my apprehensions were gone, and I asked Vera if she would arrange for a meeting with this mysterious man.

It was a few days before the disastrous coup d'état. At that first meeting Daskalos made a lasting impression on me. Unlike the ferocious sorcerer I imagined in my youth, he was a good-humored, retired grandfather with a piercing intelligence and a depth of knowledge about life. I began to wonder if he was an unrecognized Western shaman or medicine man. Unlike most of his retired peers who spent their free time playing backgammon and cards in the traditional all-male coffee houses, he devoted himself to helping people with their problems, both physical and psychological, without accepting any money. He was alleged to have special abilities or "powers" that seemed similar to the lore about Tibetan lamas, Hindu yogis, and Native American medicine men. Yet, he was a baptized Orthodox Christian living within an Orthodox Christian world. Like the *curanderos* of Mexico, who practiced their craft within the context of a Catholic Christian world, Daskalos worked within the Greek Orthodox Christian tradition with which he identified himself.

Now four years after that first encounter, I thought that Daskalos was perhaps the Cypriot equivalent of Castaneda's *Don Juan* and Doug Boyd's *Rolling Thunder*. The fact that he lived and operated from within a Christian framework was especially intriguing. Exploring his world would not be difficult. We shared the same cultural background and we spoke the same language. I could get easy entrance into his circle of practitioners and learn about his world. That fateful evening when the beam of light hit me, the idea popped into my mind that instead of spending my sabbatical writing about terrorism, I might devote it more meaningfully to the world of healers, mystics, and medicine men. I could put the terrorism project on the back burner and take advantage of my semester in Cyprus to engage in a radically different kind of research.

I talked about my new idea with my friends Stephen and Joan Marks. Joan was a reputable clinical therapist in the Bangor area. I was staying in their home in the fall of 1978, having rented out our own home for the academic year. They were the first to know about my bolt-of-light experience. Their exposure to Eastern mystical traditions through the TM practice and their familiarity with Castaneda's and Boyd's books made them supportive and interested in my changed plans.

I had three issues that I had to deal with. First, how do I study Daskalos? I was not an anthropologist with training and experience in field research. Do I study him and his circles of healers through conventional sociological methods, or do I invent a method appropriate for the reality that confronted me? This issue was quickly resolved when Joan Marks suggested, "Why not keep a journal and write down everything you observe and experience with that healer?" I thought it was a brilliant idea, and I decided that night to follow her suggestion and become a participant-observer in the circles of Daskalos, recording everything as objectively as possible.

My second issue was more challenging, and it concerned my colleagues. Will they see my shift of research focus positively, or will they find my new direction suspicious or unacceptable? My training was in political sociology and I was moving into unfamiliar territory. I would even be shelving the article I was revising for *The Journal of Terrorism*, thus denying myself the recognition I might have received for this contribution to a hot topic. Fortunately, my colleagues understood that within sociology there is a venerated tradition of participant-observation, parallel to anthropological field work and often hailed as a counterweight to mainstream, quantitative hypothesis-testing. The phenomenological, participant-observer approach I settled on was quite consonant with the old Chicago-School approach. I would simply let Daskalos explain his world as he himself experienced it, from within his own categories of understanding.

Much to my delight, my colleagues were supportive of my new line of research. It was considered a legitimate work of ethnography. I had brought to light a subculture that was hidden from view. At a university like Harvard or Berkeley, I might have encountered strong resistance to violating mainstream notions of research. I sometimes think that there is more freedom to be innovative at the periphery than at the center of a system of power. At the University of Maine periphery, I felt free to explore areas beyond the pale of conventional disciplinary boundaries.

My third issue was perhaps the most difficult and challenging. Will Daskalos allow me to study him? I had already written to Emily about my intentions. I urged her to ask Vera if she could get some advance indication from Daskalos that it would be okay for me to do the study. The news back to me was discouraging. I learned that Daskalos had not allowed anyone to interview him even for a newspaper article, so the chances of him giving permission to write a book about him were slim. Also, Emily wondered in her letter, "Why do you want to throw away your career?" Daskalos had a rather uneven reputation. For the devoutly religious he was someone who consorted with spirits that were not necessarily benign. For the secularists he was a charlatan and a trickster, a magician fooling the gullible and the naive. Among his followers he was often a miracle worker. For me, of course, he was an intriguing subject of investigation, a Christian shaman operating within the confines of a society that was both modern and traditionally religious, an enigma.

I did not give up. Before I flew to the Island to reconnect with my family and begin my sabbatical leave, I decided to contact Daskalos directly. I wanted him to take me seriously, to impress him with my academic credentials. I sent him a copy of my book on *The Rise and Fall of the Cyprus Republic*. I was not certain that he received it. Unsure of my prospects of studying his world, I prepared for the terrorism project as a backup. But two days after my Cyprus reunion with Emily and Constantine, I met with Daskalos. I told him I would not debunk or discredit him or dismiss his work in any way. I certainly did not see him as some instrument of the devil. My approach was going to be strictly objective, allowing his worldview to become known to a wider audience. I explained to him the method of participant-observation. That would mean simply hanging around with him and observing his daily life with people who sought his help. I would also sit in on his regular lectures and discussions he had with his small circle of disciples.

To my great delight and the surprise of many of my friends, Daskalos gave me the green light to do my study. For the next nine months on the island, I spent many hours and days with him recording everything. I observed and taped as many of our conversations as possible, including some vigorous exchanges between Emily and Daskalos. With her challenging questions, and her background of European secular literature and feminist thought, Emily became a catalyst as well as my best helper in extracting the intricacies of his world.

The anthropological literature on shamanism was good preparation for this work. I learned that leading scholars followed the shifting intellectual currents through the decades. Until the late fifties, for instance, when Freudian psychoanalysis was in its heyday, anthropologists defined shamanism as a form of mental pathology. Shamans were explained away as victims of infantile regression with symptoms such as auditory and visual hallucinations, as if ignorant natives had turned their madmen into prophets, seers, and witch doctors. This was a typical reductionist view of shamanic experience. Western anthropologists with a background in psychiatry routinely applied this mental-illness model to what they observed. Freudian psychiatrists saw the shaman's purported out-of-the-body journeys as nothing more than regression to an infantile, "oceanic" state of consciousness.

Anthropologists of the countercultural sixties began questioning this reductive model. The floodgates opened to the scrutiny of every established orthodoxy in medicine, politics, religion, or even science. Shamans were no longer seen as madmen but as local healers serving important "functions" in their communities, attending to the physical and mental needs of the people around them. The works of Ari Kiev in his *Magic, Faith and Healing*, and Fuller Torrey in *Witchdoctors and Psychiatrists* were emblematic of the shifting attitudes about the nature of shamanism.[14]

The war on imposed categories in the sixties also penetrated deeply into the field of psychiatry. Sociologist Erving Goffman's *Asylums* exposed the abuses of psychiatry as it was practiced in mental hospitals, implicitly attacking the field as an instrument for the oppression of the weak, the poor and the nonconforming.[15] Some psychiatrists launched a rebellion from within psychiatry itself, calling for radical changes that would deprive psychiatry of all authority. Psychiatrists are no more scientific than tribal shamans, they argued. The British psychiatrist R.D. Laing went as far as to claim that some people who have been misdiagnosed as mentally ill may be more in contact with "reality" than the psychiatrists who label them. Laing made this argument after spending a year meditating at a Sri Lankan Buddhist monastery.[16]

The seventies saw a more radical approach to the study of shamanism, one that was considered taboo until then. Some daring anthropologists decided to undergo shamanic training themselves. For Michael Harner of the New School of Social Research, it seemed that there was no other choice. Having gone to Brazil to study the medicinal culture of the Jivaros tribe in the heart of the Amazon, the shamans there refused to reveal their knowledge unless he was willing to become an initiate and undergo their schooling. Harner ended up becoming a trained shaman of the Jivaros and did not shy away from announcing his new status to his surprised colleagues when he returned to his position as chair of the Anthropology Department. After his retirement he set up the Center for Shamanic Studies.

I met with Harner in New York after my sabbatical in Cyprus, eager to get any counsel he might offer about my ongoing research with Daskalos. On the way to his office at the New School, I bumped into a colleague I knew who was teaching in the political science department. Surprised to see me, she asked what I was doing there. I replied, "I have an appointment with Michael Harner." With a puzzled look she asked, "Why on earth do you want to see *him*?" I asked, "Why does that surprise you so much?" "Well," she said, "he sort of does weird stuff."

Michael Harner did not seem weird at all, and I had a wonderful exchange with this man full of humor and wisdom, who died in 2018. He told me about his experience at UCLA as Carlos Castaneda's advisor for his undergraduate project, which ultimately became the latter's first book, *The Teachings of Don Juan*. I asked him if Don Juan was a real person. He said yes, and he regretted that he had not accepted Castaneda's invitation to meet the remarkable and talented shaman. I told him what I was doing with Daskalos. He showed keen interest, and he encouraged me to proceed without hesitation. Sometime later when I came up for full professor, he wrote a supportive letter on my behalf, focusing on the strength of my work as a form of participant-observation. Getting this validation from a leading anthropologist was important to me. He helped me to maintain a certain tenacity going forward, having allayed my fear that fellow academics will dismiss my work as nonsense.

In the middle of my visit, Harner received a call from a TV station requesting his public appearance with a critic who wanted to challenge his work. Harner set his conditions: "I will be happy to debate him if he first takes one of my workshops to experience shamanism. And by the way, tell your friend to bring along a drum." We shared a laugh about that, and Harner then invited me to join him at one of his shamanic workshops to experience what he wrote about. I declined, too scared to enter directly into the mystical realm of Jivaros shamanism, the source of Harner's training.

I decided that Harner, along with Joan Halifax and others,[17] represented a third stage in the evolution of studies of shamanism—the *Experiential* model. The shaman is neither ill (the *Mental Illness model*) nor simply a folksy, idiosyncratic witch doctor serving up useful functions for the local culture (the *Functionalist model*). Instead, the shaman is seen as a preserver and promoter of ancient wisdom about the nature of the world, a kind of master of ontology whose knowledge of his craft is independent of specific cultures.

In my study of Daskalos I followed none of the above three approaches. I refused to think of the reality that confronted me as trickery, or as a form of mental pathology (*the mental Illness model*). I also did not wish to follow the conventional *functionalist model*. Although it offered significant insights about local cultures, it too was limited by Western ways of thinking. Shamanism addresses ontologically authentic phenomena, and the functionalist perspective was tainted by an unconscious materialist and reductionist view of reality, bereft of any spiritual foundation. At the same time, I shied away from becoming, like Michael Harner did with the Jivaros, a full initiate into Daskalos' circles. Daskalos did not require me to become like him before I could study him. I honor Harner's courageous and experiential involvement with the Amazonian shamans, but it almost cost him his life when they gave him some very potent mushrooms as part of his training. I wanted to stay safe, and I also felt my work would benefit if I remained both an outsider and an insider.

In studying the world of Daskalos I chose a *phenomenological* approach, the fourth one I had identified. When I encountered Daskalos this method of research was becoming increasingly acceptable within the social sciences. It meant that I must temporarily suspend my own concepts and categories and engage my subject in a way that would reveal his reality from within his own experience and categories of understanding. It also meant avoiding all value judgments about what I was witnessing in the field. I was not there either to debunk Daskalos' worldview or to proselytize on behalf of what I was uncovering.

However, my approach led me to witness phenomena that unavoidably challenged some academic preconceptions about reality and altered my view of the world. My encounters and field observations with this Cypriot mystic during my sabbatical of 1979 were the beginning of a decade-long exploration that led to a trilogy of books on the life and teachings of an extraordinary healer. The world of Daskalos struck me as empirical confirmation of Sorokin's insistence that human beings are endowed not only with a conscious and an unconscious mind but also a supraconscious mind. It is a perspective about consciousness that has acquired momentum during the first two decades of the twenty first century, promising, I believe, to revolutionize our understanding of ourselves and our place in the universe.[18]

NOTES

1. Charles Moskos, *Peace Soldiers: The Sociology of a United Nations Military Force* (Chicago: University of Chicago Press, 1976).
2. Kyriacos C. Markides "Social Change and the Rise and Decline of Social Movements: The Case of Cyprus." *American Ethnologist,* (May 1974): 309–330.
3. Henry Benson, *The Relaxation Response* (New York: HarperTorch, Reissue edition 2000).
4. Richard Maurice Buck, *Cosmic Consciousness: A Study of Evolution of the Human Mind* (Eastport, CN: Martino Publishing 2010).
5. Bernard Haisch, *The God Theory* (San Francisco: Weiser Books, 2009) p. 32.
6. Ibid, pp. 32–33.
7. See YouTube for Sagan's famed lectures. His opening statement is particularly telling.
8. Kyriacos C. Markides, *The Rise and Fall of the Cyprus Republic* (New Haven: Yale University Press, 1977).
9. Kyriacos C. Markides, Elengo Rangou, and Eleni Nikita, *Social Change in a Cypriot Village,* (Nicosia: Cyprus Social Research Centre, 1978).
10. Fritjof Capra, *The Tao of Physics* (Boulder, CO: Shambhala, 1975).
11. Steven Pinker, *The Better Angels of Our Nature: Why Violence Has Declined* (New York: Penguin, 2012).
12. Carlos Castaneda, *The Teachings of Don Juan* (New York: Simon & Schuster, 1985).
13. Doug Boyd, *Rolling Thunder, a Personal Exploration into the Secret Healing Powers of an American Indian Medicine Man* (New York: Random House, 1974).
14. Ari Kiev, *Magic, Faith and Healing: Studies in Primitive Psychiatry Today* (New York: Collier–Macmillan, 1964); Fuller Torrey, *Witchdoctors and Psychiatrists: The Common Roots of Psychotherapy and its Future* (New York: Harper & Row, 1972).
15. Erving Goffman, *Asylums* (New York: Anchor Books, 1961).
16. R.D. Laing, *The Politics of Experience* (New York: Ballantine, 1967); See also Thomas Szasz, *The Myth of Mental Illness* (New York: Harper & Row, 1972).
17. Michael Harner, *The Way of the Shaman* (New York: Bantam Books, 1980); Joan Halifax, *Shaman: The Wounded Healer* (New York: Thames & Hudson, 1988).
18. See works like Larry Dossey, *One Mind* (New York: Hay House, 2013); Dean Radin, *Supernormal: Science, Yoga, and the Evidence for Extraordinary Psychic Abilities* (New York: Crown Publishing, 2013); Edward F. Kelly et al. *Irreducible*

Mind: Toward a Psychology for the 21st Century (New York: Rowman & Littlefield Publishers, 2010).

Chapter 4

Witness to
Extraordinary Phenomena

FAMILY MATTERS

When I entered the world of Daskalos, I was already in tune with a growing development within western culture—the decline of its enchantment with scientific materialism. As Sorokin had predicted, the historical pendulum was starting to swing back from its sensate, antispiritual phase to a resurgence of spirituality and the return of faith in all its multifaceted expressions. My encounter with Daskalos could help me become a more conscious participant in this transformation.

At the same time, career, marriage, and family provide their own challenges, with swings that sometimes take us by surprise. I was struggling to get tenure at the University of Maine, and we were raising two children. Emily now had two master's degrees in languages. With the enthusiastic support of her professors, she was a strong candidate for a Ph.D. program at stellar institutions like Columbia or Cornell. I should not have been surprised when she received letters from both of those august universities, offering her an assistantship to pursue a doctoral degree in French literature. The doctoral degree seemed a prerequisite for us having parallel academic careers, hopefully within the same university. But I felt deeply uneasy; the opportunity posed serious challenges for the stability of our family and marital life, or so I believed. Our children, Constantine and Vasia, were still young, and I could not give up my tenured position at the University of Maine to relocate to Ithaca, once Cornell had become Emily's first choice. How were we to do this in a mutually satisfying way?

I became anxious and depressed, and it was difficult for me to hide it. I had witnessed marital breakdowns and family dissolutions among couples we knew, triggered in part by incompatible career paths. I found it difficult to offer cheerful and enthusiastic support for what I felt was a perilous turn in our life together.

I was also fearful of the actual substance of Emily's Ph.D. program. I worried about the quicksand of "deconstructionism," the leading perspective at Columbia, Cornell, and other celebrated universities, an "epidemic," according to my friend Leonard Doob of Yale. Deconstructionism was an overarching worldview based on the notion that there is no such thing as truth, only subjective interpretations in need of being deconstructed. These Contemporary French *philosophes* such as Derrida and Lacan assaulted everything that had been considered holy and sacred. They reminded me of Diderot's tongue-in-cheek comment that man's freedom will arrive only when the last king is strangled with the entrails of the last priest! I worried that Emily and I would drift apart intellectually, emotionally, and spiritually. And we were both worried about Constantine and Vasia.

In my despair, I phoned Daskalos in Cyprus and explained my predicament. Should I flatly oppose her pursuit of a doctoral degree several hundred miles away from Maine? He fired back in a stern voice: "If you stop her from going to Cornell she will never forgive you!" That did it. The Delphic oracle had spoken. I would support Emily in her doctoral program at Cornell, come what may. I tried to see the situation as a spiritual exercise, a challenge that we could survive.

We decided that Emily would take Constantine with her to Ithaca. He would begin his elementary education there, while Vasia would stay with me and continue attending the prekindergarten Montessori school near our home. As a family, we would meet periodically. With a heavy heart I drove Emily and Constantine to Ithaca and helped her settle into a small university apartment. Then I drove back with Vasia, who was not yet 4.

Two weeks later, Emily sent me an S.O.S. message. She had changed her mind and wanted to return to Maine! Splitting the family, she said, was too heavy a price to pay for French literature. A doctoral degree was not worth the sacrifice, given the potential damage to the kids. The next day I drove to Ithaca. On the way back home to Maine, Emily told me that her decision was triggered by a bus-ride conversation with a Mexican woman, who told her that separating from the family was not a good idea. The anonymous woman came from a cultural background like ours, in which family bonds are at the center of people's lives.

When my friend and confidant Stephen Marks read this account, he provided an insightful psychodynamic reason for my deep angst around Emily's Cornell episode: "I'm convinced that Emily's departure to Ithaca reminded you on some deep level of your mother leaving you when you were 4. Of course, she didn't 'abandon' you, she died, but surely it felt like abandonment to a 4-year-old. The fears you were in touch with—Emily and you would grow apart, deconstructionism would steer her in a direction incompatible with your own, and so on—these things were there, but they likewise add up to fears of abandonment. Consider, too, that Vasia, nearly age 4, was about the same age you were when you lost your mother, and she was now suddenly with you while her mother was gone. No wonder she started 'regressing'! [Vasia began peeing on herself at night.] Imagine how emotionally loaded this parallel must have been for you, unconsciously. Many psychologists (psychics too) say that we often carry our parents' unresolved issues. Is it possible that Vasia was not only missing her mother when she 'regressed,' but she also was carrying some of your own feelings of abandonment? It is something to wonder about."[1]

FACING THE PARANORMAL

The crisis passed, and during the next year and a half we continued to work and raise our children together in Maine. Emily still looked ahead to a time when she could enter a doctoral program—which she eventually did pursue in the nineties at the University of Maine with a degree in counselor education that allowed her to happily teach in the peace studies program, having been for a while its interim director. In the meantime, neither of us could put aside that familiar feeling of "double consciousness." We were split—intellectually American but emotionally Greek—comfortable and at home in Maine but with lingering longings for our native island.

Those longings were intensified by our inability to honor our promise to Emily's parents that we would return to Cyprus permanently after Emily finished her education in the States. The Turkish invasion and the never ending "Cyprus problem" had radically altered our lives and careers. We decided that our best option was for Emily and our children to live in Cyprus for a few years. This plan would provide her quality time with her elderly parents before their departure from this world, and it would give our children a strong exposure to their grandparents and to Greek culture before the complexities of their teenage years. Fortuitously, it would also enable my continuing immersion in the world of mystics, healers, Christian elders, and saints who lived in that part of the world.

Between 1984 and 1988, Emily stayed in Cyprus with our children and taught at a newly established private college. I commuted to the island from Maine during summers, Christmas breaks, a sabbatical, and a semester's unpaid leave-of-absence. With such frequent visits and my long stays on the island, the temporary separation was manageable. Emily became a close partner with me in the exploration of Daskalos' fantastical world, and I devoted my alone time in Maine to research and writing.

My emerging senior status at the University of Maine was marked by two related developments. The first was my shift to the sociology of religion as my primary research interest. By now, mystical spirituality and paranormal healing had challenged all my academic notions about mind, consciousness, and ultimate reality. Daskalos' mystical world was the central catalyst, eventually opening my curiosity to the mystic tradition and practices of Eastern Orthodox Christianity, little known to the West. The second development, thanks to my frequent presence on the island, was my parallel involvement in peace work related to the Cyprus conflict, a worldly passion that I had never abandoned.

In my research, Daskalos' paranormal reality revealed itself to be a splendid exemplar of Sorokin's concept of the supraconscious. Intuition is the real source of real knowledge Sorokin claimed, different from the role of the senses and reason. I witnessed many instances of Daskalos' extraordinary abilities, and these could not be understood through any textbook notion of human physiology or psychology. I realized that the commonplace academic equation of the mind with the physical brain simply does not provide us an adequate paradigm of what we are as human beings. Several examples of his paranormal abilities that I witnessed follow.

One day as we chatted during a coffee break, Daskalos casually described to me with stunning detail and clarity the inside of our home in Maine. He suggested that we might consider installing a phone on the upstairs floor so that, as he put it, "you don't break your neck rushing down the steps to the kitchen every time the phone rings." How did he know all the details of our home, along with some of our routine habits within it, when we had never mentioned anything to him about it or shown him any pictures?

Ten days after our return to Maine from my leave, Emily had severe pain in her right knee, and she could hardly even sit in a car. She was hoping the pain would fade away without the need for medical attention. After about ten days of this we received a letter from one of his accolades: "Daskalos noticed that Emily has a problem with her right knee. We will do everything we can from here, but he recommends that she immediately have a doctor look at it." We were flabbergasted. We had not mentioned Emily's problem to anyone. Her pain went away two days later without the need for a doctor.

My friend Leonard Doob was in Cyprus again to revive his peace efforts. He joined me for a chat with Daskalos, and he was impressed with his knowledge of metaphysical and psychological issues. On the way out of the house, Daskalos called out to Leonard: "By the way, Professor, you must abstain from alcohol. You have an infection in your liver. It is a form of hepatitis. Don't worry, it is not life threatening, but you must never give blood to anyone because you will always be a carrier of the virus." Leonard whispered to me, "What on earth is he talking about? I just had my physical and I am perfectly fine." I shrugged and told him that I had no idea. Three months after we had returned to the States, Leonard called me from New Haven. "Remember what that healer of yours said about my health? Well, the doctors discovered that I have hepatitis type B."

When Leonard told his doctors about what the healer had said, they declared it impossible. They said the virus takes three months to incubate. At the time of Daskalos' pronouncement the virus must have already been there, but the doctors insisted that there was no medical means to detect the virus at its initial stage. How did he know?

Following the publication in 1985 of my book, *The Magus of Strovolos*, I received a call from a New Yorker who wished to send a photo of his wife to Daskalos. The caller wanted Daskalos to identify the cause of his wife's health problems. She had visited several specialists to no avail. I volunteered to bring the picture to Daskalos, as I would be visiting the island soon. When I gave it to him, he closed his eyes, rubbed it with his fingers for a minute, and declared that the woman's gums were all infected. She needed to have all her teeth replaced with dentures. I wrote the couple to tell them what he had said, and after I returned to Maine I received a call from the same person. He mentioned that when they received my letter, they were incredulous; they thought it was nonsense and threw it in the trash, but a week later, two of his wife's front teeth "exploded," and yellowish, infectious puss began to drip down her mouth. She immediately made an appointment with her dentist, who discovered that indeed her gums were infected. She then did exactly what Daskalos had suggested, and her health problems vanished.

A similar case involved a European ambassador and his wife. I drove the couple to his home, and after some chatting, each spouse complained of identical health problems. Their doctors were stymied. Daskalos then offered them a diagnosis and a recipe for how to heal themselves. He explained that during the ambassador's tenure in Turkey and then Japan, both he and his wife had caught a virus that was a hybrid of two different viruses they had picked up in the two countries. The new virus remained stuck in their intestines, and no medical instrument could detect it. He assured the couple that their problem was curable. He suggested ten days of eating a concoction of yogurt mixed with parsley, honey, and lemon juice. "This treatment," he promised, "will wash the virus away." And so it did. The grateful diplomat and his wife invited us to their ambassadorial home for a thanksgiving lunch.

Another incident was simply a remarkable discussion I had with Daskalos about the AIDS epidemic that was beginning to become a global menace. "I am convinced," he told me, "that the AIDS virus came from contact between human beings and a special species of chimpanzees." "How could you be so certain?" I asked. He explained that shortly after the 1974 Turkish invasion of the island he had spent a couple of years in Kinshasa, the capital city of Zaire (now the Congo). "While there, I noticed that the vibrations of certain chimpanzees were identical to the vibrations of people who suffered from that dreadful disease, the name of which I didn't know yet." At the time of this conversation, there was no public knowledge yet about the origin of the disease, but two weeks later, I read about a breakthrough in the medical understanding of the origin of AIDS. A Harvard researcher had discovered that the virus came from chimpanzees.

Perhaps the most extraordinary episode I witnessed was the healing of a middle-age woman who suffered from serious spine problems. She had visited the best doctors in Cyprus and nearby Israel, and all of them had told her that there was no cure. In desperation, her daughter sought Daskalos's help. I drove him to the patient's home, where we found her lying in bed, having been in that condition for the past six months. I watched silently as he passed his palms up and down her spine, hardly touching her bare back. While working on her, he gave us a diagnosis of the state of her spine, and he reassured her that she was going to get well. After about thirty to forty-five minutes of this treatment, he asked her to get out of bed and stretch her arms backward. The woman did as she was told, soon exclaiming, "Oh my God! I haven't been able to do this for months." Then he asked her to bend down and touch her toes. She did so. He pronounced her healed, and in wondrous excitement the woman thanked Daskalos profusely, and she hurried to the kitchen to make us coffee.

There was more to this story. The woman could hardly believe what had happened to her, so she visited her radiologist that same afternoon. The new X-rays revealed a normal, healthy spine, while her previous X-rays showed an ill-shaped one. Ten days later I asked the lady how she had felt during Daskalos' intervention. She told me that it was as if an electric current was moving up and down her spine. She felt as if myriads of tiny ants were marching along her back. She considered her healing to be nothing short of a miracle, and there was no relapse of her condition. The next time I saw her several years later, she was accompanying another woman to Daskalos' home for a spinal healing.[2]

Had I not myself witnessed the above episodes, I would have found it difficult to believe their validity. I sought corroborating evidence from reports of other observers. When I surveyed cross-cultural studies of shamanism and paranormal abilities, I soon realized that I was not alone in observing such phenomena in the field. Skeptical readers might likewise seek out this literature and draw their own conclusions.[3]

Not all Daskalos's interventions that I witnessed over the years led to healing. He himself claimed that we cannot predict whether a healing will be successful because "all healing comes from God's will." He insisted that he was simply a vehicle of the Holy Spirit's healing energy. "When I was a child," he told me, "I could see angels and other spirits and would have conversations with them. I thought everybody had those experiences that would often get me into trouble." His mother told him to stop talking about such matters, lest people think he was crazy and lock him up. Once he realized that others did not share his reality or see what he saw, he became careful about what he said and to whom he said it. He did not want to push his knowledge on anyone, nor did he want to compete with traditional medical practice, and he agreed to work on people with health problems only after they had exhausted conventional medical input. He steadfastly refused to take any money for his healing interventions, a refusal that was also true of other celebrated healers such as Edgar Cayce, the reputed "sleeping prophet" of Virginia Beach.[4]

After *The Magus of Strovolos* came out in 1985, I began to receive letters and phone calls from around the world, as well as visits to my office by people who told me that they too lived in the realities described in my book. Like Daskalos, they kept their experiences secret for fear of being misunderstood. I concluded that there is a kind of *paraculture* out there that has been missed or ignored because of deeply entrenched materialist prejudices. *Paranormal* abilities are real, and people like Daskalos may be harbingers of a new understanding of human nature and the wider cosmos we find ourselves in. Now years later, scientific literature on paranormal phenomena has grown rapidly, and it confirms the reality of what I observed in the field.

Like scientists, conventionally religious people often have their own issues with that world. Paranormal phenomena that happen outside of their religious community are *ipso-facto* suspect. People alleged to have such abilities may be shunned as heretics or as victims of diabolical traps who are now leading others astray. The problem with this assessment, of course, is that healing does happen. Daskalos and others like him have something to teach us. His living example helped me to free myself from the materialist reductionism I had internalized in my sixties education. The world he lived in could not be explained away. It extended beyond the three-dimensional universe and was not confined to the boundaries of the five senses. Textbook knowledge of reality was looking anemic by comparison, hopelessly narrowed down in scope and breadth. I am reminded of the impact that Mrs. Leonora Piper had on William James, the celebrated father of American psychology. Through her extraordinary gifts, she inspired him to abandon the materialist assumptions dominant within his field and to replace them with a vastly broader worldview grounded in a spiritual understanding of reality.[5]

Daskalos' explanatory framework seemed to me as compelling as his healing work and his other paranormal abilities. I was constantly impressed by the intricacies of the metaphysics he taught to his small circle of followers. I discovered later that his teaching was not unlike other philosophical and spiritual traditions from both the East and the West, from Plato and Pythagoras to Twentieth century mystics like Rudolf Steiner (1861–1925)[6] and George

Gurdjieff (1866–1949),[7] as well as contemporary transpersonal thinkers like Stanislav Groff and Ervin Laszlo.[8]

Daskalos taught that human beings are composed of three bodies. Most people assume that the only body we have is the one in the mirror, our gross material body. But we also have a psychic body, which is likewise material but at a higher level of vibrations. This psychic body is the body of our emotions, sentiments, desires, likes and dislikes, and so on. In fact, we are capable of feelings and emotions only because we have a psychic body.

The third body, the noetic body, vibrates at still higher frequencies. This is the body which makes possible our thoughts and ideas. Each of the three bodies is linked with its corresponding etheric double, or etheric energy field. The gross material body cannot exist by itself. It requires the other two bodies that vibrate at higher levels of reality. But the psychic and noetic bodies (together, "the psycho-noetic body") can exist without the lower, gross material body being present. This means that human beings survive after death through the psycho-noetic body, the body of feelings, thoughts, and memories—our personality. We survive as centers of self-consciousness. For Daskalos and others like him, there is no death, only transformation. Life continuous beyond the grave. The psycho-noetic body is not the soul. According to this teaching the three bodies (gross material, psychic, and noetic) are the garments through which the soul expresses itself.

A central aspect of Daskalos' teachings is the notion of *elementals*, which are thought forms. These are energies that we project outward as we incessantly generate ideas and feelings. Elementals have power, shape, and form. When we create a thought form of desiring a particular object, an automobile for example, we construct the form of that desire in our mind. We visualize, say, a Honda Accord, without any conscious effort because we know what a Honda Accord looks like. If we desire this object, we inject the idea of a Honda (the form) with our desire of owning it (the energy). The stronger the desire, the greater the energy injected into the form. Mind is the material we use to construct these elementals, as according to this teaching all creation is mind at various levels of vibration. Daskalos taught that the universe itself is a grand elemental within God's mind. Not a single atom or molecule, therefore, is bereft of mind since everything is embedded with some form of mind stuff in it, which is God's energy. Plainly, there is a theology embedded within Daskalos' metaphysics.

Thought forms that we incessantly create must be viewed as things having a life of their own. They are objects, not merely conceptual abstractions. Thoughts are like light, heat, or electricity; they can be seen by those who have developed abilities to see them. If proper instruments were in existence, they could be measured and weighed.[9]

If we conceive of elementals as objective realities, Daskalos taught, we will be able to appreciate the profound impact they exert on us. An elemental created by my strong desire will be connected to me through my subconscious and become a part of me, but also it will take on an existence independent of my consciousness. Even if I overcome my connection with that elemental, it will continue to exist in the environment and will retain a certain force of energy for a time. It is like having a stove in a room. We light the fire, it brings forth warmth. We put the fire out, but there is still a glow there. The stronger the fire, the longer the afterglow. It is the same with elementals. We create them, they have energy, and that energy remains active for a time. Depending on the strength of the source that projected it, it can affect other people's consciousness in a positive or negative way. The nature of the impact will depend on the state of consciousness of the one who created it and the ones who come under its influence.

It is the nature of any elemental that once projected outward, it sooner or later returns to its source to acquire further energy. Our desire will keep injecting it with energy and keep it alive until either the desire has been satisfied or discarded, thus de-energizing the elemental. But as long as elementals are active, they have a tendency to move in the direction of fulfillment. We are warned to be careful what we wish for, as our desires may not necessarily bring happiness or joy into our lives.

The elementals we keep energizing are part of our subconscious and they always stay with us. We own them. In fact, our subconscious is the sum total of the elementals that we have constructed. We are fully responsible for the construction of our personality because this part of ourselves is the product of the elementals that we incessantly create as individuals and as groups through the utilization of thought and emotion.

My friend Stephen Marks wondered if *all* of our powerfully held thoughts and beliefs, not just strong desires, are included in Daskalos' analysis of elementals. "Patriotic fervor," he wrote me, "is not necessarily a desire or amalgam of desires. National pride, belief in Jesus or Buddha, belief that the earth is flat or round—these beliefs are not quite the same as desires." Stephen is right: Any of our thoughts and beliefs may become elementals in Daskalos' teaching. And collectively created elementals can exert extreme power over us, depending on how intensely we fuel and refuel them with our energy. Stephen recalls that Maharishi Mahesh Yogi, who brought Transcendental Meditation to the West, often said, "Whatever we put our attention on grows stronger in our lives." Persistent attention is indeed another way of signaling how elementals operate in our lives. Stephen applied this principle in his sociological theory course. He told me, "I always stressed the importance of Randall Collins' theory of rituals. I wanted my students to be clear that nothing they think or believe, nothing they hold dear, will remain in their minds unless they revisit it and reinvigorate it through thinking about it, talking about it with other people, or celebrating it through cheers, song, prayers, chants, or whatever. If we stop thinking about something, it will soon disappear from our life. The ritual process is what keeps our beliefs alive by refueling them. This is the same thing as elementals and how they work. Powerfully held beliefs are also important elementals."[10] Precisely!

The nature of elementals to return to their source, Daskalos taught, is the dynamic that makes possible the law of cause and effect, often known as "karma." What we outwardly project eventually returns to us, good or bad. A negative elemental that we project toward an individual or a group, toward anything, will eventually come back to us. When we harm someone or think ill of them, we harm ourselves. When we do good for them or think well of them, we do good to ourselves. This is wisdom that is central to all authentic spiritual traditions, East or West. It is the wisdom that gave birth to the golden rule: "Do unto others as you would have them do unto you." It is not God who punishes us for our misdeeds. We simply punish ourselves through the effects of the elementals that we ourselves have created. Daskalos claimed that it is the law set up by a perfect God who allows us total freedom to choose whatever elementals we wish to create.

POIGNANT MEMORIES

The Cyprus Problem—that perennially powerful "elemental"—always seems to be looming, and while I was deeply engrossed in my ethnographic work with Daskalos, it once again pushed its way into my daily life. In the mid-eighties, events unfolded that sucked me back into the vortex of the Greco-Turkish dispute. My time was then divided for a while between investigating the world of Daskalos and trying my hand at some peace operations.

In 1983 I participated in a three-day Greek-Turkish peace workshop at Harvard University. The goal was to stimulate networking and forge understanding between Greek and Turkish academics teaching at American universities. We worked on drafting mutually agreeable guidelines for politicians to solve the Cyprus problem more effectively. That conference rekindled my interest in peace work, and when I returned to Cyprus the next summer, I felt I should do something more. Daskalos warned me that my chances of getting anywhere with such efforts were close to zero, but I was undeterred. My strategy was to organize an ad hoc get-together of Greek and Turkish Cypriots at the Ledra Palace hotel, simply to help crack the ice between some members of the two opposing ethnic groups. There would be no set criteria for recruitment, only that the participants should be university graduates with a mastery of English to facilitate communication.

Though perhaps quixotic and amateurish, I tried this difficult project for a variety of reasons. I was an outsider of sorts. I was a Greek Cypriot, but I was also an American professor holding an American passport. Hopefully, that would give me some cachet with local authorities on both sides. In addition, my book on the social and historical dynamics leading to the Greek coup and the Turkish invasion was greeted by reviewers as objective and dispassionate. The Turkish Cypriots liked it insofar as it was sociological and analytical, not the usual propagandistic diatribe against them. The person who helped me contact the Turks was James Holger, the United Nations representative back then who had fruitlessly circulated between the Greek and Turkish sectors in the hope of finding a solution and establishing a durable peace on the island.

Ambassador Holger, a Chilean diplomat, arranged a meeting for me with Rauf Denktash, the Turkish Cypriot leader considered by the Greeks to be their mortal enemy—the Bad Demon of Cyprus, as he was routinely portrayed on the Greek side. Greek Cypriots believed that he, more than anyone else, prepared the ground for the 1974 Turkish invasion. I had no illusions. I knew that getting his permission to recruit Turkish participants was a long shot, perhaps a mission impossible, but I had to try.

Our meeting took place on a warm August morning of 1983. I was driven in a United Nations military jeep to the Ledra Palace checkpoint, the only one available over the stretch of 140 miles of the Dead Zone, a mine-infested dividing line that separated the Turkish occupied north from the Greek-controlled Republic of Cyprus. Reminiscent of North and South Korea, the Dead Zone prevented any contacts whatsoever between the two sides, creating a fertile environment for the thriving of conspiracy theories, prejudice, stereotyped thinking, and hostile posturing. Only foreign diplomats and United Nations personnel, who monitored the Dead Zone, could cross that line.

I felt a sense of apprehension and numbness as I crossed over to the Turkish-controlled area. I passed by somber-looking armed Turkish troops, surrounded by a plethora of Turkish red flags with the white crescent in the middle. For anyone growing up Greek, these flags were symbols of fear and hatred. A large poster declared in Turkish and English, "I am Proud to be a Turk," Kemal Ataturk's motto for the forging of Turkish nationalist identity.

My numbness was so strong because of a recurring dream that had haunted me since my teenage years, when intercommunal fighting first broke out on the island two years before I left for America. I would find myself trapped on the Turkish side of Nicosia, hardly able to breathe and not knowing how to get over to the Greek side undetected. At a critical moment in the nightmare, as I was about to be captured, I would wake up with great relief. The longer I lived in America, however, the less frequently the dream would reappear. But now I was on the other side of that physical divide once again, and this was not a dream.

Mr. Denktash welcomed me into his office with a robust handshake and an offer of Turkish coffee, a protocol of hospitality shared by both Greek and Turkish Cypriots. It was the first time I had ever met him alone, face to face. I knew him only from news reports and always within the context of a negative spin: the man responsible for the tragedy of Cyprus, an enemy *par excellence* who had vowed to partition the island between Greece and Turkey.

I realized right away that he was extremely intelligent, a formidable opponent who had no hesitation in spilling out his bitterness against the Greek side, often with some jokes mixed in. In fact, I was impressed with his sharp and humorous wit. Although it had an aggressive edge, that wit must have served him well in diplomatic circles. "I have read your book," he began with a sharp tone in his voice as we settled down with coffee in hand. He paused for a few seconds and then continued. "People think you are objective in your analysis. But in my view, you are just another Greek who is very biased against Turks. Like all Greek Cypriots your deep-down desire is to see the island united with Greece and you would not hesitate if you had the power to bring it about. I have no doubts about that."

Fortunately, I maintained my cool. I was not shocked by his frontal assault. I simply looked him in the eyes with a grin as he made his pronouncements about how I felt and what I believed. Then, softening for a moment, he paused. "Of course," he continued, "I am not objective either." "Well, I am glad you recognize that," I shot back. "I have read *your* book too!"

Before I could explain my presence in his office, Mr. Denktash launched into a diatribe against Greek Cypriots in general, angrily enumerating all the terrible things Greeks had done to Turkish Cypriots. He concluded with a mantra he had been repeating publicly for many years: Greeks and Turks cannot live together again. If they were brought together into a unified state, they would soon be slaughtering one another. The only realistic way of solving the problem is a mutually agreed-upon divorce, followed by maintaining separate lives adjacent to each other.

I took it all in stride because a few days earlier I had been warned by Glafcos Clerides, who by then had served as a Greek Cypriot negotiator for many years and had come to know Denktash well: "When you meet with him, he will begin telling you all the bad things we have done to them. That's his standard introductory speech to anyone he meets for the first time. Don't be shocked; just let him get it out of his system. Then proceed to tell him the reason you wanted to see him." This was advice that I followed to the letter.

The Turkish Cypriot leader ended his anti-Greek diatribe, and then he attempted to make common with me: "Do you see what Makarios has done to us? He ruined our beautiful island." Denktash was referring to the policies of Archbishop Makarios, the Greek Cypriot nationalist leader and first president of the Republic of Cyprus in 1960. "Mr. Denktash," I responded, "with goodwill we can restore what has been damaged." I resisted the temptation to mention the part that he himself had played in that tragic historical catastrophe. "No!" he snapped angrily, whatever is done is done. We have to live in separate states." Then he made a proposal. "You Greeks think that I am a dictator here, don't you? To show you that I am not, I will introduce you to one of my severest critics who can be your escort and show you around our side." "I would love to meet your severest critic," I quipped. He then picked up the phone and made a quick call. I had no knowledge of the Turkish language, so I could not understand his end of the conversation.

As we waited for his severest critic to arrive, I asked him for permission to assemble a group of Greek and Turkish Cypriots so that they may begin to know one another, even if they will have to live separately. He did not give me a straight answer right away. His official policy at the time was separation, and what I was asking implied, perhaps, that Greeks and Turks who could come to know one another might also live together instead of separately. Denktash changed the subject and began telling me about his passion other than politics. Photography! He showed me with pride some of the black and white pictures he had shot over the years. I was impressed; I thought they were quite artistic, and I told him so. He smiled with satisfaction. We now had something in common, along with the shared background of having grown up in colonial, British-ruled Cyprus. Despite our ethnic and political differences, I felt a certain respect for this man, with his passionate and ebullient nature. In fact I was shocked to admit to myself that I liked him! I found him to be quite colorful, unlike some other politicians I had known.

Before long the "severest critic" arrived. "This is Bekir Azgin," Mr. Denktash said, introducing us. "The two of you think alike and I am sure you will get along well. I hope he has the time to show you around our state." The visitor nodded and expressed his readiness to give me a tour of the occupied north that neither I nor any other Greek Cypriot I knew had visited since the invasion nine years earlier. I mentioned that I would very much like to visit Kyrenia, where I spent my summers as a child, and later, where Emily and I had taken our honeymoon. It was a place of some of our fondest memories. When I added that this was the very day of our wedding anniversary, Denktash gave me a big smile. "Well," he said, "we will make sure that your wife can also come over and have Bekir take you both to Kyrenia. Consider it an anniversary gift from me!" My first thought was that this man has a nerve; it's like adding insult to injury. The Turkish troops invaded Cyprus, took over nearly 40 percent of its territory including Kyrenia and Famagusta (Emily's home town), stole our homes and properties, and now Mr. Denktash is generously offering us the gift of a visit to Kyrenia, whose Greek inhabitants, like the Famagustians, have become refugees living elsewhere.

The thought did cross my mind that Denktash may have set this whole thing up for propaganda purposes, including the notion that Bekir was one of his opponents. I soon realized, however, that Bekir was genuine. He was indeed a severe critic, and he paid a heavy price for it. He had a doctoral degree in social science and religious studies, but he could not get a job as a teacher in any school because he was blacklisted as a leftist, while Denktash was far to the nationalist right. So Bekir was now a freelance journalist, not a professional teacher. The maximum leader must have felt so secure and confident in his power that he felt free to act with a modicum of largesse. In any event, I thought it was a good omen for my project that Denktash organized this tour for us.

Quick arrangements were made, and Emily crossed over to the Turkish side for the anniversary-gift journey to Kyrenia. Bekir's wife Fatma, a pharmacist, also came along, and the four of us went north over the Pendadaktylos range. In no time we were in Kyrenia, my favorite town in all of Cyprus, if not the entire world. At that time, its pristine beauty had not yet gotten spoiled by the unchecked development that was to savage that picturesque town in the nineties, soon after the massive influx of settlers from Turkey.

Entering Kyrenia was a heart-wrenching excursion. With no Greek Cypriots in sight, there was nothing left to show that it was once mainly a Greek town. All the Greek signs had been replaced with Turkish ones. The homes where Greeks used to live, many of whom I knew personally, were now the residence of Turkish Cypriot refugees from the southern part of the island. There were also settlers from Turkey. Other than the buildings, it was a radically different town. Our host/drivers were refugees themselves. They had fled from the Greek side and could empathize with our unsettling emotions when we visited places filled with memories. We went outside my Aunt Polyxeni's house on Pericles Street, now renamed. We stood in front of the house in stunned silence. The vines were still covering the flat roof that offered natural air conditioning during the summer heat. The orange grove that my aunt watered and cared for with so much diligence was still intact. Thousands of cicadas rhythmically chanted their summer songs and the jasmine and rose bushes in front of the house emanated their dizzying aromas. Emily began sobbing silently and I did my best, and I fought back my own tears. Bekir and Fatma, both heavy smokers, began puffing their cigarettes with nervousness as they felt our pain. We did not dare knock on the door to peruse the inside of the house that I knew so well.

We then traveled west along the coastal road on the way to Karavas and Lapythos—citrus-producing villages, built at the slopes of the Pentadaktylos range with winding, picturesque roads leading to the beaches below. They suffered the same fate as Kyrenia. All their inhabitants who survived the invasion escaped south before the Turkish troops arrived. We stopped at

Pente Mili (Five Mile Beach), a cove that Emily and I used to visit during our engagement. At that time, we knew the owner of the restaurant, a woman named Pagona (Peacock). It was a great place to eat fresh fish after a good swim. She had proudly told us a few weeks before the invasion of her plans to expand her business for the increasing influx of tourists. The restaurant, far away from any built-up area, overlooked a most magnificent sandy beach. This was, alas, the beach where Turkish generals chose to land their invading army. Pagona woke up that morning from the noise of the invasion. While the Turkish navy started shelling the area around the beach, she rushed her family into the car to flee south. It is said that a shell hit them the moment their car began moving, killing everyone inside. As for the restaurant, it is now run by a Turkish family.

On the way back to the Ledra Palace checkpoint, Bekir shared his own story as he fled Potamia, a mixed village of Greeks and Turks and a paragon of good neighborly relations and interethnic amity. When fighting broke out around the island his family felt unsafe, and before the invasion they moved to the Turkish side of Nicosia. Bekir was fluent in Greek and had many Greek Cypriot friends. "Growing up in our home," he told us, "we spoke only Greek. My mother knew no Turkish at all, and she felt very embarrassed when relatives visited, and she could not understand them." But her ignorance of the Turkish language proved to be invaluable, Bekir told us. During a skirmish between Greek and Turkish paramilitary gangs, a group of armed Greek vigilantes came to Potamia from another village looking for Turks. They broke into their home, and Bekir's mother, alone and terrified, hid under a table and screamed in Greek, *"Panagia mou tha mas skotosoun!"* (Holy Mother of God they will kill us). Her screams saved her life. The potential killers left, believing that it was a Greek home.

Later, Denktash gave his reluctant permission for us to have the first meeting ever of ordinary Greek and Turkish Cypriots. I assumed he did so after getting permission from the Turkish military. He probably believed that such a meeting would have no effect, and it would only reinforce his belief that Greeks and Turks cannot live together in peace.

We met at the Ledra Palace just once, and what we accomplished was disappointing, as Daskalos had warned. It quickly turned into a shouting match between the two groups, who could do no better than to point fingers at each other. Moderating voices were clearly a minority. Leading the charge that set the confrontational tone was Raif Denktash, the eldest son of Rauf Denktash. In his mid-twenties, he was being groomed to succeed his father as a leading politician in the north. Much of the meeting was spent listening to Raif's angry outbursts against Greek Cypriots, pretty much copying his flamboyant father in style and substance. It was as if Denktash senior had sent his son to prove that Greeks and Turks are like oil and water, unable to mix.

I felt at the time that the only gain from that exercise was to establish a bond between Bekir and Fatma and us that would last a lifetime. An interesting sidelight, however, is that the recurring nightmare that had haunted me over the years—being stuck on the Turkish side, unable to get back to the Greek side undetected—has never reappeared. The actual experience of finding myself in the occupied north with Bekir and Fatma, and perhaps my contact with the fiery Denktash himself, were sufficient to heal me from that affliction.

PEACE WORK

I was again on the island in the summer of 1985 when my old friend and mentor Leonard Doob returned to Cyprus to restart his peace-mediation efforts. He asked for my assistance to bring together Greek and Turkish Cypriots with the aim of creating a bridge between the two communities. The hope was to break the chronic stalemate. Eleven years had passed since the Turkish invasion, when Leonard was rescued from the island by the American Sixth Fleet. It had been two years since my failed attempt to enlist Rauf Denktast's help in bringing together some Greek and Turkish Cypriots to start them talking. Nothing had changed.

I was still absorbed with issues of nonmedical healing, metaphysical queries, and tales of extraordinary psychic feats, but I gladly volunteered to participate in this new peace initiative. Leonard was interested in the recruitment of a selected group of intellectuals—journalists, academics, writers, and opinion makers—who would meet regularly to discuss ways of breaking the impasse between the two sides. The venue for the meetings would be Ledra Palace, the Nicosia hotel taken over by the United Nations peacekeeping force and used since 1974 as their headquarters. The rare meetings between Greek and Turkish Cypriot officials over the years had to be held at that bullet-riddled and militarized former five-star hotel, which had the misfortune of being situated at the dividing line between the Greek and Turkish Cypriot part of Nicosia. It was a place that experienced heavy fighting and was now surrounded with barbed wire.

It was not difficult to recruit Greek Cypriots for this peace project. I had several friends who fit the requirements, and they helped me to identify others. The more challenging problem was recruiting Turkish Cypriots. Bekir Azgin, my host for the Kyrenia revisit two years before, was the obvious choice for putting together the Turkish team. I trusted that he would choose individuals with a track record of commitment to an amicable resolution, eager to embrace the challenge of creating a reunified island state.

With the help of the United Nations authorities, Leonard contacted Bekir, who agreed to assemble the Turkish team. I did the same on the Greek side. The problem now was to get permission from the two sides to carry out these meetings during the fall of 1985. Meetings would continue for as long as needed. Coincidentally, I had my second sabbatical during that semester, and therefore I could remain as part of the team until December.

The Greek Cypriot authorities, although somewhat suspicious of Leonard, could not legally prevent us from carrying out our project. The official policy was to encourage contacts between the two sides, even while they continued to blame the Turks for the separation and the division of the island. The bigger challenge was to get cooperation from the Turkish side. With the help of James Holger, the United Nations mediator, Leonard finally secured permission from Rauf Denktash and indirectly from the Turkish military.

The United Nations officials in Cyprus were only too happy to facilitate Leonard's project, formally nicknamed "*Operation Locksmith*." Leonard presided over the first couple of meetings to help set the ground rules and objectives of the peace effort. Then he left Cyprus, planning to return at the end of the process that he had set in motion. At the outset we agreed on certain rules. A most important one was that to generate trust among us, we should not discuss with outsiders the content of our proceedings. We agreed that we would not hold any press conferences, write any articles, or give interviews about who said what and when. We would maintain confidentiality. We wanted to feel free to bring out ideas without the fear of public resistance or intrusion from the political parties on either side.

At the start of the first meeting, I thought our new attempt was doomed. Of the eight Turkish Cypriots that Bekir chose, the most dominant presence was Raif Denktash, the son of the maximum leader and the person I thought responsible for spoiling my previous attempt at mutual understanding. But I could not believe my ears! Raif was a transformed human being. He was the most enthusiastic among the Turkish Cypriots in promoting Greco-Turkish friendship and finding a peaceful resolution of the ethnic problem. For an instant I thought that he was playacting. Perhaps he was a spy for his father. I was wrong. During our first break I told him, "I am really curious, Raif. What happened during the last two years that turned you into such an enthusiast for a solution?" Sporting a bushy black beard, Raif smiled and explained his radical transformation. "I spent two years at Oxford University studying for my master's degree in international relations. I met and befriended a group of Greek Cypriots there, and I was stunned to realize that we were so much alike. I then vowed to work for peace."

"I am so pleased to hear that," I said. "But how is it that your father is following the exact opposite policy on the Cyprus problem?"

"I am willing to take risks," he replied. "My father is not."

In fact, following his return to Cyprus from Oxford, Raif had created his own party, different from the conservative one headed by his father. But I was reassured by Bekir, who knew the politics of the Turkish side, that they were still close as father and son. The elder Denktash was hoping that his son would eventually succeed him as leader of the Turkish Cypriots, despite their differences about how to deal with the Greco-Turkish dispute.

Our meetings went smoothly for a couple of months. We met three times per week. We were getting mixed but mostly negative coverage by a suspicious press on both sides. The typical concern was the question of who was behind our efforts. Who decided on the makeup of the two committees? Who gave us the right to represent our respective communities? And so on. We simply responded that it was a nonpartisan, citizens' initiative and that no person or political party was guiding us. We insisted that we had no power to solve the Cyprus problem. Some interpreted our refusal to give details as sure evidence that we were organs of foreign powers trying to impose an unacceptable solution to the problem. Lurking behind us, someone claimed, was the invisible hand of the American CIA. We got a barrage of hostile editorials in both the conservative press and the pro-Soviet oriented communist newspaper, which smelled the scent of American imperialism everywhere.

After two months of meetings, we thought it was time to become bold; we should host visits to each other's communities for social get-togethers. Given the omnipresent tensions, this was risky business. We decided that the Greek Cypriots would first host the Turkish Cypriots for a tour of the southern part of the island controlled by the Republic of Cyprus. After that it would be the Turks who would host us somewhere in the north. The Cypriot government gave us the green light, and Raif's participation gave us the confidence that the Turkish Cypriots would get permission to cross over to our side.

We were concerned about security. There were still many fanatics on both sides who might have caused serious problems, so we requested discreet and unseen police protection. The police should wear in plain clothes and stay at some distance from the rest of us. Our plan was to devote the morning to traveling around the island and then have lunch in Platres, a traditional resort town on the pine-covered Troodos Mountains, a place our Turkish friends wished to visit. It should all be done in a low-key fashion, free of publicity.

Excitement mixed with some anxiety was mounting as we finished all the preparations. A historic event was about to happen: For the first time in eleven years, a group of Turkish Cypriots would cross over and visit the south. We arranged for a minibus to take all sixteen of us around the Greek-controlled area of the Republic. But the day before the crossing was to happen, I received a disturbing call from Raif, who served as the de facto liaison for the Turkish Cypriots. I was serving in that capacity for the Greek Cypriot team. "Unfortunately," Raif said, "we cannot cross over. We were unable to get permission." He then informed us that the Turkish Cypriots could no longer participate in our weekly meetings either. Our efforts for a peace opening came to an abrupt and inglorious end. We found out later that the obstacle was the Turkish occupying army. We never understood their refusal, given the fact that they had given us the green light to have the regular meetings at the Ledra Palace.

The collapse of the peace process was soon compounded by a horrendous tragedy a week later. Raif, who was an enthusiastic proponent of Greco-Turkish cooperation and the likely successor to his father, was killed in an auto accident. He was speeding on the Famagusta-Nicosia road when he apparently lost control of his car and crashed into a motionless Turkish military truck that had broken down and was sitting in the middle of the road. Raif, the man in a hurry, apparently took chances not only in working for a solution but also in his driving.

We got permission from the Turks to cross over and offer our condolences to Raif's father and attend the funeral. That was the first and last crossing of our team after over two months of regular contacts. Our original crossover plan had been pitched as a pleasant social get-together with the Turkish team. Instead, we were crossing for the funeral of the man who could have played a major role in working for peace on the island.

There was an eerie atmosphere when we entered Denktash's office, escorted by members of the Turkish team, along with the usual plain-clothed police following behind us. We had stitched on to our chests the picture of the deceased, as was the custom for Turkish funerals. Rauf Denktash's office was filled with high-ranking members of the Turkish military, the very generals who had carried out the invasion eleven years before. It was surreal. The office was covered with photographs of Raif taken by Rauf Denktash himself. The flamboyant and aggressively humorous politician that I had known from a couple of previous meetings was deeply distraught, looking at us with watery eyes as we offered our sympathies.

We were not allowed to attend the actual funeral at the mosque, apparently for security reasons. After we offered our condolences to the elder Denktash, we were whisked back to the Ledra Palace checkpoint for our return to the Greek side. The following day a hardline nationalist Greek Cypriot newspaper displayed a photo of one of our members with Raif's picture on his chest. It thundered against our group for "kissing the ass" of the Turkish invaders.

On the surface, this second attempt to bring about understanding between the two sides went nowhere, as Daskalos had prophesied, but I want to believe that our efforts were not in vain. They created a sense of possibility that such encounters might happen. We got negative publicity from both sides, but none of the participants suffered any negative consequences in their careers or their standing in society. Two of the members of the Greek team ended up as ambassadors, one to Paris and then London, and the other to Moscow and then Washington. The precedent we created encouraged others, and they experienced less resistance from their respective communities.

The cultural milieu was becoming less restrictive. Committees were set up for ongoing dialogues. By 2003 several crossings were agreed upon by both sides, allowing ordinary Greek and Turkish Cypriots to visit each other's sector on a routine basis. And based on a mutual agreement, the UN force began removing 27,000 mines that were planted across the 140 miles of the Dead Zone. By 2017, a new leader on the Turkish side was elected on a prosolution platform. Like my friend Bekir, and unlike the late Rauf Denktash, who died in 2012, he seemed genuinely interested in uniting the island within the context of a bizonal, bicommunal federation. Unfortunately, he was defeated in 2020 at a contested election by a hardliner of the Denktash persuasion. But I do want to believe that our first attempt at reconciliation played a miniscule part in the ultimate goal of reunification and peace.

After Raif's funeral, Leonard returned to Cyprus a final time. He loved the place, and like many mediators who preceded or followed him, he got emotionally entangled in the island, its people, and its problems. Despite all the disappointments around our mediation efforts, my connection with Leonard Doob was a wonderful gift. I have fond memories of our conversations beyond the practical issues of organizing the workshops. He mesmerized me with stories of his life in Berlin as a foreign student, the decade before the Nazis took power. He went to Germany to study sociology because at that time Germany was a leader in graduate education, attracting young American academics among others. When the Nazis came to power, he had to give up his studies and return to the US, switching to social psychology because his doctoral advisor, the great Karl Mannheim, had fled to England. It was a sheer delight to hear firsthand stories about Mannheim, a Hungarian Jew and one of the leading sociologists of the twentieth century, whose ideas were required reading in my own graduate program, and later, in my teaching. Leonard died in 2000 at the ripe age of 91.

Years later, I found out some interesting details that we were unaware of during *"Operation Locksmith"* at the Ledra Palace. Our meetings were carefully monitored by both sides. Denktash knew in detail about the ongoing discussions, not via his son Raif but from another member of the Turkish team who was feeding him detailed information. Likewise, a Greek Cypriot equivalent who was connected to the foreign ministry dispatched similar reports to the government on the Greek side. Given the tension-laden context of our meetings, none of this should have been surprising. I also learned that

Raif accidentally came across a final report sent to his father's office by the "mole" in our group who was sympathetic to Denktash senior's intransigent line that the two sides must remain separate. When Raif read it he was furious, not only because it was a violation of our pledge of secrecy but because it was a distortion of what was being said and who had said it. Ideas put forward during the meetings by Raif were attributed to Bekir, the left-leaning progressive who worked for peace and reconciliation. Raif confronted his father, demanding that the report should be at least corrected. His father allegedly replied, "Unfortunately, it is too late now"; the report had already been sent to the foreign ministry of Turkey. Further information revealed that the abrupt termination of our meetings may have stemmed more from our success in reaching a consensus about how the Cyprus problem could be solved than from objections to the planned visits across the two sides. At one point, I had made a remark after we had reached an agreement, marveling that these were the same conclusions reached at the Harvard University workshop that I had participated in two years earlier. As I said that, the "mole" on the Turkish side, commissioned to provide the secret reports to the Turkish Cypriot authorities, turned toward one of the Greek members and murmured "I wish Kyriacos would not say that. This may terminate our meetings." I cannot say that there was a cause-and-effect relationship between my innocuous comment and the reaction of our Turkish participant-spy. But if the official policy on the Turkish side was the partitioning of the island into two independent states, then the abrupt termination of the meetings made sense.

The mystics whom I have studied and encountered in my life all teach that we do not live within a lifeless, dead universe. Nothing in it, no thought, no feeling, no action is ever lost. Deeds that promote right values, even if they appear to lead nowhere, will always be registered within what some call Universal Memory, ready to bear fruit when the conditions are ripe. That is how I want to think of *"Operation Locksmith."* The Ledra Palace meetings of 1985 were the final chapter of my involvement with the politics that had begun with my entanglement as a young teenager in the anticolonial underground movement, and had continued in my academic work related to the Cyprus problem. After *Operation Locksmith* I turned my focus almost exclusively to the exploration of spiritual and paranormal realities, leaving direct political activism behind while retaining an undiminished interest in the vicissitudes of the island's and America's politics.

The eighties, the Ronald Reagan years in America, completed my divorce from the stranglehold of philosophical materialism, thanks in large part to my decade-long encounter with the awesome world of Daskalos. That radical turn in my life was reinforced by the publication of my first book on the Cypriot healer. Its positive reception by critics and readers brought about a happy convergence of my spiritual and my academic interests. Emily herself, who was at first concerned about the new direction of my work, soon became an active supporter and participant. The philosophical discussions we had together with Daskalos solidified a lifelong partnership in the pursuit of a deeper, integral vision of reality, the kind of vision that Sorokin had promoted so passionately in much of his work.

The publication of my three books on Daskalos had further consequences in my life. It brought me into contact with a wide range of people who had similar interests and resonated with the ideas presented in *The Magus of Strovolos* and in my subsequent volumes. Michael Lewis was one such person. I had known Michael before as an esteemed professor in the Art Department and a celebrated artist in the state of Maine, but I began to see him regularly when his art studio was relocated to the attic above my office in Fernald Hall. We discovered that we shared parallel interests. I learned that while I was working on my dissertation in Detroit and undergoing intensive Freudian psychoanalysis, Michael was painting semi-abstract images with Freudian themes. And while I was beginning to question the efficacy of Freudianism and scientific materialism in general, Michael was giving up Freudianism in his art and shifting his focus to Jungian notions of the collective unconscious. This shift resonated neatly with my own preoccupation with Sorokin's notion of the supraconscious.

It was during this latest turn in Michael's artistic and spiritual exploration that we began to deepen our relationship. It coincided with Emily's stay in Cyprus with the children while I commuted to the island during breaks and sabbaticals. During those four years of my feverishly working on the Daskalos material, Michael became the first reader of each chapter I completed, offering me invaluable feedback and sharing my excitement along the way. The connection grew still stronger after Michael visited me in Cyprus and met with Daskalos himself. It was an event that changed Michael's life and work, ushering in some of his more mystical paintings that characterized the latter part of his academic career. Both of our careers seemed to reflect the monumental transformations that were happening within modern American society at large—the increasing rediscovery of the spiritual among large numbers of people disenchanted with extreme rationalism, materialism, and organized, dogmatic religion.

NOTES

1. Personal communication with Stephen Marks, April 11, 2018.
2. More details are found in my trilogy: *The Magus of Strovolos* (New York: Penguin, 1985); *Homage to the Sun* (New York: Penguin, 1987); *Fire in the Heart* (New York: Penguin, 1990).

3. Dean Radin's work *The Conscious Universe: The Scientific Truth of Psychic Phenomena* (San Francisco: HarperOne, 2009) offers compelling evidence of the reality of the "supernormal."

4. Sidney D. Kirkpatrick, *Edgar Cayce: An American Prophet* (New York: Riverhead Books, reissue edition, 2001).

5. Mark B. Ryan, "The Transpersonal William James," *Journal of Transpersonal Psychology*, 40, no. 1 (2008): 20–40.

6. Rudolf Steiner, *How to Know Higher Worlds* (East Sussex, UK: Anthroposophic Press, 1994).

7. George Gurdjieff, *In Search of Being: The Fourth Way to Consciousness* (Boulder, CO: Shambhala, 2013).

8. Stanislav Groff, *When the Impossible Happens: Adventures in Non-Ordinary Realities* (Louisville, CO: Sounds True Publisher, 2006); Ervin Laszlo, *The Immortal Mind: Science and the Continuity of Consciousness beyond the Brain* (Vermont: Inner Traditions, 2014).

9. Kyriacos C. Markides, *Riding with the Lion* (New York: Viking Press, 1995), p. 48. Quoted in Yogi Ramacharaka, *Fourteen Lessons in Yogi Philosophy* (Chicago: Yogi Publication Society, 1903), p. 78.

10. Personal communication with Stephen Marks, April 11, 2018.

Chapter 5

Meetings with Remarkable People

ALTERNATIVE THERAPIES

I found myself sitting next to Etel De Loach at the 1992 conference for the inauguration of the Office of Alternative Medicine (OAM) at the National Institutes of Health. She was a humble and unassuming grandmother from Atlanta with a national reputation as a leading psychic healer and medical intuitive. I learned that she had appeared on national television news several times and lectured at the medical school of Johns Hopkins University.

We spent several hours together discussing her extraordinary life, and I shared stories of my own experiences with Daskalos, the Cypriot healer I had studied the previous decade. While having dinner, she told me of a profound visionary experience she once had with a short, stocky man who suddenly "appeared" one evening in her living room. "I am," he said to Etel, "Saint Thomas Aquinas, and came here to offer you my blessings and a lesson on the nature of God."

I asked Etel what she had known previously about Saint Thomas Aquinas, and she said she had "never heard of the guy." She repeatedly mentioned the physique of her uninvited visitor. I knew that Thomas Aquinas, the thirteenth-century Dominican Italian friar, was short and rotund. His classmates at the University of Paris teased him about his obesity. After an ecstatic experience he once had during a liturgy, he announced that all he had written about God over the years was irrelevant, like "a straw mat," compared to his experience in that ecstatic state. He never wrote another word.

Etel wrote down everything St.Thomas had dictated to her during her vision. She gave me a copy, along with permission for me to publish it in my book, *Riding with the Lion*.[1] Etel herself was neither a scholar nor a theologian. I felt confident that her experience was genuine, consistent with similar experiences that gifted people have had through the ages, often impacting history in major ways.[2]

My chance encounter with Etel was entwined with a string of developments going back to the life and times of President Richard Nixon, whose surprise visit to China was a monumental turning point in international affairs. I remember vividly that October day in 1972, witnessing on live television Nixon smiling and blissfully toasting with his arch enemies Mao Ze-dong and Zhou Enlai. What I did not realize back then, at the start of my teaching career, was that Nixon and Kissinger's mission to China was also a cultural watershed. It opened the way for westerners to legitimize ancient Chinese philosophy, medicine, and related exotic arts from the Far East. Acupuncture, Tai Chi, Qigong, Reiki, Feng Shui, and a variety of martial arts have increasingly become part of the American landscape and experience.

The first encounter of the American public with acupuncture occurred during Nixon's visit, when a major American television channel broadcast a brain operation taking place in a Peking hospital. The surgeons were watched by millions as they operated inside the open skull of a woman. She was fully conscious and being interviewed by stupefied American journalists while the operation was in progress. The only anesthetic the doctors applied was topical, along with the insertion into her face of acupuncture needles.

The Chinese doctors demonstrated that day the value of blending Western medicine with ancient Chinese practice. The breathtaking spectacle likely contributed to the eventual acceptance of acupuncture by the American medical establishment and by medical insurance companies. Perhaps it also paved the way for the creation in 1992 of the OAM at the National Institutes of Health, which provided the context for my encounter with Etel.

The extraordinary experience of congressman Berkley Bedell from Iowa likewise helped to undo the resistance to nontraditional practices. His physicians had given him just a few months to live, and at the urging of a friend, he visited an alternative healer and therapist in Canada. After a month's stay, he returned to Washington fully recovered, and he was convinced that the American public should be alerted to these alternative healing modalities. With the help of his friend and fellow Iowan Senator Tom Harkin, a bill was passed in Congress that created the OAM, later renamed "The National Center for Complementary and Integrative Health." Of course, powerful medical lobbies stood ready to oppose nonmedical healing, seeing it as nothing but dangerous superstition. The official aim of the OAM, however, was quite modest: simply to make possible the actual scientific study of these alternative practices and make the results known to the public.

Because of my published work on healers, I was privileged to be included in the discussions that led to the establishment of that national office. It was a thrilling experience. At the conference were about a hundred specialists from a variety of fields—from medicine to engineering, from nursing to space science, from cultural anthropology to alternative therapies coming from a variety of traditions, including Native American shamans or medicine men, and medicine women like Etel Delock.

Aware that I was the lone sociologist, I felt duty-bound to represent my field. In addition to sharing information about my own research on unconventional healers, I emphasized the importance of social and cultural factors in the prevention and treatment of disease. This position was grounded in well-established studies dating back to the Nineteenth century, ultimately leading to the burgeoning field of the sociology of medicine. For example, accumulated evidence has confirmed the therapeutic power of strong communal ties. I also emphasized the role of poverty and inequality in the onset of disease, another well-established fact within sociology.

There was excitement, high expectation, and energy in these meetings. Everyone was attuned to the historic nature of the event, keenly aware that the new organization could help reverse a century of prejudice against non-medical healers. I took away several experiences that had long lasting consequences for my personal and academic life. For example, I listened to several talks about how our thoughts can affect the "matter" of bodies, so much so, Dr. Larry Dossey suggested, that doctors who do not pray for their patients may be depriving them of healing energy![3] Dossey and all the other leading participants claimed that the mind is nonlocal; it is not confined to the physical brain. Having spent ten years observing an unconventional healer in the field, I had no problem accepting the accumulated empirical evidence supporting that proposition.[4]

In addition to attending talks by pioneers in the field of alternative therapies, I connected with some leading practitioners of unconventional healing arts. Dr. Effie Chow, a Chinese woman living in San Francisco, was a world-renowned Qigong grandmaster, energy healer, and acupuncturist. With a group of five other participants, she generously demonstrated the power of Qi energy—the foundational principle of Chinese medicine. We retreated into a private room for an impromptu demonstration. First, she asked that we stand firm as she tried to push us backward, one at a time, simply using her physical strength. She instructed us to resist her pushing with all our muscular power. We were all men, some of us large, and although she pushed with all her might, none of us budged.

Huffing and puffing, Dr. Chow then announced that she was going to marshal her Qi energy. For about half a minute she focused on the center of her solar plexus, and without harnessing any apparent physical effort, she pushed each one of us off balance with a force that we could not resist. Each of us stumbled backwards, anywhere from one to three feet. Following this extraordinary demonstration, Dr. Chow gave us a talk about the Chinese understanding of the Qi energy that permeates the universe and can be mastered through simple meditation practices for healing purposes. She described Qi energy in much the same way that I heard Daskalos describe "etheric vitality" ten years earlier. She told us that her dream was to help integrate Chinese and western medicine, and this led her to establish the East West Academy of Healing Arts. It was after the OAM conference that then President Bill Clinton appointed her and 14 others as advisors on alternative medicine.

Dr. Chow claimed that what she demonstrated could be done by anyone who knew how to concentrate, and I was eager to try it out in one of my classes when I got back to Maine. I recruited a few volunteers for a classroom experiment on Qi energy, and I then followed Effie Chow's instructions. To my amazement, I had the same results! Students could not maintain their balance after I barely pushed them with just two fingers. But that night I got a severe case of the flu and was out of work for several days. I cannot be certain of any connection between the classroom experiment and my illness, but I felt that perhaps I had dealt with power that I was ill equipped to handle. Serious spiritual teachers discourage their followers from focusing on mastering power for this very reason, urging instead that they put their attention on how to overcome their narcissistic proclivities. Extraordinary abilities come naturally, according to my informants, as the individual peels away layer upon layer of egotistical desires. These are gifts of the Holy Spirit. Sages through the ages teach that psychic powers must be used only for healing purposes, and without fanfare or bravado.

FURTHER WITNESSES TO THE MIRACULOUS

A few weeks after the conference, Dr. Wayne Jonas, physician at the Walter Reed Hospital and future director of the Office of Alternative Therapies (1995–1998), invited several participants to his home for an informal mini conference on the subject. Each of us guests had carried out field research in various parts of the world on paranormal medical interventions. The agenda was to present cross-cultural field material on unusual and often controversial medical phenomena. The presentations were mesmerizing. The venue was idyllic. The home was in the lovely Shenandoah Valley in Virginia, romanticized in the Civil War ballad *Shenandoah,* which was in the entertainment we were treated to by a group of local musicians during an evening meal.

My suspicion was growing that cutting-edge knowledge about the nature of reality remains hidden, a casualty of censorship imposed by the gatekeepers and guardians of the established orthodoxies from medicine, religion, and science. The late Professor of Psychiatry at Harvard John Mack almost lost his job because he studied people who claimed they experienced abductions by extraterrestrial beings. Although he followed strict scientific methodologies, his colleagues apparently felt that the subject matter itself of his investigation was a threat to their reputation as Harvard scholars.

During the nineties, challenges to any remnants of my materialist assumptions intensified. My world was becoming more mysterious, more extraordinary, more fascinating, and more spectacular. After the Shenandoah gathering, I received a call from a Mr. Henry Belk. He had read my book *The Magus of Strovolos*, and he invited me to South Carolina to share his twenty-five-year exploration of unconventional therapists around the world. He was a man of independent means, and he traveled widely. He had first-hand information about extraordinary, paranormal phenomena, such as the feats of psychic surgeons in the Philippines. He told me that if I accepted his invitation, he would fly me to Charlotte so that we could go over his archives and compare notes.

I met Mr. Belk at the Charlotte airport on March 20, 1993. He was an amicable Southern gentleman in his mid-70s. He drove me to his quite modest home, the rooms covered wall to wall with books on healing and spirituality. He had found hardly anyone who was interested in his accumulated work. Several of his relatives were deeply troubled by his interests, fearing that he might be tampering with demonic forces. Given my published work, he hoped that I might become a rare ally.

After a few hours of sharing stories, Belk agreed to my request to do a videotaped interview. The next morning, he told me that his interest in psychic phenomena started in 1939 when he was enrolled as a psychology major at Duke University. There, J.B. Rhine was immersed in his pioneering parapsychological work and was determined to establish that focus as a branch of psychology. Rhine's ambition did not sink roots in a field then dominated by behaviorists, but it did capture Belk's imagination.

Over time, Henry Belk fortified his conviction that paranormal phenomena are quite normal. He learned of Peter Hurkos, a Dutchman who fell off a ladder, injured his head, and became psychic. Belk brought Hurkos to America in 1955. In collaboration with medical investigator Dr. Andrija Puharich, the goal was to find out which part of Hurkos' brain had been injured, and to learn how his psychic abilities may have been triggered by the injury. Dr. Puharich himself confirmed Hurkos' abilities under carefully controlled experimental conditions, although his skeptical colleagues rushed to debunk his findings.

I learned that before Hurkos's death in 1988, he purportedly served as a medium for then President Ronald Reagan. Although unconfirmed, this was not a far-fetched notion, as Nancy Reagan was known to have consulted astrologers as a way of advising her husband about the timing of major decisions. Belk also mentioned that because Hurkos could read other people's minds, he was recruited by the CIA as a spy against the Russians. It is well-documented that the CIA experimented secretly with psychics for such purposes. It was called Stargate Project, and it went on for 17 years, from 1978–1995.

Peter Hurkos' gifts apparently included some impressive healing abilities, and one recipient was Belk's brother Henderson, who had broken his Achilles heel. Henderson was healed instantly, Belk claimed. Hurkos was merely the medium for "someone invisible. The windows were shut, and the door was locked so whoever entered the apartment came through the walls. That episode really caught my attention. I would say it was a turning point in my life."

Sometime later, Belk flew to the Philippines to observe psychic surgeons there. He told me, "These people do not cut with a knife. They open and shut bodies with their bare hands, they discard pieces of flesh such as tumors, and they leave no trace on the body of the patient." He then treated me to his own stunning videos of these surgeries. Material such as this can now be watched on YouTube, perhaps a further sign of a paradigm shift in our understanding of reality.

I asked Belk how we can be certain that these healing phenomena are not fraudulent. "Fake phenomena are done for entertainment purposes," he answered. "These phenomena will never be accepted until academics, doctors, scientists, and scholars begin to take them seriously, observe and study them. I don't have the credentials to be taken seriously." Unfortunately, even the conventional medical doctors who witnessed the psychic surgeries in the Philippines would not go public. "They told me they were afraid that their reputations would be ruined," Belk said.

Belk told me about his encounter with the Brazilian healer Arigo, whose gifts became known to a wide audience through John Fuller's book *Arigo: Surgeon of the Rusty Knife.*[5] I had recently read the book and had seen Belk's name mentioned as a member of the team that watched Arigo perform extraordinary paranormal surgeries. Fuller's account of *Arigo* is perhaps the most spectacular story of nonmedical healing in the Twentieth century. In Brazil, Arigo is more famous and generates deeper emotions than Pele, the legendary soccer champion, but his name is hardly known by North Americans and westerners in general. Arigo's work is verified by medical doctors and documented with photographs, newspaper clippings, names of persons healed, and dates of the healing episodes. It is also documented by a respected American researcher and writer. Nevertheless, frustration with scientific dogmatism is a perennial problem for serious researchers of paranormal phenomena experience. Cases like Arigo's are normally dismissed *a priori* on the assumption that what is reported must surely be the result of human error or charlatanism.

Before I left South Carolina for Maine, I asked Henry Belk what conclusions he has drawn about the nature of reality after his years of exposure to human beings with extraordinary healing abilities. "I have concluded," he replied, "that the origin of all major religions is based on contacts between humans with realities beyond the physical universe. I call a person who makes such a contact a *contactee.* Jesus had contact with his heavenly father. So did Moses and the other Jewish prophets. Joseph Smith started Mormonism through his own kind of contact. The uneducated Mohammad had contact with what he believed to be Archangel Gabriel. Now a thousand years later, the outcome of that contact becomes a myth, and people add and subtract to the story. But you can say that the origin of all religions is *contactee* business. Someone had contact with spirit beings or supernatural realities that are invisible to our ordinary sight and common understanding. That was also true of the Philippine surgeons, and Peter Hurkos, and Arigo. What I don't understand is why religious people often fight this instead of embracing it?"

Like his mentor Dr. Rhine at Duke University, Henry Belk was ahead of his time in suspecting that the human mind is non-local; it is not confined to the walls of the physical skull. Belk's conclusions parallel my own field observations. In addition, a small but highly trained group of experimental scientists have demonstrated time and again that human beings have hidden within themselves abilities that transcend our five senses. Dr. Russel Targ, for example, physicist and co-founder of the Stanford Research Institute, has been studying the psychic abilities of his subjects. He concluded that such abilities as telepathy, precognition, remote viewing, clairvoyance, and similar phenomena are real.[6] In fact he claimed that the evidence for such abilities is stronger than that aspirin prevents heart attacks.

The works of physicist Russell Targ, psychologist Charles Tart, and others have been important to me. In controlled experiments, they show that psychic abilities are real.[7] They point to the presence of a spiritual realm, accessible more by revelation or by what Sorokin calls intuition than by rational intellect or perception through the five senses. The last decade of the twentieth century was perhaps the harbinger of a new Enlightenment, more holistic in its outlook and more attuned to the paranormal, spiritual, mystical realm as the foundation of true knowledge of reality. This process is still unfolding. It will continue to reverberate into medicine as well as other sciences. Developments during the '90s such as the creation of OAM are part of it. I was beginning to feel that the new century might herald the end of the war between science and religion that began with the French philosophers' assault on religion in the seventeenth and eighteenth centuries. Perhaps Pitirim Sorokin's Integral vision, which so fascinated me during my graduate years, will be fulfilled. We might see a more mature understanding of how the major religions of the world share common truths. The peace of the world and the long-term survival of humanity may be at stake.

My involvement with the OAM has also been a great bonus to my life with Emily. It triggered her interest to pursue her doctoral education at the University of Maine in counselor education, focusing on alternative therapies.

It is as if the establishment of that prestigious office in Washington gave the green light to her professors to allow her to work on a first-of-its-kind dissertation dealing with the women healers of Maine. It was an additional blessing for our life together and opened up a career opportunity for her to play an important role in the Peace Studies program of our university.

PARLIAMENT OF RELIGIONS

I was noticing more and more synchronicity in my life. Following the establishment of the OAM, another event of great historical importance took place—the Second World Parliament of Religions. The mainstream media simply ignored it, and I learned about it only because that same weekend in 1993, I was offering an all-day workshop at the Oasis Center in Chicago, a human potentials venue. Participants at the workshop alerted me to it, and they shared literature and information about what was happening just a short distance from our workshop.

The World Parliament of Religions has a notable history. Exactly one hundred years earlier, the first World Parliament of Religions was held in Chicago. Representatives gathered from around the world in 1893 to begin a process of interreligious dialogue for the purpose of global understanding and world peace. It was a public and open dialogue between representatives of the world's religions, and it included Christians, Jews, and Moslems as well as Hindus, Buddhists, and representatives of other far eastern religions. For the first time ever, large numbers of westerners, who in past centuries were cut off from the rest of the world because of oceans, deserts, and mountain ranges, were now exposed to religions and civilizations beyond the West.

The presence at the 1893 parliament of Swami Vivekananda, the influential and charismatic yogi from India, played a decisive role in introducing the Vedic tradition of India to a western audience. Like Nixon's visit to China some eight decades later, the Swami's speech was a cultural watershed. An increasing number of western writers, poets, intellectuals, and other seekers found a new source in the wisdom traditions of India.

About a decade after the first World Parliament, a series of books appeared in Chicago, presenting with extraordinary clarity the essentials of Indian spirituality and philosophy. The books were written by Yogi Ramacharaka, a Chicago lawyer and an initiate of the Hindu religious tradition.[8] Still in print, these books along with several others, were instrumental in bringing Indian philosophy to the West. They were also important for my own exposure to the wisdom traditions of the Far East.

The turn towards the East continued slowly but steadily over the decades. Several mystical movements were important early in the twentieth century, including the Theosophical Society of Madam Blavatsky and Henry Olcott, and its offshoot the Anthroposophical society, led by the German mystic and psychic Rudolf Steiner. Some of these esoteric groups have continued to the present, despite being denounced at times by mainstream religious organizations. In the sixties and after, fascination with the East accelerated with the arrival in America of Maharishi Mahesh Yogi and the introduction of meditation and yoga as regular practices to an increasing number of Americans, particularly the college educated. The emerging popularity in the West of Chinese medicine was a parallel part of this process.

It took a span of time that included two world wars, several communist revolutions, the Cold War, and the 1979 Islamic revolution in Iran for the second World Parliament of Religions to convene. Representatives came from the historical religions of East and West as well as from tribal religions. There were also several Native American shamans.

The keynote speaker was none other than the Dalai Lama of Tibet. The latter's reputation as a man of peace was by then solidified, some three decades after the Chinese communists took over Tibet and forced him and 100,000 of his followers to seek refuge in India. Not surprisingly, the theme of the 1993 conference was world peace through dialogue and understanding among the world's religions. The underlying assumption was that the religions of the world must reach a consensus on key moral principles that should govern interreligious, interethnic and interracial relationships.

A "Manifesto for a Global Ethic" was drafted at the end of the conference and the signatories vowed to promote its principles. The Manifesto drew on understandings common to all the participants regarding ethical and moral issues. They avoided the theological disputes that have so often plagued interreligious dialogue. I found the Manifesto compelling, a refreshing antidote to the polar extremes of relativistic postmodernism on one side and rigid religious fundamentalism and xenophobic ethnocentrism on the other.

In the preamble to the "Declaration," the authors begin by pointing out that the world is in peril and agony. The sources of that agony are the abuse of the Earth's ecosystems, poverty, the social disarray of nations, the disregard for justice, and the "insane death of children from violence." The Declaration also denounces the incitement of aggression and hatred in the name of religion, and it soundly rejects the extreme relativistic position that there are no objective ethical truths: "There already exist ancient guidelines for human behavior which are found in the teachings of the religions of the world and which are the condition for a sustainable world order." The Manifesto then lays out the following principles, which deserve quoting in full:

We Declare:

We are interdependent. Each of us depends on the well-being of the whole, and so we have respect for the community of living beings, for people, animals, and plants, and for the preservation of Earth, the air, water, and soil.

We consider humankind our family. We must strive to be kind and generous. We must not live for ourselves alone, but should also serve others, never forgetting the children, the aged, the poor, the suffering, the disabled, the refugees, and the lonely. No person should ever be considered or treated as a second-class citizen, or be exploited in any way whatsoever. There should be equal partnership between men and women. We must not commit any kind of sexual immorality. We must put behind us all forms of domination or abuse.

We commit ourselves to a culture of nonviolence, respect, justice, and peace. We shall not oppress, injure, torture, or kill other human beings, forsaking violence as a means of settling differences.

We must strive for a just social and economic order, in which everyone has an equal chance to reach full potential as a human being. We must speak and act truthfully and with compassion, dealing fairly with all, and avoiding prejudice and hatred. We must not steal. We must move beyond the dominance of greed for power, prestige, money, and consumption to make a just and peaceful world.

Earth cannot be changed for the better unless the consciousness of individuals is changed first. We pledge to increase our awareness by disciplining our minds, by meditation, by prayer, or by positive thinking. Without risk and a readiness to sacrifice there can be no fundamental change in our situation. Therefore we commit ourselves to this global ethic, to understanding one another, and to socially-beneficial, peace-fostering, and nature-friendly ways of life.

We invite all people, whether religious or not to do the same.

Given at the 1993 Parliament of the World's Religions September 4, 1993 in Chicago, Illinois, United States of America.

I have tried to counter the dominance of relativism in the modern university by alerting my students to these principles. Their response was always overwhelmingly positive, perhaps a sign of the exhaustion of materialism as a viable compass for human existence. For their part, the organizers of the Parliament pledged not to wait for another hundred years to convene another such conference, recognizing the urgency to save humanity from possible annihilation, nuclear or environmental. Similar parliaments were repeated in various cities around the world in 1999, 2004, 2007, 2009, and 2016. And in February of 2017, the World Parliament of Religions collaborated with the United Nations on a "World Interfaith Harmony Week," offering a series of live-video webinars. The aim was for religions and spiritual communities to take action on behalf of a more peaceful, just, and sustainable world order.

The Parliament's stirring "Declaration" of 1993 convinced me that something profound was happening in the realm of ideas in the nineties. Perhaps non-ordinary abilities and ways of seeing were not so uncommon after all. Even the U.S. government had given a surprising stamp of approval to the

new Office of Alternative Therapies, despite virulent opposition from orthodox medical authorities.

Several new institutions contributed outlets for these new ways of thinking and were prominent in broadening my worldview. The Association of
Transpersonal Psychology was created in the late sixties by psychologists
who felt that their discipline had neglected types of awareness that extended
beyond the rational ego. They advocated bringing spiritual, mystical, and
other paranormal experiences into psychology, leading to a more holistic
understanding of the psyche. This idea had long ago been promoted by
mavericks such as Carl Jung, and before him, William James. It was time
to birth a new field, and luminaries such as Abraham Maslow and psychiatrist Stanislav Groff played leading roles. They inaugurated *The Journal of
Transpersonal Psychology* in 1969, and in 1972 it became the official journal
of the Association.

I became enamored of transpersonal psychology in the early nineties, when
I began reading authors who published in the journal or put out books that
dealt with these new ideas. Philosopher Ken Wilber was an especially strong
influence. He mapped regions of the self that are transegoic, states of consciousness that may manifest through spiritual practice but may also emerge
in unexpected ways, as in the mystical experience of St. Paul on the road
to Damascus or the epiphanies of great saints within the world's religions.
Wilber specifies three phases of the self: a pre-egoic state of oneness experienced by infants, an egoic or ordinary state of consciousness, and a transegoic state of mystical illumination. He warns psychologists not to reduce the
transegoic experience to a simple regression to the pre-egoic phase, as Freud
did in his reckoning of the "oceanic" feeling reported by mystics. But Wilber
also cautions against mistaking real mental illness for mystical illumination.[9]

Another inspiring new institution was The Institute of Noetic Sciences, an
outgrowth of the mystical epiphany of Dr. Edgar Mitchell on his return trip
from the Moon during the Apollo 14 space mission. He reports being overwhelmed by an intense feeling of universal interconnectedness. Mitchell's
lifelong ambition was to explore the external physical universe, but after
his mystical epiphany, his way of seeing the world evolved: "I realized that
the story of ourselves as told by science—our cosmology, our religion—
was incomplete and likely flawed. I recognized that the Newtonian idea of
separate, independent, discreet things in the universe wasn't a fully accurate
description. What was needed was a new story of who we are and what we
are capable of becoming." By 1973 Mitchell had inaugurated the Institute
of Noetic Sciences.[10] The Institute has since become a pioneering center for
research on inner space that could free science from its Nineteenth century
mechanistic assumptions.

A TRANSPERSONAL SOCIOLOGY?

Inspired by the pioneers who launched transpersonal psychology and the Institute of Noetic Sciences, I collaborated with my colleague Steve Cohn on a publication to alert the wider community of sociologists to this innovative perspective. Our goal was to spark interest in a new branch of our discipline, a sociological equivalent of this already established branch of psychology. Our starting premise was that the prevailing paradigm in sociology is based on an unexamined assumption: that reality is only physical, and mind is a byproduct of matter. This paradigm rules out the possibility of transmaterial realities, realities beyond gross matter. We argued that empirical evidence about paranormal experiences such as remote viewing, telepathy, and clairvoyance suggest a mind that is independent of the physical body and the brain. And among these nonordinary varieties of experience, one particularly stands out, the religious experience itself. Religion will often be a focus within this new subfield, just because it is a social location in which transcendence has often made an experiential appearance.

Unfortunately, in the history of sociology, religious phenomena have too often been seen through the lens of the materialist paradigm. Religion is simply part of the social machine, a social production maintained by socially created rituals, and lacking any transcendental origin or referent. This approach rules out a transpersonal sociology, which, like its counterpart in psychology, assumes that there are spiritual stages of human development beyond the rational and the sensate.

My observations of healers and mystics convinced me that what is primary in matters of religion is spiritual transcendence and mystical revelation. The rituals that the "social machine" then might create to celebrate it are secondary. This conclusion is not unlike Henry Belk's notion of "*contactee* business," discussed earlier. All religions began with the ecstatic experiences of a founder or founders. One can argue that without Paul's mystical epiphany on the Road to Damascus there would have been no Christianity as we have known it. The same applies to Judaism with the experiences of the prophets, Islam with Mohammad, Buddhism with Prince Gautama during his prolonged meditation under the Bodhi Tree, and shamans with their journeys out of the body.

Steve Cohn and I proposed a set of axioms drawn from the major spiritual traditions of the world:

1. There is a reality toward which religions point that is both nonphysical and nonsocial.

2. People have an inner spiritual component—a facility for transcendence—that enables them to reach toward this reality.
3. This spiritual component may influence and sometimes drive human behavior and human values; that is, human personalities may be influenced by more than heredity and environment.
4. Human freedom lies outside of the realm of social and biological conditions; therefore, the explanatory power of the social, physical, and biological sciences is necessarily limited.

To summarize, the religious experience—mystical, transcendent, ecstatic experience—is an ever-present potentiality within human nature itself. There will always be human beings who have such experience, and under certain historical conditions this experience may spawn movements that culminate in institutional religions. Mystical transcendence could never be eradicated by secularization, and religion could never be annihilated from human history. Even within the most totalitarian, atheistic societies, mystics will appear, pointing to realities beyond the material and physical world and serving as exemplary models of what human beings might be. The Nietzschean notion of the death of God is nothing other than a Nineteenth century fiction, widely and uncritically accepted by the secular establishment. In the words of Aldous Huxley, "The mystics are channels through which a little knowledge of reality filters down into our human universe of ignorance and illusion. A totally unmystical world would be a world totally blind and insane."[11]

My collaborator Steve Cohn and I knew that it would be difficult to publish our article in a sociology journal. Indeed, an angry reviewer pointed out that sociology is methodologically atheistic and what we were proposing was theology, not sociology. Our work did find its way into a regional literary journal, but this was hardly the venue to catch the attention of sociologists. Fifteen years later, our article was rediscovered by a Polish sociologist who was editor of an English language journal. He wished to republish it after some updating in a special edition of the *International Journal of Transpersonal Studies.* That journal devoted an entire issue to Transpersonal Sociology![12] Perhaps the twenty-first century will welcome the arrival of a new subfield in sociology, one that will include spirituality as foundational for human development. Pitirim Sorokin surely would have seen this development as faithful to his "Integralist Truth."

A VISIT WITH HUSTON SMITH

We were excited that Huston Smith would be visiting us. He was a world-renowned philosopher and sage of comparative religions. His classic work on the world's religions remained a best seller for decades after its original publication in 1958.[13] That work helped me to see that despite their differences, the various religions share a common core of spiritual wisdom, quite compatible with the consensus that emerged in the World Parliament of Religions of 1993.

Huston Smith always preferred to explore those aspects of religions that have nurtured the loftiest yearnings of humanity. His approach reminded me of what Pitirim Sorokin used to say, that the social sciences draw conclusions about human nature by studying primarily what is pathological; it focuses excessively on deviants and criminals while ignoring saints and sages. Smith would agree with Sorokin that in order to truly understand the depths of human nature, we must focus on those individuals who have reached great heights of altruism, selflessness, and creative wisdom, people who point the way to what we might be, and show us the reason why we are here in this life.

Growing up in China, the son of Methodist missionaries, Huston Smith had a profound appreciation of Abrahamic religions—Judaism, Christianity, and Islam—as well as all those religions outside the sphere of western influence. He remained a practicing Christian, but he explored other religions with equal zeal and discernment, both intellectually and experientially, from Native American sweat lodges to Zen retreats, and to Christian Eucharistic services. During his stay in our home and before his scheduled talk, Emily was surprised to find the venerated professor emeritus standing on his head! It was part of the yoga exercises he engaged in every morning after his Christian prayers.

As professor of philosophy, Huston Smith was at the very center of an era of spiritual transformation in America during the sixties, seventies and beyond. By the time he visited us in the nineties, he was retired and living with his wife in Berkeley, while remaining actively engaged as a pillar of the vibrant human potentials movement. We were fascinated by stories of people he knew personally, including the Dalai Lama and other luminaries of the world's religions. He was critical of the shortcomings of some of the gurus coming from the East during the sixties and seventies, but he also lamented the failure of American divinity schools to address the experiential, mystical side of religion. Regardless of disclaiming any such mystical episodes of his own, he identified himself as an intellectual mystic.

Huston Smith regretted his lack of success in introducing spiritual perspectives within academia. He tried valiantly to do so while teaching philosophy for many years at the Massachusetts Institute of Technology. As a philosopher, he was often merely tolerated by colleagues who thought religion and even philosophy were leftovers of a prescientific era. Such attitudes sometimes made the life of the great philosopher less than ideal.

When he was about to board the plane back to California, I gently mentioned that in his classic work on the world's religions, I found his treatment of Eastern Orthodox Christianity to be a bit thin. I suggested that perhaps in a new revision, he might elaborate on this part of the Christian movement that has been neglected by western scholars. He smiled widely, and pointing his finger at me, he said lightheartedly, "Why don't *you* do that!" I smiled back, thinking that this was not on my plate. Huston Smith died in 2016, but back when he made that offhand suggestion to me, I never could have imagined how prescient it was, as developments were soon to emerge that would throw me into that very focus on Eastern Christianity.

NOTES

1. Kyriacos C. Markides, *Riding with the Lion* (New York: Viking Penguin, 1995), pp. 59–60.
2. Arthur Hastings, *With the Tongues of Men and Angels: A Study of Channeling* (New York: Holt Rinehart and Winston, 1991).
3. Larry Dossey, *Healing Words: The Power of Prayer and the Practice of Medicine* (New York: HarperOne, 1995).
4. Charles Tart, *The End of Materialism: How Evidence of the Paranormal is Bringing Science and Spirit Together* (Oakland, CA: New Harbinger Publications, 2009); Pim van Lommel, M.D. *Consciousness Beyond Life: The Science of the Near-Death Experience* (New York: HarperOne, 2010).
5. John G. Fuller, *Arigo: Surgeon of the Rusty Knife* (New York: Thomas Y. Crowell Company, 1974); See a more extended version of this story in my *Riding with the Lion* op. cit. pp.131–137.
6. Russell Targ, *The Reality of ESP: A Physicist's Proof of Psychic Abilities,* (Wheaton, IL: Quest Book 2012).
7. Dean Radin, *The Conscious Universe: The Scientific Truth of Psychic Phenomena* (San Francisco: HarperOne, 2009).
8. A couple of these books are: *Advance Course in Yogi Philosophy* (Chicago: The Yogi Publication Society, 1904; *Lessons in Gnani Yoga* (Chicago: The Yogi Publication Society, 1906).
9. Ken Wilber, *Eye to Eye: The Quest for the New Paradigm* (New York: Anchor Books, 1983).
10. Edgar Mitchell, *The Way of the Explorer: An Apollo Astronaut's Journey Through the Material and Mystical Worlds, Revised Edition* (Newburyport, MA: New Page Books, 2008); Edgar Mitchell, *Earthrise: My Adventures as an Apollo 14 Astronaut* (Chicago: Chicago Review Press, 2014).
11. Dana Sawyer, *Huston Smith: Wisdomkeeper* (Louisville, KY: Fons Vitae, 2014), p. 38.

12. "Religion and Spiritual Experience: Revisiting Key Assumptions in Sociology" (with Steven F. Cohn--revised), *International Journal of Transpersonal Studies,* special volume on Transpersonal Sociology. 32(2), 2013, pp. 34–41.
13. Huston Smith, *The World's Religions* (San Francisco: Harper One, 2009).

Chapter 6

The New Millennium

SPIRIT AND THE NEO-ATHEIST OPPOSITION

My class on the Sociology of Mental Illness was over for the day, and I began walking across campus towards my office in Fernald Hall. It was a perfect, cloudless morning. The lush forests that cover most of Maine would soon be changing their dark green color to multiple hues of reds and yellows. As always, visitors from around the world would be arriving to relish the stunning cornucopia of autumn colors. I was in an upbeat mood. My latest book would soon appear in the bookstores, and my editor at Random House had arranged a media push to promote it as widely as possible.

No one foresaw the sinister plot that was now unfolding, causing death and destruction, and haunting the lives of generations to come. As I was about to enter my building, a colleague came out looking terribly distraught. "Are you aware of what's going on in New York?" she asked me breathlessly. She quickly told me, and I rushed to the sociology office upstairs and joined others watching on live television. There was a collective "Oh-my-God" moan as we saw the second plane hitting the Twin Towers in lower Manhattan. Further gasps followed as we witnessed the macabre spectacle of people jumping to their deaths from the two skyscrapers consumed by fire. It was September 11, 2001, a day that will remain in infamy in American history.

Hours earlier, two of the terrorists who hijacked the planes and flew them on their murderous mission had driven from Canada along Maine's I-95, passing just a hundred meters from our home in Stillwater. They then boarded a southbound plane at the Portland airport for their fateful connecting flight. A chilling coincidence was the fact that the St. Nicholas Greek Orthodox Church, situated under the shadows of the Twin Towers, was obliterated by the collapsing skyscrapers. My new book was about the mystical spirituality of the Greek Orthodox Church.[1]

As scheduled, *The Mountain of Silence* appeared in the bookstores the day after 9/11, when the entire country was in a state of shock and terrified of more such attacks. Three thousand people were dead, and everyone remained riveted to their televisions. Understandably, there was no media outreach for newly published books. The country was mourning its dead. The publicity manager at Random House was out of commission for over a month, struggling to recover from the loss of her closest friend, who perished under the rubble of the World Trade Center where she worked.

By training, temperament, and habit, I tried to understand how this tragedy was affecting people all over, my way of emotionally coping with it. I noticed two developments taking place. The first was a sociological observation, and it centered on the social solidarity in the aftermath of the tragedy. Far from creating chaos, the attack rallied people to support their government and each other. They focused on the heroism of the first responders—the hundreds of firemen and policemen who lost their lives trying to rescue victims—and on the altruism of ordinary people. New Yorkers whose demeanor was typically blasé or self-protective among strangers on the streets became caring and generous with one another. The sense of community paralleled the aftermath of the "Blitz" in World War II London when that city was under relentless bombardment by Nazi Germany. The external threat created internal cohesion, a phenomenon I also witnessed after the Turkish invasion of Cyprus in 1974. In times of extreme stress, we often rediscover our better angels. American flags were everywhere on display. Even Democrats and Republicans in Congress embraced one another.

A second consequence of the tragedy was a spontaneous turn towards religion and spirituality. Some brought out their family Bibles and read St. John's *Apocalypse*, the last section of the sacred book. Even nonpracticing believers and agnostics, along with the occasionally religious, went off to churches, synagogues, and mosques to pray, light candles, and support each other.

But the question *"Where was God on September 11?"* can also provoke an antireligious answer. That very question brought forth a cottage industry of religion-hostile books with titles such as *"The God Delusion," "God is not Great," "The End of Faith,"* and so on. The terrorist attack spawned a virulent neo-atheist movement that branded religion as the root of all evil. Leading neo-atheists—biologist Richard Dawkins, journalist Christopher Hitchens, neuroscientist Sam Harris, and philosopher Daniel Dennett—thundered against belief in the supernatural as the very thing that breeds fanaticism and threatens peace.[2]

The frontal assault on religion was heralded by fellow atheists and agnostics as a brilliant triumph of reason, in opposition to the ignorance and irrationality that paved the way for the horrors of 9/11. The neo-atheists certainly had critics of their own, but I welcomed their war on religion because it stimulated so many brilliant, scholarly, and readable reactions that otherwise would not have been written.

Perhaps truth emerges in history dialectically, through challenge and response. Unchallenged beliefs can easily become rigid dogmas that silence critical thinking, breed intolerance, undermine creativity, and stultify the growth and evolution of human consciousness. The clamoring of the neo-atheists stimulated a more mature and authentic understanding of the nature of faith and religious phenomena.

The work of Jonathan Sacks—Chief British rabbi and philosopher—is a case in point. He writes that the new atheists' program consists of criticizing religion without understanding it "abusing, mocking, ridiculing, caricaturing, and demonizing religious faith and holding it responsible for the great crimes against humanity."[3] Sacks echoes the views of leading sociologist of religion Peter Berger, arguing that it is not the presence but the absence of religious anchoring that has created the worst calamities for humanity.[4] "The cure for bad religion is good religion, not no religion," Sacks insists. A purely secular worldview invites a nihilistic outlook and a vacuum of meaning that can lead to unspeakable evil: the French guillotine, the Stalinist gulags, the slaughter-houses of Maoist China and Pol Pot's Cambodia, not to mention the archetypal horror of the Holocaust, rationally planned and executed by the Nazis.

Perhaps the greatest provocateur among both the debunkers and the supporters of religion was Dr. Francis Collins, a leading geneticist and later director of the National Institutes of Health (NIH). A devout, nonfundamentalist Christian, Collins's best-selling book offers a spirited defense of a theistic view of reality that honors the best insights from science.[5] In so doing he provoked fury from the debunkers of religion, who demanded his resignation as head of NIH, but he also angered some traditional believers through his equally spirited defense of evolution. For Collins as for many modern believers, evolution is the mechanism through which God brings about his creation; it is not a negation of Spirit.

Collins reminds us that the position of leading scientists on the Big Bang theory of the Universe is virtually identical to the opening paragraph of the book of Genesis in the Bible. One might say that the Universe was created through an unfathomable grand miracle. Collins quotes the colorful comment made by astrophysicist Robert Jastrow in his book *God and the Astronomers*: "For the scientist who has lived by his faith in the power of reason, the story ends like a bad dream. He has scaled the mountains of ignorance; he is about to conquer the highest peak; as he pulls himself over the final rock, he is greeted by a band of theologians who have been sitting there for centuries."[6]

What added insult to injury for the neo-atheists was the defection of one of their own, prominent atheist and British philosopher Antony Flew. Known as an "evangelist of atheism," Professor Flew was a fellow of an organization set up to combat belief in God and spirituality. But two years before his death in

2010, his final book flashed a shocking title: *There is a God: How the World's Most Notorious Atheist Changed his Mind.*[7] Why did Flew change his mind?

It was reason and science, Flew explains, that eventually led him to God, not blind faith. "The biggest discovery of modern science was the discovery of God!" Flew had become increasingly alienated from fellow atheists such as Dawkins, Harris, and Hitchens, and he now mocked their best sellers. The authors "sound like hellfire-and-brimstone preachers warning us of dire retribution, even of apocalypse, if we do not repent of our wayward beliefs and associated practices. There is no room for ambiguity or subtlety. It's black and white."[8]

Flew had decided that the Universe was created by an infinite Intelligence. The Universe's complex laws express what scientists have called the Mind of God. Life and reproduction originate from a divine source. This is the world picture, he claimed, that has emerged from modern science. It points to God. And "I have also been helped," Flew added, "by a renewed study of the classical philosophical arguments."[9]

CAN RELIGION BE LIFE-ENHANCING?

The neo-atheist movement and the reaction against it coincided with my emerging interest in the mystical spirituality of Christianity, as preserved in the traditions of the Eastern Orthodox Church. Once I discovered it, particularly its monastic legacy, I had to revise my negative view of organized religion. The sixties had turned me into an agnostic, while the seventies led me to become skeptical of my skepticism. The eighties led me to think of myself as spiritual but not religious, and the nineties completed my pendulum swing: I began to see myself as both spiritual and religious. At the same time, I continued to identify myself as a critical sociologist, fully aware of the dark side of organized religion's history.

My former prejudice against organized religion had grown out of my sixties education. Most of my professors were implicitly anticlerical and antireligious, and they too often highlighted the dark side of religion. It took me a long time of inner struggle to see beyond these treatments, in large part because the western intellectuals I studied were aligned with the Enlightenment's antireligion beliefs, much like my professors. The neo-atheists had simply extended that tradition, seeing the church-attending faithful as intellectually challenged, lacking in rational acumen, and victims of incredulous beliefs, myths, and superstitions. Reaction against the historical dominance of the Catholic Church often generalized to all "men of the cloth." Scandals unveiled in the media and in films featuring clerics as villains continue to fuel these sentiments.

My shift of perspectives accelerated when I took over my department's sociology of religion course, which prompted me to learn more about the history and substance of religions. By then I was eager to stand on the shoulders of sociologists who, like philosopher Huston Smith, have focused on the positive functions of religion. Durkheim, a founding father of sociology mentioned earlier, centered one of his most celebrated works on how religion strengthens moral values.[10] Karl Mannheim, a classical sociologist who narrowly escaped Nazi Germany, believed that both religion and family serve as bulwarks against the atomization he considered to be the breeding ground of totalitarian mass movements such as Nazism and Communism. Eric Fromm[11] and Eric Hoffer[12] shared Mannheim's conviction that unattached, atomized human beings are vulnerable to manipulation by charismatic demagogues.

But the question remains: How can we know the difference between authentic and inauthentic spirituality, between life-enhancing and life-denying expressions of religiosity? My answer is that beliefs and practices that foster intolerance towards out-groups and uncritical devotion toward the rituals and dogmas of the in-group are supporting inauthentic forms of spirituality. Religious beliefs that are life-denying espouse an insular xenophobia. The "other" gets defined as less than human, less favored by God's grace, and less likely to inherit the kingdom of heaven. Outsiders are denounced by religious zealots as heretics who are on the wrong side of God's throne. Only the officially sanctioned dogmas are tolerated. Critical thought is discouraged, and censorship of alternative ideas is used to repel the miasma of apostasy.

Historically, inauthentic spirituality led to religious wars, abuse of human rights, and genocidal pogroms. The history of humanity is full of tragic examples: the militant Islamic terrorists of today; the extermination of the people of Canaan in the Old Testament; the longstanding prejudice against Jews that culminated in the Nazi Holocaust; the human sacrifices by the Aztec priests; the sacrifice of Iphigenia in the Iliad. Perhaps all religions in today's world could stand some soul-searching to cleanse themselves of rituals, dogmas, and behaviors that are life-denying and life-destroying. None of the historical religions has been immune to these tendencies.

In contrast, authentic spirituality cultivates love and compassion towards all of Creation including human beings. It sees reality as friendly and life-enhancing, and its core attributes are infinite love, infinite wisdom, and infinite power. It makes available a set of practices for cultivating virtues such as love, humility, *metanoia* (repentance), compassion, and mercy. And perhaps most important, authentic spirituality includes an experiential component that fosters direct contact with the ineffable reality behind Creation, variously referred to as God, the Ultimate Ground of Being, the Eternal Tao, unbounded awareness, and so on. In every generation there are spiritual leaders who embody authenticity and who can serve as role models. Among the luminaries of today I can think of the Dalai Lama of Tibetan Buddhism, Pope Francis of Roman Catholicism, and Patriarch of Constantinople Bartholomew of Eastern Orthodoxy—the "Green Patriarch," so named because of his activism in saving the planet from environmental catastrophe.

When I speak to religiously diverse audiences, I am often asked to explain the differences between Roman Catholicism, Protestantism, and Eastern Orthodoxy. Following the same model of Huston Smith, my preference is to focus on the most positive and life-enhancing contributions of each branch of Christianity to the world. I shall start with Catholicism.

The derogatory term "the Dark Ages" is a misnomer, we know now through the work of historians and sociologists. This period was a broad advance beyond the economically stagnant Greco-Roman world, maintained through the brutality of slavery. In fact, the sack of Rome by the barbarians gave rise to technological innovation and expanded trade markets. The "dark" centuries also planted the seeds of the scientific revolution, and the Catholic Church played a key role in this development. Its theology encouraged the study of nature as a legitimate way of knowing God's work. The rational intellect was honored as a divine gift to humanity from the Almighty so that humans may come to know their Creator. Unlike in the East, monks in Catholic monasteries were encouraged to study and experiment with nature to understand God's handiwork. In addition, the Catholic Church kept Western Europe together when the imperial political institutions collapsed as a result of the tribal invasions from the north. Protestantism's most enduring contribution to human life-enhancement was a political culture that nurtured modern democracy. The United States was itself a creation of the Protestant Reformation, and it set the template for democratic governance around the world. The founding fathers were all nurtured within the context of Protestant culture and tradition. They championed free and critical thinking—indispensable traits of mind for the thriving of democracy. Liberal Protestantism played a leading role in promoting the civil liberties enshrined in the American constitution as "inalienable rights," leading eventually to the abolition of slavery and the liberation of women from their status as second-class citizens. The Civil Rights Movement was propelled, after all, by the passion for justice of black Baptist ministers like Martin Luther King. We often forget these facts when critics of today blame religion for the reactionary excesses of Protestant fundamentalism.

To summarize: Catholicism rescued Western European culture from falling into chaos and obscurity, and it helped foster the scientific revolution and the appreciation of nature. Protestantism set the foundations for representative government, free markets, critical thinking, and universal civil rights. What, then, is the unique contribution of Eastern Orthodoxy? My answer is that it cultivated, developed, and preserved a mystical pathway to fulfillment that was sought elsewhere by disenchanted western poets and writers of the Twentieth century—in the ashrams of India and the lamaseries of Tibet. To be sure, Catholicism is likewise replete with mystics, from St. John of the Cross and Hildegard of Bingen to Padre Pio of Italy. Similarly, one also finds Protestant mystics, such as the German Meister Eckhart, within and outside of denominational boundaries. It is within Eastern Orthodoxy, however, that mystical theology is the central focus, and there are historical reasons why this is so.

Cut off from western developments after the Islamic takeover of areas formerly controlled by the Eastern Roman Empire, Orthodoxy turned inward. It became more otherworldly, seemingly indifferent to the workings of the external world. Instead of trying to understand God through the study of nature, it focused on the cultivation of spiritual methodologies to directly experience God. Whereas western theology developed a more rational and contemplative approach to God, the East invented forms of prayer meditation. The Jesus Prayer, for example, led practitioners to experience the Uncreated Light, which the fathers of the Orthodox Church considered to be the very manifestation of God within the human heart. Put simply, the West pursued God by placing greater emphasis on reason and the mind, whereas the East favored tuning the heart for direct experience of divine energies and realities.

MYSTICAL CHRISTIANITY

My discovery of Eastern Christian spirituality within the boundaries of organized religion was the result of a fateful coincidence. My friend Antonis, a Cypriot businessman, urged me to join him on a pilgrimage to Mt. Athos during Easter of 1991. In his letter from Cyprus, he said that if I wished to meet real saints I should join him in that pilgrimage. My immediate reaction was lukewarm if not downright negative. The notion of traveling to Greece and then to that remote peninsula in the north of the country to spend time with monks was not appealing. Living in a mainly Protestant country for many years, I had absorbed a cultural prejudice against monasticism, considering it to be a backward, reclusive lifestyle. That prejudice seemed further justified when I learned that no woman since the ninth century was permitted to step on Mt. Athos. The emperor of Constantinople had reserved it for male hermits and monks, providing them a haven from the advancing armies of Islam. The restriction against women was simple confirmation of monasticism's backward traditionalism. What could these monks possibly offer to a modern seeker of spiritual knowledge and wisdom?

I owe it to Emily's compelling counterarguments that I finally sent Antonis a positive reply, a decision that changed my life as well as hers. I flew to Athens, and together with Antonis and one of his friends, we drove to Ouranoupolis (Heavenly City) eight hours to the north, where we could get the ferry for the two-hour journey to Daphni, the disembarkation point on Mt. Athos. There was no other way of getting there, a place where close to two thousand monks in twenty monasteries and many hermitages and *sketes* (small communities of monks attached to a major monastery) were struggling for their salvation through continuous prayer.

It was at Vatopedi, a tenth-century monastery and the first one I visited at Mt. Athos, that I first met Father Maximos, a 32-year-old monk who struck me as a person of extraordinary spiritual gifts. While casually conversing with him, I began the gradual process of revising my negative views about monasticism. I realized that in those isolated monastic communities, there was a different Christianity: vibrant, mystical, experiential, and unknown to the world. Athonite spirituality was the kind that many disgruntled intellectuals in the West, fatigued with rationalism and the cynical shallowness of materialism, sought in the ashrams and lamaseries of the Far East.

With the help of Father Maximos, I began to learn that Orthodox experiential spirituality was an integral part of the organized church. The highlight of my first visit to Mount Athos was my introduction to Elder Paisios, who lived in the Athonite wilderness as a hermit, a miracle worker with extraordinary spiritual gifts, continuously praying for the good of the world and offering spiritual counsel to pilgrims. I could not have imagined that after his death in 1993, the venerated elder would be officially canonized as a saint of Orthodoxy, the "Saint Paisios of the Holy Mountain." Years later, I attended the sanctification of a Greek Orthodox Church in honor of this latest saint. I watched the faithful stand in line for their turn to make the sign of the cross and reverentially kiss the icon of the somber-looking saint. To my knowledge icons that depict smiling saints are never found, thus lending the impression that saints were somber in their real life. That was not the way I remember Elder Paisios. He kindheartedly cracked one hilarious joke after another, interspersed with spiritual advice and wisdom.

Through Father Maximos, Elder Paisios sent me a message before his death that I still cherish: If I wished to understand Orthodox spirituality and benefit from its fruits, I should fully immerse myself in it and avoid distractions. I tried my best to follow his advice by regularly attending church services, participating in the sacraments, having Father Maximos as my spiritual guide, remembering the Jesus Prayer, and learning how to chant, an art that I found spiritually uplifting. I know that my efforts have been woefully inadequate and sophomoric, compared to the spiritual virtuosi whom I encountered on the Holy Mountain. Alas, I could not resist the temptations of other, more trivial and worldly preoccupations.

My first pilgrimage to Mt. Athos was a turning point in my life, although at first I was not fully aware of its importance. I was impressed with young Father Maximos' theological knowledge and his extraordinary capacity to emanate Christian love, but it did not yet occur to me to write books about him. A year before his repose Elder Paisios, however, told Father Maximos to prepare his luggage and leave Mt. Athos at once. He insisted that he return to his native Cyprus to revitalize the monastic tradition that was rapidly disappearing from the island. For Athonite monks, an elder like Paisios spoke with the authority of Heaven, so regardless of his own wishes, Father Maximos had to obey his spiritual father. Within a year he reluctantly found himself abbot of the Panagia monastery, a historic and ancient institution in the Troodos Mountains of Cyprus.

That same year (1993), my friend Theofanis Stavrou, a fellow Cypriot and professor of Russian history, invited me to join a team of academics to advise the Cyprus government on promoting social research. It required to visit Cyprus twice a year, all expenses covered. It was like a divine gift. I could be in Cyprus for a week during summer and Christmas breaks, a great opportunity to continue my involvement with the island, maintain contact with friends and relatives, and keep in touch with Father Maximos. Then for my next sabbatical leave, I would spend time at his monastery as a participant observer and study his world.

It never crossed my mind to become a monk myself, although I stayed at the monastery for a large portion of my sabbatical leave, and I became the temporary chauffeur of the young abbot, who did not know how to drive. This responsibility gave me easy access and time for many conversations as I drove him around for his various errands. The net result was my book, *The Mountain of Silence.* It was the start of a new chapter in my academic career and personal life.

When people ask me about the essential features of Orthodox spirituality, I often begin by pointing out three salient characteristics. First, it is a healing tradition; its goal is to heal the soul. According to Orthodoxy the inner purpose of all human beings is to reestablish their unity with God, which was originally shattered because of the mythic fall of Adam and Eve. Second, Eastern Orthodoxy is a miracle tradition, in that those who are known to sustain a direct connection with God become vehicles of the Holy Spirit. They can cause miracles to happen, even on the physical level. In fact, miracles are the hallmark of what is required before one can be declared a saint. And these miracles must take place both while the saint is alive and after he or she departs from this world. The culture of Mount Athos and Orthodoxy in general is filled with stories of miraculous healings and paranormal phenomena of great variety. Elder Paisios himself was reputed to be a miracle worker, curing people from cancers, being seen in two places at the same time, demonstrating clairvoyant gifts, befriending wild animals and the like, all of which were strongly denied by him as idle rumors.

Third, in Eastern Orthodox mystical spirituality, the desert plays a prominent role in both its theology and its spiritual practices. Elder Paisios' spiritual yearnings led him to live alone in the Sinai desert near the monastery of St. Catherine for two years before he migrated to the "desert" of the Holy Mountain. Unlike the Sinai, this desert is lush green. It is called a desert because the hermits' isolation fosters their exclusive focus on prayer, which will open their hearts to God's presence. Cultivating the heart—love and compassion—is at the core of Eastern Orthodox spirituality, superseding every other virtue.

When Christianity became the official religion of the Roman Empire in the fourth century, the new martyrs and living witnesses to the faith were hermits, like the Great Anthony, who abandoned the comforts of city life in Alexandria and entered the desert to find God through ceaseless prayer, contemplation, and spiritual exercises. This tradition is preserved to the present day in ancient monasteries like Mount Athos, which cultivate inner silence so that the practitioner may hear the voice of God unencumbered by the distractions of ordinary life. The way to reach God and unite with Him is to create within ourselves an inner desert, free of egotistical passions and desires. Within that silence, God's voice will echo into the depths of our hearts. The full-time practitioners of this inner silence are the ascetics from whose ranks came most of the leading saints and the great theologians of Eastern Christianity. These holy elders provided the foundations of the healing tradition and its mystical theology.

I learned from Father Maximos and other elders that the hallmark of Eastern Orthodox mystical spirituality is what may be called *The Three-Fold Way.* They teach that the reestablishment of the shattered unity between human beings and God proceeds in three identifiable stages: *catharsis,* the purification of the soul; *fotisis,* the enlightenment of the soul; and *theosis,* union with God. There is a universality to these stages, as they are found in a variety of mystical traditions.

The premise upon which *The Three-Fold Way* rests on the notion that human beings since time immemorial have fallen from Grace. They have shattered their connection with God and live their lives in a state of exile from their true homeland. This is the meaning of *Original Sin* as understood by the mystical holy elders of Eastern Christianity. A key precondition for union with God is that the individual undergoes deep *metanoia* (change of heart and mind, repentance), leading to the process of catharsis and purification of the soul from egocentrism. The story of Genesis in the Old Testament and the parable of the prodigal son in the New Testament allude to this fundamental existential truth about human origins and destiny. In Jesus' parable, the prodigal son leaves the palace of the loving Father and cuts himself off from his spiritual roots. He squanders his divine inheritance by indulging in various passions and temptations of the material world. His human nature becomes distorted; the passions he was given to celebrate the creator are now employed for the satisfaction of lowly desires. For example, the capacity of the soul for anger, given to the soul as a power to resist temptation and sin, becomes a source of discord among human beings, both individually and collectively. Similarly, pride in one's divine lineage becomes pride in one's possessions, along with cravings for attention, fame, and power over others.

Eventually, the prodigal son becomes miserable, his life cut off from God, and he yearns for the palace. He returns after great difficulties and tribulations, and the Father embraces him and orders a feast to celebrate. Clearly, the story is allegorical. It is the story of every human being who yearns for a connection with God and begins the process of metanoia and catharsis. The palace, the inner kingdom, is always within us and within reach but we do not recognize it because it is covered up by layers of contaminants: poor habits, inattention, worldly desires, and lowly passions. The prodigal son never stops being a prince even while living among the pigs. It is easy to see parallels in this story with Plato's parable of the cave and Prince Gautama's adventures outside the palace of his father in search of enlightenment.

The Christian elders, both East and West, teach that the healing and restoration of the soul requires arduous spiritual struggle and effort. This point is also made by modern religious thinkers. It is a point often lost on a culture that values instant gratification. The monastic tradition of Christianity, rooted in the lives, experiences, and teachings of its great saints and holy elders, provides a methodology for how to heal the soul, free the self from egotistical desires, and reestablish the connection with God. This methodology is called *askesis,* which means exercise.

Among the set of practices that form askesis is regular participation in the sacraments of the Church: confession, communion, charitable action in the world, fasting, ceaseless prayer, systematic study of sacred texts and the lives of saints, cultivation of deep humility, and communal worship. Charity—material and nonmaterial giving and caring for the other—should be offered freely and humbly. It is a way of forgetting our own self-absorption and our tendency to imprison our hearts and minds in the things of this world. Similarly, fasting trains the soul to master the lower passions; unless we gradually learn to overcome small temptations, we will not develop the power to resist greater temptations that unavoidably assault our everyday existence. Confession, through the spiritual guidance of an experienced elder, enables us to address our sinful actions and to become conscious of our *logismoi,* the negative thought-forms we generate that create layers of separation between ourselves and God. We are called to replace these logismoi with systematic and ceaseless remembrance and contemplation of God through prayer. A most important practice is the incessant repetition of short prayers, foremost of which is the Jesus Prayer: *Lord Jesus Christ, Son of God, Have Mercy on Me*, or Saint Gregory Palamas' shorter variant, *Lord, Enlighten My Darkness*. The practitioner is instructed to repeat this prayer as much as possible. It can be recited even while engaging in worldly activities such as waiting at a bus stop or washing dishes. The purpose of this practice is to minimize the creation of negative thought-forms and replace them with the memory of God. It is a method of returning to paradise, which can be attained amid one's present life. In addition, reciting long-established prayers like the Psalms, reading about the lives of saints, and attending regular communal services will eventually bear fruit in the life of the practitioner.

For any soul who engages in askesis and the release from worldly passions, *fotisis* will eventually follow. At this stage, divine providence may offer the soul extraordinary gifts, such as prophetic vision, healing abilities, phenomena of levitation and bilocation, and the like. These gifts are deeply buried within human nature and may manifest only after the purification of the soul. What we call paranormal phenomena become normal at this second stage, gifts that are reported in the lives of saints who serve as models of what we might be. The most prized gift of the Spirit is the vision of the Uncreated Light, the mystical perception of God's presence that floods the soul with exquisite joy. It is the point when the heart opens to God's grace and love, liberated from lowly worldly passions and addictions.

Those who are offered such gifts of the Spirit must accept them in utter humility, never as a source of self-promotion or self-aggrandizement. In fact, such gifts may become cravings that can lead to a spiritual fall. That is why great saints use them only sparingly, solely to help fellow human beings fulfill their spiritual, psychological, and medical needs. The desert fathers have been called *nyptic*, meaning vigilant. Healing abilities and gifts should never be flaunted to impress an audience, as too often happens today within certain New Age circles. I recall the strong reaction of Elder Paisios when I naively asked him about his reputed abilities to heal people. He emphatically denied such "rumors." He told me that all he does is pray for people, and whatever healing takes place is the result of God's Grace and Providence. Back in Maine, rumors of his reputed friendship with wild animals had reached me before I ever met him, and this was the reason for my query. In Orthodox spirituality, the God-realized individual may reestablish that harmonious relationship with nature that was characteristic of life before the fall. Hence the legends of saints who lived among wild beasts without fear of being harmed. It is this understanding that led Patriarch Bartholomew of Constantinople to begin a global campaign to save the Earth from environmental degradation. In his championing of the spiritual need for a harmonious relationship with nature, he was instrumental in adding environmental degradation to the list of sins that wayward humans may commit. That commitment earned him the appellation "Green Patriarch."

The third stage in the spiritual development of the self is the attainment of *theosis*, the ultimate destination of the human soul and its restoration of oneness with God. It is the true healing of the soul. Like the previous stage of *fotisis, theosis* lies totally in the hands of Providence. Human beings cannot reunite with God strictly of their own accord. Our will can be involved only at the first stage, the stage of *Catharsis*. The other two stages follow naturally as God's rewards for our struggles to purify our hearts. Attempts to get gifts directly, such as trying to develop psychic powers without struggling to free our soul from egotism, is tantamount to stealing from God.

All the great sages have pointed out that oneness with God—*theosis*—is beyond human description or comprehension. Its attainment does not imply that the soul loses its autonomy. In Christian spirituality, the self does not get diluted into the All. What is annihilated is the totality of our egotistical passions and desires, not our uniqueness as persons created in the image of God. The end of spiritual development could never be the obliteration of personhood, a form of spiritual nihilism. The God-realized human being will continue to work for the salvation of others, and do so from this side of the divide, still uniquely alive and active in this world.

CRITICS AND SUPPORTERS

My work on Eastern Orthodoxy, starting with *The Mountain of Silence,* was well received among ecclesiastical circles in Europe and America, and in the monasteries of Mt. Athos. However, it also triggered a virulent reaction among some men of the cloth who did not find it Orthodox enough or even Orthodox at all. One young monk, an ordained priest, produced a strident, five-and-a-half-hour CD denouncing my books as heretical and dangerous for Orthodoxy. "Lucifer penetrated the Orthodox Church," he thundered. I told Father Maximos that at first I was fired up enough to pay the good father a visit, but I had changed my mind because I wasn't certain that I could confront him with equanimity and in a spirit of Christian love. "That was wise," Father Maximos nodded with a grin. "You can't change the mind of such people with words and arguments."

Some of my academic friends who were already convinced that religion equals superstition felt deeply uncomfortable with my new line of inquiry. An Indian colleague, who had given up his Hinduism in favor of western rationalism, exasperatedly blurted out, "It is your right to believe that the moon is made out of Swiss cheese, if you so wish!" Similarly, a Cypriot friend was angry that I had offered academic legitimacy and cover to an institution that he considered disastrous for the island. Like most contemporary Greek and Greek Cypriot intellectuals, he blamed the Church and its hierarchy for the ethnic mess the island found itself in. It simply reinforces irrational beliefs that distort the politics of Cyprus and prevent a solution to its ethnic problem. "It puzzles me," he told me, "how a rational human being like yourself can believe in such nonsense." It was impossible for him to see that there was another side to the Orthodox Church, a mystical, esoteric, and deeply spiritual side.

An anonymous critic, a peer reviewer of one of my papers on Eastern Orthodox mystical spirituality, identified himself as a former monk as well as a sociologist. He wrote that he is not at all opposed to monasticism, only to my overly idealized version of it. He claimed that I leave out the negative aspects of monasticism, some of which he experienced himself as a former monk.

I responded to this reviewer's concerns by adding some comments to the published version of the paper. It would be a mistake, I acknowledged, to assume that the Athonite elders, abbots, and monastics are perfect human beings. They are not, and they are certainly not infallible or all-knowing. They have a shadow side. They make mistakes, sometimes even appalling ones. They can be misguided by the limitations of their formal education and their cultural conditioning. Narrow-mindedness and superstition can exist side by side with great spiritual wisdom, even among the greatest of saints of the Christian tradition, past and present. Expecting perfection can quickly lead to disappointment, and then we may deprive ourselves of whatever accumulated wisdom is preserved and active in these ancient religious institutions.[13]

Fortunately for my self-confidence, my colleagues in the sociology department thought well of my work on healers and on Christian monks and mystics, and they gave me maximum support and encouragement. The University of Maine functioned like a protected harbor, from which I could tackle controversial ideas without resistance from well-meaning friends, agitated denouncers, fundamentalist clerics, or doctrinaire skeptics.

SYNCHRONICITY, OPPORTUNITY, AND BELOVED COMMUNITIES

I was delighted when I received a letter of acceptance for the coveted Fulbright Scholarship program. Emily and I were both excited by the prospect of spending a year in Greece, where I would teach and do research for several months. But a month later, a second letter arrived informing me that the selection committee had made a mistake; the letter of acceptance was intended for a different applicant! Although I was dismayed, I stoically accepted the verdict without protesting the reversal, which had probably never happened to any applicant in the history of that program. I would like to think I was influenced by Father Maximos and the spiritual tradition he laid open to me: Accept whatever comes your way, positive or negative, as a gift from heaven. Do not waste your energy in futile and self-destructive recriminations. Exploit spiritually whatever happens to you. Turn it into an opportunity to come closer to God. Here, however, I do wonder if my surrender to the reversal had less to do with getting closer to God than with my lifelong aversion to conflict with others. It was the same aversion that probably rendered me the least qualified recruit for urban guerrilla warfare when I was a teenager.

Not much later, I received a surprising invitation from Boston University to become a visiting professor for the spring semester of 2004 at the Institute of Culture, Religion and World Affairs. I was elated. My responsibilities would be to offer a weekly seminar on religion and international affairs to a small class of graduate students in political science. I would present one formal colloquium on a topic of my choice to the faculty of the Institute, and I was to use the rest of my time for research and writing, the central focus and mission of the Institute. My work conditions at BU would be far more favorable to my writing than being in Greece on a Fulbright scholar program, where my teaching responsibilities would have left little time for research and writing.

The Boston apartment where Emily and I stayed was on the second floor of the home of the director of the Institute. He was none other than Peter Berger, a leading sociologist of religion and a legend in modern sociological theory. I had read most of his books, and I felt honored when I received the invitation via his assistant. I was stunned when I noticed the name of the previous occupant under the second-floor entry buzzer. It was Thomas Luckmann, the Austrian sociologist and close friend and collaborator of Peter Berger. Everywhere, students in sociology were assigned the Berger and Luckmann classic, *The Social Construction of Reality,* one of the most influential books in modern sociology.[14] And here I was with Emily in the very same house! I felt a mixture of pride, humility, and self-doubt. I was certainly not in the same league as these bigwigs of the sociological tradition. Is this another painful experience of mistaken identity?

The visiting scholar program at the Institute had begun the previous year with Thomas Luckmann as the first invitee. I was the second, but also the last. For reasons unknown to me, the funds to continue the program would soon dry up. I had flirted with the idea of postponing my visit, and had I done so, someone else would have taken my place and there would not have been a third invitee the following year. The twists and turns of fate that incessantly move our lives never fail to amaze me.

It turned out that the winter of 2004 at Boston University was one of the most intellectually gratifying semesters of my academic career. My seminar with the bright and motivated graduate students felt like a weekly exchange of ideas with colleagues. It was a treat to meet frequently with Peter Berger and his wife Brigitte, a well-known and respected sociologist in her own right. We chatted about everything—grandchildren, world politics, religion, problems plaguing contemporary sociology, anything. Living in Boston was an additional bonus. We were within walking distance of our favorite cafe near Harvard Square, where we had coffee and stimulating conversation with friends, old and new. Most importantly the semester at Boston University allowed me to finish my *Gifts of the Desert.*[15] None of this would have happened if the Fulbright award and the year in Greece had been mine to keep.

I recall an exchange I had with Huston Smith during his brief stay at our home in the 1990s. "I marvel," I said to this premiere scholar of comparative religions, "at how full you must feel spending your entire life exploring the world's wisdom traditions." With beaming eyes, he replied: "That's exactly how I feel!" Years later now, I feel likewise about my own experience and academic career. The twists and turns in my life, the uncanny synchronicities that brought me to the University of Maine thrust me into a full and meaningful life, unimaginable in my teenage years in Cyprus during the troubled fifties. No doubt, a lifetime of shared experiences with Emily and our children Constantine and Vasia provided the foundation I needed. On that bedrock, we were blessed with an ever-expanding community of supportive connections, beginning with our colleagues at the University of Maine and our friends and acquaintances within the Greek Orthodox community in the Bangor area.

Later, with the publication of my books on healers, spiritual guides, and Christian mystics, a new layer of relationships emerged from outside the boundaries of Maine, strengthening our roots in our adopted country. I received frequent invitations to give lectures and workshops at various church organizations, particularly Eastern Orthodox congregations situated throughout the Eastern coast, the Midwest and Canada.

Eventually I became a regular presenter at several nondenominational human potential and holistic centers, all promoting a worldview that incorporates Spirit as central to understanding reality. It is a worldview that strives to integrate the best of science with the best of religion, a vision that I first encountered as a young graduate student in the work of Harvard sociologist Pitirim Sorokin. At these centers, I had repeated contact with a wide spectrum of people: readers of my books, other writers, charismatic religious virtuosi from diverse traditions, artists, and world-renowned scholars. These were connections that enriched our life enormously.

Three of these holistic centers were especially important to Emily and me. One was the International Institute of Integral Human Sciences of Montreal

(IIIHS). I first heard of it when I visited Henry Belk to learn about his lifelong interest in the activities of unconventional healers around the world (see Chapter 5). He told me about his participation in the annual IIIHS conference, and he urged me to do likewise. Not long after I returned to Maine, that conference's organizers invited me to give a presentation. I soon learned that it was not Henry Belk who made the invitation happen; it came to me through one of those bursts of synchronicity that have shaped my life.

Dr. John Rossner, Professor of Comparative Religions, had read my first book about the healer Daskalos, and he wanted me join them at their upcoming conference. He and his wife Dr. Marilyn Rossner, Professor of Child Psychology, were responsible for setting up IIIHS. An affiliate of the United Nations, the organization has served for over forty years as the nucleus of a network of scientists, scholars, religious leaders, and professionals involved in mind-body research. Its aim is to bring forward new paradigms for the reconciliation of science and spirituality.

For over twenty years Emily and I have been attending and presenting at the IIIHS conference—Emily on peace and ecological sustainability, and I on Eastern Christianity and mysticism. John Rossner, an ebullient, goodhearted, and passionate scholar with a keen sense of humor, was also an ordained Anglican priest with a strong personal affinity for Eastern Orthodox theology. His wife Marilyn Rosser has been a world-renowned medical intuitive, gifted with unusual psychic abilities. She was instrumental in sensitizing her husband to transcendent realities, much like Daskalos opened up my own horizons. Our long friendship was unsettled by John's repose in 2012, but it continues with Marilyn, who soldiers on with the IIIHS organizing committee.

A second beloved community for Emily and me is the Sivananda Yoga Retreat on Paradise island in the Bahamas. Sivananda began its operations in 1968, a few years before the creation of IIIHS, and it has similar if not identical aims. Both John Rossner and Marilyn Rossner maintained close ties with the Sivananda organization, and many presenters at one institution were also presenters at the other, including Emily and me. We always enjoyed our respite from the Maine winter and the extraordinary beauty of the setting in the Bahamas, and we benefited from hearing the work of other presenters from around the world.

A third beloved community has been the New York Open Center, where I have given regular talks and workshops. It was established in the 1980s and was founded on the same holistic vision that inspired the other two institutions. One of its founders was Walter Beebe, a Wall Street lawyer who donated the property that houses the Center. Beebe and his friends Ralph White and Sandy Levine were eager to create a holistic center in the heart of New York City. As Ralph White points out, their goal was to create a haven for spirituality, a vibrant alternative to the secular materialism prevailing within the mainstream intellectual establishment.[16] Through my lectures at the Open Center and my friendship with the people who set up the organization, New York acquired a more personal meaning for me.

Like John Rossner, Ralph White contacted me to present at the organization after he read my first book on the healers of Cyprus. Our connection grew stronger, and in 2013 he brought a group of American spiritual seekers to Cyprus, where they had a memorable encounter with Father Maximos, the elder from Mt. Athos and now Bishop of the Orthodox Church. I was honored to serve as guide and translator.

Through these three institutions, Emily and I have been privileged to meet a great diversity of presenters from different religions: Tibetan Lamas, Sufis of Islam, Swamis from India, Cabbalists from Judaism, and medicine men and women known to be elders of various North American Indian tribes. We have sat shoulder to shoulder with pioneering scientists and scholars who have made an indelible mark on the spiritual resurgence view foreseen by Pitirim Sorokin and other visionaries. Their successful careers in academia enabled them to forsake the established boundaries and think outside the box. They comprise a long list, including such luminaries as Cambridge biologist Rupert Sheldrake,[17] quantum physicist Amit Goswami,[18] Harvard psychiatrist John Mack,[19] Columbia scholar and director of Indo-Tibetan Studies Robert Thurman,[20] theologian Mathew Fox,[21] and medical doctor, professor of Philosophy and discoverer of the near death experience, Raymond Moody.[22] We established a deeply gratifying friendship with Moody through repeated encounters at the IIIHS and by sharing mutual interests, including his love of ancient Greek philosophy.

With the guidance radiating from these and other pioneers, we are witnessing a new vision of reality that sees Spirit as foundational. Our own experience of the world has been radically transformed by this vision. The legacy of narrow identity, cultural insularity, and avoidance of contact with outsiders is receding. Diversity becomes a blessing. We might finally stop demonizing one another on the basis of differences and see one another as sparks of divinity. Institutions like IIIHS, the Sivananda Yoga Retreat, The New York Open Center, the Office of Complementary Medicine at the NIH, the society of Transpersonal Psychology and the Center for Noetic Studies are exemplars of this emerging integral vision of reality.

NOTES

1. Kyriacos C. Markides, *The Mountain of Silence: A Search for Orthodox Spirituality* (New York: Random House, 2001).

2. Richard Dawkins, *The God Delusion* (Boston: Mariner Books, 2008); Christopher Hitchens, *God is not Great: How Religion Poisons Everything* (New York: Twelve Publishers, 2009); Sam Harris, *The End of Faith* (New York: W.W. Norton, 2005); Daniel Dennett, *Breaking the Spell: Religion as a Natural Phenomenon* (New York: Penguin Books, 2007).
3. Jonathan Sacks, *The Great Partnership: Science, Religion, and the Search for Meaning* (New York: Schocken Books, 2011).
4. Peter Berger, *Pyramids of Sacrifice: Political Ethics and Social Change* (New York: Anchor Books, 1976).
5. Francis Collins, *The Language of God: A Scientist Presents Evidence for Belief* (New York: Free Press, 2007).
6. R. Jastrsow, *God and the Astronomers* (New York: W. W. Norton, 1992), 107. Cited in Collins op cit., p.76.
7. Antony Flew, *There is a God: How the World's Most Notorious Atheist Changed his Mind* (New York: HarperOne, 2008).
8. Antony Flew, Ibid xvi-xvii
9. Antony Flew, Ibid xvi-xvii
10. Emile Durkheim, *The Elementary Forms of the Religious Life* (New York: Free Press, 1995 [1912]).
11. Eric Fromm, *Escape from Freedom* (New York: Holt Paperback, 1994).
12. Eric Hoffer, *The True Believer* (New York: Harper & Brothers, 1951).
13. Kyriacos C. Markides, "The Healing Spirituality of Eastern Orthodoxy: A Personal Journey of Discovery," *Religions* (June, 2017), pp. 1–14.
14. Peter Berger and Thomas Luckmann, *The Social Construction of Reality: A Treatise in the Sociology of Knowledge* (New York: Anchor, 1967).
15. Kyriacos C. Markides, *Gifts of the Desert* (New York: Random House, 2005)
16. Ralph White, *The Jeweled Highway: On the Quest for a Life of Meaning* (Studio City, CA: Michael Wiese Productions, 2015), p. 117.
17. Rupert Sheldrake, *Science Set Free: Ten Paths to New Discovery* (New York: Deepak Chopra Publisher, 2013).
18. Amit Goswami, *God is not Dead: What Quantum Physics Tells us about our Origins* (Newburyport, MA: Hampton Roads Publishing, 2012).
19. John Mack, *Passport to the Cosmos* (New York: Crown Publishers, 2002).
20. Robert Thurman, *Inner Revolution* (New York: Riverhead Books, 1999).
21. Mathew Fox, *The Coming of the Cosmic Christ* (New York: HarperOne, 1988).
22. Raymond Moody, *Life After Life* (New York: HarperOne, 2015).

Chapter 7

A Summing Up

WHY FAITH?

Early in my Cyprus youth, I began to ponder the perennial questions: Is God a reality or an illusion? Is death the end of life? Is there a Heaven? I was haunted by a need for answers, and my 1960s higher education in America complicated everything. That decade was my secularization period, shattering my traditional faith and my comfort within Orthodox Christianity. Sociology was my new path and a replacement for God. I became a skeptic and an agnostic, needing rational evidence to believe in anything. None was offered for traditional faith within the corridors of academia. With the sole exception of Sorokin, the thinkers to whom I was exposed all pointed toward atheism and agnosticism. Faith was for the gullible, the naïve, and the undereducated. From the leading minds of the nineteenth and twentieth centuries, I learned that rational philosophy and empirical science are the superior alternative to religion. God is long dead. Religion is the opiate of the people, Marx declared. It is an infantile fixation and regression, Freud added. From the pioneers of sociology I learned that God is a creation of society, not the other way around. "I am not religiously musical," said Max Weber, a giant pillar of sociological theory who spent most of his life studying the role of religion in society.

But times have changed. Now in my twilight years, it is clear to me that the secularist dismissal of God and religion is itself laden with illusion, and perhaps these memoirs have shown you that I have splendid company in that conviction. With a lot of help from like-minded questers, I came back to faith, but one that is rooted in the discoveries of both secular science and enlightened, mystical religion. As a capstone to this spiritual and intellectual journey I will summarize my case.

This is surely a contradictory epoch in the ways that people in the West think about spirituality. Surveys show higher rates of atheism and agnosticism than ever before, especially among the university-trained "millennial" generation. Contrariwise, however, this may be the most privileged time for

141

spiritual questing in human history. Persistent seekers can find myriad signposts pointing toward a divine reality behind the realm of physical matter. The choice for seekers today is not between blind faith in religious dogma and no faith at all. There is an expansive middle ground that is transforming rationality itself. At the dawn of the third millennium, science is becoming the leading witness for the reality of Spirit. Whether we call this divine reality the "implicate order" of physicist David Bohm, the "Ground of all Being" of philosopher Aldous Huxley, the God of our fathers and mothers, or something else, a grand peace accord between the two traditional adversaries—religion and science—is in full bloom.

When Antony Flew abandoned his longstanding atheistic philosophy (see chapter 6), he offered scant elaboration of his new position that the biggest discovery of modern science "is the discovery of God." What science did he have in mind? How did it happen that theology, which doctrinaire rationalists had dismissed as irrelevant, is boldly returning to center intellectual stage?

Several seminal developments in science were pivotal for my own return voyage to a spiritual understanding of the world. They include the Big Bang theory of the Universe's origins; the relationship between mind and sub-atomic particles, as shown by several quantum physicists; the nonordinary ability of some human beings to see and know things through extrasensory perception, as shown by pioneering experimental psychologists; and the exploding research in thanatology as it relates to the near-death experience (NDE). I will touch on each of these developments.

I vividly remember how enthralled I was to encounter the "Big Bang" theory, which is the dominant cosmological view among leading astronomers since the mid-1960s. No specialized knowledge was needed to appreciate its theological implications. Up to that point, celebrated thinkers from David Hume, Karl Marx, and Friedrich Nietzsche to Jean-Paul Sartre, Bertrand Russell, and Sigmund Freud all took for granted the Steady State theory of the Universe. The notion was that the physical, material universe is all there is. It has always been there, and it does not require a creator to explain it. Religions are therefore purveyors of ignorance and superstition. The sooner they are replaced by science and rationality, the better for the future of humanity.

The Big Bang cosmology changed all that. Suddenly, the Universe we inhabit had not always been there. It was born a mere 13.7 billion years ago, the result of an unimaginable cosmic explosion. This extraordinary new understanding *sounded much like the scientific equivalent of* Genesis in the Old Testament, for as soon as we decide that the Universe had a beginning, the question arises, where did it come from? Who or what caused it?

Additional discoveries boggled more than a few minds. The Milky Way is not the entire Universe. It is simply one of 100 to 200 billion galaxies that scientists estimate are out there, each of them housing billions of solar systems like our own. For all practical purposes, the material universe appears to host an infinite number of galaxies. Think about that, along with the shocking revelation that these billions of galaxies make up only about 3 percent of the estimated total matter of the cosmos! The other 97 percent is "dark matter" that we know nothing about and that may well be unknowable. Who or what is behind this stupendous physical reality to which modern science has alerted us?

Some cosmologists conclude that the Big Bang could not be explained as a magnificent accident. The Universe is not a closed system, and therefore it cannot be explained by itself. As a leading astronomer once put it, to consider the Universe accidental is the equivalent of assuming that a tornado zoomed through a vast junk yard, causing the creation of a jet plane. What is the mathematical probability of this happening? What is the probability that this fine-tuned Creation that brought 200 billion galaxies into existence, including ourselves, is just a freak and bizarre occurrence?

Could science be a kind of divine revelation, unrecognized as such by its acolytes and practitioners? That question swirled in my mind when Emily and I visited the Kennedy Center at Cape Canaveral in Florida. I remember having a quasi-mystical moment, awed by the fact that we were standing on hallowed ground. We live *at* a moment when self-conscious beings can harness eons of evolution and reach for the stars. Here we stood, billions of years after the Big Bang brought this world into existence, right at the spot where several human beings broke through their earthly cocoon and reached the moon! How does that happen?

If the Big Bang theory raised questions about a possible creator, the findings of quantum physics intensified my wonderment, and I began to ponder their philosophical implications. As infinite as the macrocosm of galaxies appears to be, the microcosm of the subatomic realm seems to be equally so, an intuition that led some ancient sages to the well-known aphorism, "as above so below." Contrary to the great Democritus, atoms are not the final building blocks of reality. Leading scientists today claim that "all the way down," one discovers empty space! Furthermore, based on controlled experiments it appears that the mind plays a causal role in how subatomic matter behaves. It acts as particles if the experimental scientist expects to find particles and it behaves like waves if she expects them to behave as waves. In other words, consciousness affects matter and not just the other way around. Mind, according to leading quantum physicists like Amit Goswami, is not a byproduct of matter but an agency affecting matter.[1] The human brain is not the equivalent of mind but a mere vehicle for it. Are the billions of galaxies a physical manifestation of Mind at large? Of God? And is quantum physics the last nail in the coffin of materialism that mesmerized the western mind for over three hundred years?[2]

I showed in previous chapters that some people who are otherwise "ordinary" have some extraordinary abilities that bypass the confines of the five senses. I witnessed these abilities during my own field studies and observations; I have no doubts about their authenticity. Parapsychologists have identified and categorized them: clairvoyance, telepathy, precognition, and telekinesis are several examples. I will not repeat the arguments and the evidence for these abilities, discussed earlier, but I want to underscore the extraordinary blindness to such abilities on the part of the gatekeepers of scientific orthodoxy. People who invest their identity in rationality and no-nonsense logic are prone to dismissing any evidence of these abilities as charlatanism, soft-headedness, and superstition. Sadly, I can speak from experience as I have shown earlier.

The literature on the NDE has likewise unsettled the dismissal of Spirit. Thanks to modern science, we now have evidence suggesting that conscious-ness can exist outside the body. Raymond Moody has been heralded as a contemporary Christopher Columbus for his discovery of the NDE, and there is now a veritable cottage industry of studies about this phenomenon. Out of body experiences of people who were apparently dead but who came back to tell their story are not new. They are recorded anecdotally in diverse cultures and times from around the world—for example in Plato's *Republic* and in the graphic accounts of Carl Jung in his autobiography.[3] What is new since Moody's pioneering breakthrough is the scientific study of such phenomena, documenting how widespread they are and laying out their importance for understanding the connection between mind and body.

Today NDE phenomena are reported more frequently than ever before. Modern medical science can easily determine that someone has "flatlined," and it can also bring them back with state-of-the-art medical equipment. What some of these people report when they return to their bodies is stunning. Many tell stories of their NDE, and they give information that they could not have known when they were presumed dead, having shown no sign of life functions. Not only do they claim that they were fully conscious when they were presumed dead, but they reveal information about what was happening in and around the very hospital where they were being treated.[4]

Is there life after death? Can conscious human experience continue when we are separated from our corporeal body, or put more boldly, after our body is permanently gone? Life after death, although not proven, does seem to be scientifically supported, and those who have gone through an NDE almost always claim that what they experienced was real. They felt totally separated from their body; they were even able to observe it in its moribund condition, and seeing that their awareness continued in this state, they lost all fear of death in the aftermath. They became transformed into more caring and lov-ing human beings. They report that the NDE taught them the real meaning of their physical existence: to learn, to develop their consciousness, and to grow in their capacity to love. This is what happened to brain surgeon Eben Alexander, a nonbelieving materialist who, after his own NDE, became an apostle of the reality of life after death.[5]

A NON-DENOMINATIONAL CREDO

Along with my own life-experience, the foregoing scientific developments lead me to suggest the following emerging paradigm as a guide to how we might view reality. My goal here is to integrate the best of science with the insights of the great religious traditions, East and West. Again, this was the kind of "Integralist Truth" the classical sociologist Pitirim Sorokin had advocated during his Harvard years and until his death in 1968 (see Chapter 2).

- We live within a Great Mystery, a living Reality that defies any understanding based solely on the thinking mind or pure reason alone. Like some of you, I call this Great Mystery "God," but if you prefer "the Ultimate Ground of Being," "The Tao," "The Great Spirit" or something else, it is worth remembering that whatever word we use is a distortion. Our world is a true *hierophany*, a sacred manifestation of the Great Mystery and a very tiny fraction of it, like the tip of an iceberg with submerged and unknown boundaries. That is, there is a living Reality infinitely vaster than the physical world we currently apprehend, or than any other world we might possibly imagine. It is the womb giving birth to everything existent. We are an integral part of this Mystery. Our lives have an ultimate purpose within that larger context, however dimly we may be aware of it.
- We do not live within a lawless world. There are laws that govern the physical universe, and there are also spiritual laws that govern our inner and outer lives based on the thoughts, feelings, and actions we constantly generate. Reality is not haphazard or chaotic. Just as there are consequences of ignoring physical laws, there are also consequences of violating spiritual laws, laws of cause and effect, and the laws related to the dynamics of love and compassion. There are no accidents, but we are free to align or to refuse to align ourselves with the rules that govern the physical as well as the infinitely vaster spiritual universe. Based on this understanding the sages of the world religions have intuited the "Golden Rule," the principle of "Do unto others as you would have them do onto you." This ethic is prescriptive, but it is also protective, for whatever we do to others we do to ourselves. This is how the spiritually grounded

Universe apparently functions. We live within a reality of complete interdependency, moral efficacy, and absolute justice.

- This ultimate Mystery and its laws of interdependency are deeply personal, not impersonal. Indeed, it often appears to human apprehension as a Person. It is totally loving, omniscient, omnipresent and all powerful. It is the foundation of all existent things. My unequivocal answer to Albert Einstein's existential query, "Is the Universe friendly?" is a resounding "Yes, it is!" We are in good hands. Ultimately, there is nothing to fear.

- We are born into a particular family, a particular culture, and a specific historical period to learn two interrelated lessons: First, to grow in our capacity for love and compassion, and second, to expand our ability to know as much as we can about ourselves, the world around us, and the Great Mystery. These two destinations—compassionate love and knowledge—are the foundation of all authentic religions. Life is a journey of self-discovery. The Socratic dictum that the unexamined life is not worth living says this plainly and clearly. If we ignore the real meaning of the journey, we miss the point of encountering pleasures and pains, triumphs and tragedies, light and darkness, and good and evil. Without these polarities to push through, we could never have the experience to help us develop our self-awareness and the virtues of love and knowledge.

- The ultimate destination of every human being is reunion with God, the Great Mystery, out of which we began our journey. Jesus' Parable of the Prodigal Son is the story of every human being (see my discussion in the previous chapter). It resonates with similar stories from other traditions: the Adam and Eve myth of the Old Testament, Plato's parable of the Cave in *The Republic*, Odysseus' yearning for Ithaca, Gautama's journey beyond his father's palace that led him to his enlightenment under the Bo Tree, and countless others.

- Death is not at all a tragedy as it is commonly understood. It is not oblivion and it is not the end of our self-consciousness. Rather, it is the continuation of life by other means. That is why Christian saints, great yogis and lamas, and sages like Socrates have shown both courage and indifference as they faced the end of their physical existence. "Hell," that bugaboo of fundamentalist religion, is ultimately an illusion. A loving God could never have created an eternal place of torment for unruly subjects! The ultimate destiny of human beings is that of the Prodigal Son, the return to the palace of the loving Father. How soon we get there is our personal, individual project. We ourselves create our hells and paradises in this life. True Paradise is our reunion with God, our real homeland and ultimate destination. Any worldly passion (nationalism, success, power, fame, wealth) that is not permeated with Spirit is idolatry. We can always escape from our hellish prisons, but we must first learn the lessons that govern the return to the Palace: love, selflessness, compassion, metanoia, and humility. No one enters the Kingdom bereft of these virtues, and authentic religion offers opportunities and methods to develop them.

- Evolution is not the enemy of Spirit but the framework through which spirituality unfolds. As souls we are at different stages of that evolutionary trajectory. There are no inferior and superior human beings. Adults are not superior to babies; they have simply matured. Deep down we are all God at various levels of spiritual development and of self-awareness. We are beings in evolution. The ultimate destiny of the human soul is not oblivion but its eternal ascent within God's providential realm. Evolution proceeds at all levels of reality—cosmic, physical, biological, psychological, moral, economic, sociocultural, political, and so on. I am not the same "me" today as I was as a teenager in 1960 arriving on a boat at the docks of New York. Yet I am still the same "I Am." This "I Am" is the only reality that does not evolve. What evolves is our individual and collective consciousness. It is the increasing awareness of our origins and destiny. Science plays a key role in this spiritual adventure, and any rejection of evolution is a real tragedy that pits religion against science.

ON BEING CHRISTIAN

As human beings we cannot live within a social vacuum. We are products of our culture and we experience the world through its filters. If the "nondenominational" principles I suggested above come into our experience, they get dressed in the symbols and myths of the traditions that we are born into, or that we happen to identify with.

My own way of experiencing the spiritual is through the lens of Eastern Orthodoxy. I find spiritual fulfillment and solace within its rituals, ethos, mystical theological formulations, artistic creations, and Byzantine chants. It is a religious tradition little known in America. As a Christian denomination it is lumped together with the rest of American Christianity, which has come to play a diminishing role in the modern university. Nowadays, the favored religions among university students and faculty who are not atheists or agnostics are the religions of the Far East, such as Buddhism and Hinduism.

During the last few decades Christianity has suffered from negative apprehensions outside the university as well. There is a reluctance to profess Christian beliefs and practices. Younger generations of Americans coming from a Christian background drift away from their cradle religion and become atheistic, agnostic, or they explore other spiritual options. Contemporary Christianity is routinely equated with fundamentalism, top-down patriarchal authoritarianism, intolerance of diversity, support for the death penalty, opposition to gender equality, homophobia, and anti-abortion legislation. Religions such as Hinduism, Buddhism (particularly Zen), shamanism, and Native American spirituality are more positively viewed, and courses about them are often available in many liberal arts departments. Courses on Christianity are rarely offered, and if they are, they may be terminated with the retirement of the faculty who taught it. Many professors will speak with a dismissive and sneering tone if the topic of Christianity comes up in a conversation with colleagues, reflecting the common American association of Christianity with extreme right-wing politics.

This anti-Christian animus is an astonishing development, considering that Protestant Christians made such stunning contributions to universal human rights in both early and continuing American history, as discussed in chapter 6. Indeed, Christianity played a key role in shaping western civilization itself. There is a significant lacuna in understanding the social and historical forces that shaped the world we live in, owing to these negative attitudes towards Christianity. I often see a tendency to focus only on the darker side of Christianity, as if the Crusades, the Inquisition, colonialism, and the bombing of abortion clinics by fanatical born-again zealots represent the core of its history and legacy.

It is certainly important to call out the ugly face of religion, those pseudo-expressions that led to holocausts, jihads, ethnic cleansing, and other persecutions done in the name of religion, or done simply in opposition to out-group religions. But we must also keep alive for future generations the truer, life-enhancing expressions that are available from religion. After all, the origin of all authentic religion springs from mind-expanding, life-affirming inspiration.

Speaking for myself as a nontheologian, I draw ample inspiration from the great gems of Christian wisdom, gems that are relevant to all peoples of the world regardless of their religious affiliations or identity. I was born into an Orthodox Christian culture, and had I been born within a non-Christian world, no doubt I would have felt equally blessed. As a Tibetan I would feel proud to have the Dalai Lama as my spiritual and political leader. As a Hindu I might eagerly practice the teachings of the great yogis and rishis of India as I struggle to escape from the Wheel of Samsara and unite my individual Atman with Brahman. As Jewish, my mystical inclinations might find solace within Judaism's prophetic tradition, including the Kabbalah, and in the rituals prescribed by the Torah, as Jesus did during his earthly incarnation as a Jewish Rabbi. As a Muslim I might join a Sufi order to practice the art of compassion so that I could attain my deliverance in the bosom of Allah. And as Native American, I might eagerly sit at the feet of my shamanic grandmothers and grandfathers, taking part in sweat lodge rituals and joining others in rhythmic dancing meditation, hoping to make contact with the Great Spirit.

My faithfulness to Eastern Orthodoxy is fully compatible with a profound respect for these other spiritual traditions. I am enriched by their teachings. Today we have an unparalleled opportunity to expose one another to different approaches to Spirit. This ecumenical aspiration is completely compatible with the best of Christian teachings and is particularly appropriate for the radically pluralizing world in which we find ourselves. An Eastern Orthodox principle of faith suggests that God *economizes* the salvation of every human being, regardless of gender, race, ethnicity, or religious affiliation. That is, God does not discriminate. The medieval tendency to separate people between "us" the chosen ones and "others" the heretics is simply too destructive for an increasingly interdependent world. Alas, that tribal tendency too often lingers on within the religions of the world.

Below I look at some Christian teachings that speak to my insistence on universal applicability. Here are six that support a more peaceful and harmonious future for all of humanity: the opening paragraph of John's Gospel; the parable of the Good Samaritan; the Sermon on the Mount; the story of the Doubting Thomas; the parable of the Prodigal Son; and Apostle Paul's elegy on love.

The sociologist of religion Peter Berger claimed that the opening paragraphs of the Gospel of John in the New Testament contain the most revolutionary and consequential ideas in the literature of western civilization. The core theme is that the Christ as the Logos is the light that lightens every human being that comes into the world. It underscores the radical equality of all human beings. We all share in the same divine spark; we are all children of the one God. This was the seed that eventually led to the end of slavery. It was the platform upon which the abolitionists launched their struggle to end the slave trade and free the African American population from bondage. It was also the fundamental belief that is enshrined in the American Constitution, and that later sparked the Civil Rights movement along with other rights movements that exploded during the sixties and continue today. It was incorporated into the charter of the United Nations in terms of the universality of human rights. Implicitly, it was a stunning renunciation of the prior notion that there are superior and inferior human beings by nature.

The Parable of the Good Samaritan is another teaching that undermines tribalism and what sociologists call ethnocentrism: the feeling that one's culture, race, or ethnicity is superior to every other. It is told by Jesus in the Gospel of Luke. A traveler is beaten up and left half-dead on the side of the road. First a priest and then a Levite come by, and both avoid the injured man. Then a Samaritan arrives, and he goes out of his way to offer help. Jesus tells this parable in response to the question from a lawyer, "And who is my neighbor [that we should love]?" The neighbor figure in the parable is the man who shows mercy to the injured man—that is, the Samaritan. Jesus offers that parable at a time when otherwise religious people refused to touch or break bread with anybody outside their own tribe, the Samaritans being the most detested. In this nuclear age, the parable teaches the virtues of empathy and understanding of others. The survival of humanity may depend on how quickly we can dismantle the walls of separation that plague humanity, and the Good Samaritan is the archetypal story of the global citizen.

Jesus' injunction to "turn the other cheek" in his Sermon on the Mount is the paean that inspired writers and activists from Leo Tolstoy and Henry David Thoreau to Mahatma Gandhi and Martin Luther King. The injunction resonates with my revulsion toward all forms of violence. It is a restraining order to mollify vengeful feelings toward those we consider our enemies or those we believe have wronged us. Turn the other cheek—Jesus' blessings for the peacemakers—is like water that extinguishes fire, a recipe for a more peaceful and sane world. I remember the reprimand of one of my professors in graduate school when I questioned the motives and actions of Che Guevara, who left his family in Argentina to join Fidel Castro in the Cuban revolution and to kill people in the service of his burning rage against economic exploitation and inequality. My professor, who was himself swayed by Che's iconic status among revolutionaries around the world, was deeply annoyed with me for questioning Che's purity of motives.

The thrust of the Doubting Thomas story is to discourage blind belief. Jesus did not reprimand Thomas for doubting that he was real when he miraculously appeared in front of the disciples after his resurrection. He simply invited Thomas to place his hands on the scars left on his body from the wounds of the crucifixion. I see this story as encouragement to explore and verify the truths of religious as well as secular authorities, an invitation to become experiential scientists. It points toward a reconciliation of religion and science. At the dawn of the third millennium, when most people are literate and when many of us have been exposed to university training, demands for blind faith are the surest way to turn people away from religion.

The parable of the Prodigal Son has always been my favorite for understanding our relationship with God, and I explored it in some detail in chapter 6. The story is an allegory about our relationship with God. Briefly, the son leaves the palace of the loving father to experience nameless, narrow, earthly pleasures, forsaking his inheritance. Eventually, he grows weary of this quest and returns to the palace, his loving father welcoming him with open arms and a feast of celebration. One moral of the story is that no experience is ever wasted: The journey led to a deeper awareness of the polarities of good and evil, light and darkness, and it therefore gave rise to a richer appreciation of what it means to live in fullness.

Finally, Apostle Paul's words on love have been heralded as the most eloquent paean for God's love ever written or spoken, and they have been recited through centuries of Christianity in myriads of nuptial vows and ceremonies:

> If I speak in the tongues of men and of angels, but have not love, I am a noisy gong or a clanging cymbal. And if I have prophetic powers, and understand all mysteries and all knowledge, and if I have all faith, so as to remove mountains, but have not love, I am nothing. If I give away all I have, and if I deliver my body to be burned, but have not love, I gain nothing. Love is patient and kind; love is not jealous or boastful; it is not arrogant or rude. Love does not insist on its own way; it is not irritable or resentful; it does not rejoice at wrong, but rejoices in the right. Love bears all things, believes all things, hopes all things, endures all things. Love never ends (1 Corinthians 13:1–8).

I have experienced the energy of this vibrant love embodied in the lives of some contemporary elders of Eastern Christianity. Father Maximos, of course, is foremost on the list, and I hope I show this in my trilogy on his life and teachings.[6] Through him I met elders like Paisios, who is now officially declared a contemporary saint of the Greek Orthodox Church.[7] I also learned about the extraordinary lives of other elders who embodied the love that Apostle Paul writes about. These would include Saint Silouan the Athonite,[8] Elder Sofrony Zacharof,[9] and Elder Porphyrios,[10] all three, like Elder Paisios, canonized as twentieth-century saints of the Eastern Orthodox Church. Mother Gavrilia is another great twentieth-century eldress who exemplifies the purest form of Christian love.[11] None of these great ones are known to the West except by some members of Orthodox congregations. The life and works of some contemporary members of the higher clergy have spiritually enriched me as well. Archbishop Anastasios of Albania and Archbishop Makarios of Kenya are also models of ecumenical Christian love. Of course, Apostle Paul's love is certainly not confined to the boundaries of Eastern Orthodoxy. It is expressed and celebrated throughout history in the lives of sages who speak in a variety of tongues and come from different cultural and religious traditions.

The Patriarch of Constantinople Bartholomew deserves special mention in this context. Known as the "Green Patriarch," as I mentioned earlier, his relentless efforts to raise global awareness of the looming environmental Armageddon evince a different expression of Apostle Paul's love.[12] After his ascent to the patriarchal throne in 1991 he officially established as sinful any action that harms the environment, and he reserved September 1 as a day for prayer and the celebration of Creation in the Orthodox liturgical calendar.

The Green Patriarch's symposia program is uniquely ecumenical. Representatives from diverse religious traditions are invited, along with environmental scientists, ecologists, and scholars representing the humanities and social sciences. The symposia take place on a boat, sailing in environmentally threatened areas such as the Baltic Sea, the Amazon, and the Arctic. These voyages have been publicized on the internet for maximum effect in dramatizing the plight of the Earth. It was heartwarming for me to watch the Patriarch on YouTube, exchanging ritual blessings with an Amazonian, feathered, native shaman who sprinkled water over the head of the Patriarch. This would have been unthinkable in earlier centuries or even a few decades ago when native peoples were viewed as savages in need of forcible conversion to Christianity.

The 9th patriarchal symposium took place on a ship in the southern Aegean Sea during the first week of June 2018. This was yet another attempt on the Patriarch's part to bridge the gap among the religions of the world and between religion and science. Emily and I were among the 200 or so invited participants from around the world, included, perhaps, because of Emily's credentials as an environmental activist and mine as a writer of books on Eastern Orthodoxy. Traveling around the "wine dark sea" for four days on a boat with the Patriarch and his global guests was a delight to the senses and an extraordinary intellectual and spiritual experience. The sobering presentations of the environmental scientists were complemented by religious representatives who advocated understanding and love between the world's religions as a necessary recipe for saving humanity from self-destruction. A most memorable presentation was the impassioned plea for the love of humanity presented by Rabbi Awraham Soetendor, the Dutch founder of The Soetendorp Institute. The Institute's mission is to bring religiously diverse people together to create just and sustainable communities "in which the divine in all of us and in all creation is revered, respected, and cherished."

It was a scene to behold: a rabbi speaking about the universality of love in front of the Eastern Orthodox Patriarch of Constantinople in a boat room full of scientists, religious leaders, academics, and journalists! His talk brought us to tears, as he narrated his life and his journey of forgiveness and love for all of humanity. He was born in Nazi-occupied Holland in 1943. When he was an infant, SS troops came to the house and arrested his parents and relatives. The officer in charge was reluctant to condemn a mere infant, so he handed him off to a German Catholic woman who became his adopted mother. His biological parents perished in the gas chambers but he himself survived, thanks to the SS officer and the charity of the Catholic neighbor. This experience marked him for life, turning him into an apostle of forgiveness and an advocate of universal love and compassion. His poetic, riveting delivery was equal to the stunning facts of his biography. Filled with authentic love and compassion, his message touched the heart of every participant. It reminded me of the words of his ancient ancestor when he drafted his classic epistle to the Corinthians.

NOTES

1. Amit Goswami, *The Self-Aware Universe: How Consciousness Creates the Material World* (New York: TarcherPerigee, 1995).
2. A most exciting work for understanding the trajectory of western philosophical thought from ancient times to the present is Richard Tarnas's classic *The Passion of the Western Mind: Understanding the Ideas that have Shaped Our World* (New York: Harmony Books, 1991).
3. Carl Jung, *Memories, Dreams, Reflections* (New York: Vintage, 1989).
4. In addition to Raymond Moody's classic work *Life after Life* (New York: HarperOne, 2015), I suggest studies like Jeffrey Long's and Paul Perry's *Evidence of the Afterlife: The Science of Near-Death Experiences* (New York: Harper One, 2010).
5. Eben Alexander, *Proof of Heaven: A Neurosurgeon's Journey into the Afterlife* (New York: Simon & Schuster, 2012).
6. *The Mountain of Silence* (New York: Random House, 2001); *Gifts of the Desert* (New York: Random House, 2005); and *Inner River* (New York: Random House, 2012).
7. Hieromonk Isaac, *Saint Paisios of Mount Athos*, (The Holy Monastery of Saint Arsenios the Cappadocian, 2016); see also my *Riding with the Lion* (New York: Viking, 1995), pp. 286–307 (In this book I used the name "Vasilios" to protect the identity of then living Elder Paisios).
8. Archimandrite Sophrony (Sakharov), *Saint Silouan the Athonite* (New York: St. Vladimir's Seminary Press, 1999).
9. Archimandrite Sophrony (Sakharof), *We Shall See Him as He Is* (Essex, UK: Stavropegik Monastery of St. John the Baptist, 1988).
10. Elder Porphyrios, *Wounded by Love* (Limni, Evia, Greece: Denise Harvey, 2005).
11. Nun Gavrilia, *The Ascetics of Love* (Thessaloniki, Greece: Series Talanton, 1999).
12. John Chryssavgis, *Bartholomew: Apostle and Visionary* (Nashville, TN: W Publishing Group, 2016).

Praise for Markides' Other Books

"A profound and exciting work of major importance. [Markides] has had the courage to address possibilities which are for the most part ignored in much of contemporary thought. It may be that Professor Markides and others like him who have the courage to explore, are on the brink of remarkable discoveries about the nature of man."—Dr. Raymond Moody, author of *Life After Life*

"A vast source of spiritual knowledge, understanding, and practice, that is largely unknown to us."—Dr. Jacob Needleman, Professor of Philosophy and author of *What Is God?*

"A really marvelous book. One of the most extraordinary accounts of a 'magical' personality. I think that this series of his is one of the most fascinating and absorbing that has been published in the past twenty years."—Colin Wilson, author of *The Outsider*

"Markides succeeds where Carlos Castaneda came up short. This is a book every man, woman, and child must become familiar with."—Antonio T. de Nicolas, Professor of Philosophy, SUNY

"A spiritually enlightening and penetrating book."—Dr. Geddes MacGregor, Professor of Philosophy and Theology

"Markides continues to explore the fascinating world of the mystical and deftly interprets its connections not just to Orthodox Christianity, but to all spirituality."—Professor Harvey Cox, Harvard Divinity School

"This is a book of marvels. Markides has gifted us with his remarkable grasp of the implications of the philosophy and practice of those who would reenchant the world."—Dr. Jean Houston, author of *A Mythic Life*

"A penetrating insight into profound spiritual truths. It is written with the critical eye of a scholar and the courage of a true spiritual adventurer."—Dr. Larry Dossey, author of *One Mind*

"A compelling glimpse into the heart of mystical Christianity. It sparkles with the wisdom of modern saints."—Dr. Joan Borysenko, author of *Minding the Body, Mending the Mind*

"A wondrous bridge between shamanic consciousness and the so-called reality of the everyday world. Under the sacred spirit of Mount Athos, Kyriacos Markides transforms ordinary vision."—Lynn Andrews, author of *Love and Power*

"I was most interested in the text, and I have learned many things from it. It forms an excellent overview of traditional Orthodox ascetic and spiritual teachings, in a lively style that may reach many people who would not read a more 'ecclesiastical' presentation."—Bishop Kallistos Ware

"Through his superb dialectic skills, Markides blends reason with faith . . . stirring the heart and mind of the reader in a spiritual journey of self-discovery."—Dr. Christos Ioannides, Queens College

"Professor Markides is a true philosopher and an inspired writer. If you want to know yourself and live to the fullest, this book is truly a must, a priceless jewel!"—Dr. Peter Roche de Coppens, East Stroudsburg University

"The insights that he communicates with such enthusiasm are timely ones: here at last is a writer who challenges the seeker after mystical understanding and Eastern spirituality to discover Christianity."—Dr. Elizabeth Theokritoff, Eastern Orthodox Theologian

"Markides' work is an excellent resource for spiritual seekers of all levels, answering questions about Christianity in general and Eastern monasticism in particular."—*Publishers Weekly* (Star review)

"A fascinating narrative that is . . . dialogue and meditation, history and politics, theology and travelogue . . ."—*Los Angeles Times*

"Spirituality with refreshing honesty. . . . Markides' book calls attention to the existence of an ancient form of mysticism within the bounds of modern Christianity."—*Booklist*

"Reminiscent of Bill Moyers's now famous interviews with religionist Joseph Campbell. . . . Markides serves . . . as the spiritual seeker's muse."—*Library Journal*

"Markides' path is the way of the Western mystery tradition, a rich expression of esoteric mystic Christianity liberally cross-pollinated with Hinduism and Buddhism. It's a somewhat neglected inner yogic tradition practiced for millennia here in the West, and . . . it's an underappreciated path that could be of considerable benefit to many. . . . In his three books [Magus, Homage, Fire] Markides has carefully laid out the teachings of Daskalos and Kostas in a rational, non-sensational manner strongly reminiscent of the old Platonic dialogues, where questions and answers are interspersed with anecdotes, stories, and experiences."—Richard Leviton, *Yoga Journal*

"When word gets out that Kyriacos Markides has published a new book, bookstores from Berkeley, California, to Ithaca, New York, are inundated with requests for it. A launch or signing invariably leads to hundreds of requests to meet the author. Well known in the world of spiritual publishing. . . . Markides has struck a chord in many who want to gain a more expansive view of spirituality."—Ellen Pontikis, *Odyssey*

"The importance of this book is potentially immense. The Mountain of Silence introduces a world that is entirely new to many Western readers, and unveils a Christian tradition that reveres the mystical approach to God as much as the rational . . ."—Michael Joseph Gross, Editorial Review, *Amazon*

"Compelling. . . . It presents an excellent overview of the main themes common to all Orthodox spirituality while avoiding the dullness of typical textbook treatments by the intensity of the author's personal search and by vivid vignettes from mount Athos. I recommend it to all Christians—Catholic, Protestant and Orthodox—who desire to grasp more deeply our common Christian spiritual roots."—Richard J. Hauser, *America*

"The books delve deeply into many spiritual topics with a frankness and clarity that is rarely found in print elsewhere . . ."—Peter Stekl, with Laurie Webster, *Convergence*

". . . a consummate scholar whose writings are so very accessible. . . . His informed, detailed, and engaging writing style makes one feel present in the conversation. Markides' writing holds the potential to transform one's very way of navigating life."—Dr. Marcie Boucouvalas, editor of *Journal of Transpersonal Psychology*

"His viewpoint is extremely radical in nature, and has great breadth in its implications. . . . These are great questions and this book poses them in a very calm and palatable way. . . . The tone is even-paced and the text is never heavy or hard to read. For one thing, the author is generous in his descriptions of his surroundings where all these discussions occur. . . . The presentation is . . . persuasive, but always dispassionate. It is, above all, brave."—Dr. M. Bockris, Dist. Prof. of Chemistry Texas A&M University, *Journal of Scientific Exploration*

"Extraordinary work. The author's enthusiasm for his search . . . gives this book its special momentum and vibrancy."—Frederic and Mary Ann Brussat, *Spirituality & Health*

"An astounding book, heart-warming and an ingenious source of inner illumination. . . . Anyone seeking to ponder the deeper truths of life will find a paradise in this intimate journey of discovery. It reveals once-buried secrets with immense clarity. . . . Realistic and down-to-earth, yet inspiring with a brilliance that comes from higher realms . . . a rare find."—*Leading Edge Review*

"A guide to a different world. . . . Markides writes in a comfortable, easy style that manages to convey his ideas simply, yet without trivializing them. The result is an interesting and thought-provoking book."—*West Coast Review of Books*

"Until now, the esoteric teachings and shamanistic practices . . . have been exclusively identified with Hinduism and Tibetan Buddhism. Thus, this is the first study to ground them firmly in Western culture. Through engaging dialogues, amusing stories, experiential vignettes and humor, Kyriacos Markides makes the abstruse not only accessible . . . but also thoroughly entertaining. Capturing a world of mystic healing and magical personalities unrivaled since the early works of Carlos Castaneda . . . will appeal to readers of New Age Literature, students of psychology and comparative religion, and all who strive to know the true meaning of reality."—*The Bookwatch*

"An excellent read . . . as far as I know, this material doesn't appear anywhere else. . . . This book and others in the trilogy present a college course in the nature of . . . reality, the nature of the human soul, and the great potential for healing ourselves, others and our planet."—N. Susan McClees, *Albuquerque Journal*

"This is a gem . . . for those who are comfortable with or curious about the applications of psi, and especially of psi healing, in the real world."—Daniel J. Benor, *Journal of the American Society for Psychical Research*

"The vision . . . is consistent with the highest traditions of esoteric Christianity, Neoplatonism and Eastern philosophy . . . full of dialogue, is as easy to read as any popular novel."—John Dreghorn, *Healing Review*

"Markides emerges as a combination participant-observer, interviewer and phenomenologist. He is an engaging, sensitive and perspicacious inquirer."—Dr. Robert Sollod, *The Common Boundary*

". . . captivating and extraordinary . . . will illuminate the thoughts of any student of healing . . . unique synthesis. . . . Highly recommended."—*Cooperative Connection*

"This is an excellent documentary of the life of . . . a healer with whom you are left in no doubt as to his efficacy. The author has come to grips with a difficult subject area which portrays in a convincing way."—*Creative Mind*

". . . well above average for its kind. . . . The narrative is an uplifting, interesting and provocative account of a somewhat unique magical reality and of the man who inhabits it. Well written . . . a coherent and persuasive cosmology that has elements from both Eastern and Western tradition. . . . This book is a must."—*The Unknown*

". . . it will appear familiar to lovers of Carlos Castaneda's books, but being closer to home and more consistent it is harder to dismiss as a wonderful fantasy."—*Lighting Flash*

". . . remarkable . . . very readable dialogue. [Markides] has avoided the turgid text we often meet when profound philosophical topics are being presented."—*Healing Review*

"Markides' style of writing has an easy, friendly flow, one not overly cluttered by a scientist's tendency towards intellectual jargon"—Jane G. Meyer, *The Handmaiden: A Journal for Women Serving God Within the Orthodox Faith*

Bibliography

Alexander, Eben. 2012. *Proof of Heaven: A Neurosurgeon's Journey into the Afterlife.* New York: Simon & Schuster.

Benson, Henry. 2000. *The Relaxation Response.* New York: HarperTorch.

Berger, Peter. 1963. *Invitation to Sociology: A Humanistic Perspective.* New York: Anchor.

———, Thomas Luckmann. 1967. *The Social Construction of Reality: A Treatise in the Sociology of Knowledge.* New York: Anchor.

———. 1976. *Pyramids of Sacrifice: Political Ethics and Social Change.* New York: Anchor Books.

Boyd, Doug. 1974. *Rolling Thunder: A Personal Exploration into the Secret Healing Powers of an American Indian Medicine Man.* New York: Random House.

Buck, Richard Maurice. 2010. *Cosmic Consciousness: A Study of Evolution of the Human Mind.* Eastport, CN: Martino Publishing.

Capra, Fritjof. 1975. *The Tao of Physics,* Boulder, CO: Shambhala.

Castaneda, Carlos. 1985, *The Teachings of Don Juan.* New York: Simon & Schuster.

Chryssavgis, John. 2016. *Bartholomew: Apostle and Visionary.* Nashville, TN: W Publishing Group.

Cohn, Steven and Kyriacos C. Markides. 2013. Religion and Spiritual Experience: Revisiting Key Assumptions in Sociology. *International Journal of Transpersonal Studies,* 32 (2), 34–41.

Collins, Francis. 2007. *The Language of God: A Scientist Presents Evidence for Belief.* New York: Free Press.

Dawkins, Richard. 2008. *The God Delusion.* Boston: Mariner Books.

Dennett, Daniel. 2007. *Breaking the Spell: Religion as a Natural Phenomenon.* New York: Penguin Books.

Dossey, Larry. 1995. *Healing Words: The Power of Prayer and the Practice of Medicine.* San Francisco: HarperOne.

———. 2013. *One Mind.* New York: Hay House.

Durkheim, Emile. 1995. *The Elementary Forms of the Religious Life.* New York: Free Press.

Durrell, Lawrence. 2009. *Bitter Lemons.* Edinburg, VA: Axios Press.

Flew, Antony. 2008. *There Is a God: How the World's Most Notorious Atheist Changed his Mind.* New York: HarperOne.

Fox, Mathew. 1988. *The Coming of the Cosmic Christ.* New York: HarperOne.

Frankl, Viktor. 2006. *Man's Search for Meaning.* Boston: Beacon Press.

Fromm, Eric. 1965. *The Sane Society.* Hollywood, CA: Fawcett Books.

———. 1992. *The Anatomy of Human Destructiveness.* New York: Holt.

———. 1994. *Escape from Freedom.* New York: Holt.

Fuller, John G. 1974. *Arigo: Surgeon of the Rusty Knife.* New York: Thomas Y. Crowell.

Gavrilia, Nun. 1999. *The Ascetics of Love.* Thessaloniki, Greece: Series Talanton.

Goffman, Erving. 1961. *Asylums.* New York: Anchor Books.

Goswami, Amit. 1995. *The Self-Aware Universe: How Consciousness Creates the Material World.* New York: TarcherPerigee.

———. 2012. *God is not Dead: What Quantum Physics Tells us about our Origins.* Newburyport, MA: Hampton Roads Publishing.

Grivas, George. 1964. *Guerrilla Warfare and EOKA's Struggle: A Politico-Military Study.* London: Longmans, Green.

Groff, Stanislav. 2006. *When the Impossible Happens: Adventures in Non-Ordinary Realities.* Louisville, CO: Sounds True Publisher.

Gurdjieff, George. 2013. *In Search of Being: The Fourth Way to Consciousness.* Boulder, CO: Shambhala.

Haisch, Bernard. 2009. *The God Theory.* San Francisco: Weiser Books.

Halifax, Joan. 1988. *Shaman: The Wounded Healer.* New York: Thames & Hudson

Harner, Michael. 1980. *The Way of the Shaman.* New York: Bantam Books,

Harris, Sam. 2005. *The End of Faith.* New York: W.W. Norton.

Hastings, Arthur. 1991. *With the Tongues of Men and Angels: A Study of Channeling.* New York: Holt Rinehart and Winston.

Hitchens, Christopher. 2009. *God is not Great: How Religion Poisons Everything.* New York: Twelve Publishers.

Hoffer, Eric. 1951. *The True Believer.* New York: Harper & Brothers.

Isaac, Hieromonk. 2016. *Saint Paisios of Mount Athos.* Mount Athos: The Holy Monastery of Saint Arsenios the Cappadocian.

Jastrsow, R. 1992. *God and the Astronomers.* New York: W. W. Norton.

Johnston, B.V. 1995. *Pitirim A. Sorokin: An Intellectual Biography.* Lawrence: University Press of Kansas.

Jung, Carl. 1965. *Memories, Dreams, Reflections.* New York: Random House.

Katz, Fred E. 1993. *Ordinary People and Extraordinary Evil: A Report on the Beguilings of Evil.* Albany: State University of New York Press.

Kazantzakis, Nikos. 1965. *Report to Greco.* New York: Simon and Schuster.

Kelly, Edward F. et al. 2010. *Irreducible Mind: Toward a Psychology for the 21st Century.* New York: Rowman & Littlefield.

Kiev, Ari. 1964. *Magic, Faith and Healing: Studies in Primitive Psychiatry Today.* New York: Collier–Macmillan.

Kirkpatrick, Sidney D. 2001. *Edgar Cayce: An American Prophet.* New York: Riverhead Books.

Laing, R. D. 1967. *The Politics of Experience.* New York: Ballantine.

Laszlo, Ervin. 2014. *The Immortal Mind: Science and the Continuity of Consciousness Beyond the Brain.* Vermont: Inner Traditions.

Linkon, Sherry Lee, John Russo. 2002. *Steel-town U.S.A.: Work & Memory in Youngstown.* Lawrence, Kansas: University Press of Kansas.

Lommel, Pim van MD. 2010. *Consciousness Beyond Life: The Science of the Near-Death Experience.* New York: HarperOne.

Long, Jeffrey and Paul Perry. 2010. *Evidence of the Afterlife: The Science of Near-Death Experiences.* New York: HarperOne.

Mack, John. 2002. *Passport to the Cosmos.* New York: Crown Publishers.

Markides, Kyriacos C. 1974. Social Change and the Rise and Decline of Social Movements: The Case of Cyprus. *American Ethnologist,* (May 1974), 309–330.

———. 1977. *The Rise and Fall of the Cyprus Republic.* New Haven: Yale University Press.

———, Elengo Rangou, and Eleni Nikita. 1978. *Social Change in a Cypriot Village.* Nicosia: Cyprus: Social Research Centre.

———. 1985. *The Magus of Strovolos.* New York: Penguin.

———. 1987. *Homage to the Sun.* New York: Penguin.

———. 1990. Fire *in the Heart.* New York: Penguin.

———. 1995. *Riding with the Lion.* New York: Viking Press.

———. 2001. *The Mountain of Silence: A Search for Orthodox Spirituality.* New York: Random House.

———. 2005. *Gifts of the Desert.* New York: Random House.

———. 2012. *Inner River.* New York: Random House.

———. 2017. The Healing Spirituality of Eastern Orthodoxy: A Personal Journey of Discovery. *Religions.* (June, 2017), 1–14.

Mitchell, Edgar. 2008. *The Way of the Explorer: An Apollo Astronaut's Journey Through the Material and Mystical Worlds.* Newburyport, MA: New Page Books.

———. 2014. *Earthrise: My Adventures as an Apollo 14 Astronaut.* Chicago: Chicago Review Press.

Moody, Raymond. 2015. *Life After Life.* New York: HarperOne.

Moskos, Charles. 1976. *Peace Soldiers: The Sociology of a United Nations Military Force.* Chicago: University of Chicago Press.

Pinker, Steven. 2012. *The Better Angels of Our Nature: Why Violence Has Declined.* New York: Penguin.

Porphyrios, Elder. 2005. *Wounded by Love.* Limni, Evia, Greece: Denise Harvey.

Radin, Dean. 2009 *The Conscious Universe: The Scientific Truth of Psychic Phenomena.* San Francisco: HarperOne.

———. 2013. *Supernormal: Science, Yoga, and the Evidence for Extraordinary Psychic Abilities.* New York: Crown Publishing.

Ramacharaka, Yogi. 1903. *Fourteen Lessons in Yogi Philosophy.* Chicago: Yogi Publication Society.

———. *1904. Advance Course in Yogi Philosophy.* Chicago: The Yogi Publication Society.

———. *1906. Lessons in Gnani Yoga.* Chicago: The Yogi Publication Society.

Ryan, Mark R. 2008. The Transpersonal William James. *Journal of Transpersonal Psychology.* 40 (1) 20–40.

Sacks, Jonathan. 2011. *The Great Partnership: Science, Religion, and the Search for Meaning.* New York: Schocken Books.

Sakharov, Archimandrite Sophrony. 1988. *We* Shall See Him as He Is. Essex, UK: Stavropegik Monastery of St. John the Baptist.

———. 1999. *Saint Silouan the Athonite.* New York: St. Vladimir's Seminary Press.

Sawyer, Dana. 2014. *Huston Smith: Wisdomkeeper.* Louisville, KY: Fons Vitae.

Sheldrake, Rupert. 2013. *Science Set Free: Ten Paths to New Discovery.* New York: Deepak Chopra Publisher.

Simmel, Georg. 1955. *Conflict and the Web of Group Affiliations.* New York: Free Press.

Smith, Huston. 2009. *The World's Religions.* San Francisco: HarperOne.

Sorokin, Pitirim A. 1957. *Social and Cultural Dynamics.* Boston: Sargent Publishers.

———. 2002. *Ways and Power of Love: Techniques of Moral Transformation.* West Conshohocken, PA: Templeton Foundation Press.

Steiner, Rudolf. 1994. *How to Know Higher Worlds.* East Sussex, UK: Anthroposophic Press.

Szasz, Thomas. 1972. *The Myth of Mental Illness.* New York: Harper & Row.

Targ, Russell. 2012. *The Reality of ESP: A Physicist's Proof of Psychic Abilities.* Wheaton, IL: Quest Book.

Tarnas, Richard. 1991. *The Passion of the Western Mind: Understanding the Ideas that Have Shaped Our World.* New York: Harmony Books.

Tart, Charles. 2009. *The End of Materialism: How Evidence of the Paranormal is Bringing Science and Spirit Together.* Oakland, CA: New Harbinger Publications.

Thurman, Robert. 1999. *Inner Revolution.* New York: Riverhead Books.

Torrey, Fuller. 1972. *Witchdoctors and Psychiatrists: The Common Roots of Psychotherapy and its Future.* New York: Harper & Row.

Watts, Alan. 1975. *Psychotherapy East and West.* New York: Vintage.

Weber, Max. 2003. The *Protestant Ethic and the Spirit of Capitalism.* Mineola, NY: Dover Publications.

White, Ralph. 2015. *The Jeweled Highway: On the Quest for a Life of Meaning.* Studio City, CA: Michael Wiese Productions.

Wilber, Ken. 1983. *Eye to Eye: The Quest for the New Paradigm.* New York: Anchor Books.

About the Author

Kyriacos C. Markides is an internationally respected authority on mystic Christianity and unconventional healers and sages. He has written many books translated in fourteen languages and appeared on national and international radio and television programs. His books include a trilogy on Christian spirituality: *The Mountain of Silence, Gifts of the Desert, and Inner River.* Dr. Markides is Professor Emeritus of Sociology and the recipient of the 2002 Best Professor Award in Arts and Sciences at the University of Maine and the 2006 Presidential Research and Creative Achievement Award of the same university. He lives in Stillwater, Maine with his wife Dr. Emily Markides, Adjunct assistant professor in Peace Studies.